IMAGES
of America

ST. JAMES TRADE SCHOOL AND BROTHER JAMES COURT

The following individuals and families have graciously and generously provided financial support for the first order of books purchased by Brother James Court. We thank those who helped make these first books available.

Brother James Court Families and Friends:

Michael Leahy in Memory of Daniel F. and Mary N. Leahy
Mark and Pamm Collebrusco
Walter and Joan Righton
Michael Carr
The Kulbida Family
Joan A. Landolt
Emily J. Kuelbs
Dale and Gloria Levitt
Dr. and Mrs. Dennis and Linda Hayes
Josiah and Muriel Smith
Joan Barnhorst
Cathy Gremley
The Trstensky Family
Joseph and Loretta Stapleton
Kathleen and Bill Rountree
Jim and Maggie Jenkins in Memory of Lucille Shepherd
Pauline Britz and Family
Rose (Britz) Blasko and Family
Robert and Christine Doty
Jean (Churchill) Blockyou and the Churchill Family
The Family of Donald Harada
The Grover Herring Family
Jeffrey and Shirley Vien
anonymous
Ron Wampler
The Landers Family
Patrick Sheehan and Jason Sheehan in Loving Honor of Our Uncle, Tom Shepherd
Honoring Tim Kiesow, from His Family
Charlotte Dormal in Loving Memory of My Husband Edward Dormal
The Stapleton Family
anonymous

St. James Trade School Alumni and Friends:

Jay Adams, Class of 1960
Mike Trenary, Class of 1962
John "Red" and Linda Leonard, Class of 1962
Joseph W. and Ruth Meny, Class of 1955
Chuck Hetzel, Class of 1962
Phil and Betty Shadid, Friends of St. James
Ralph J. "Jim" and Gina Vespa, Class of 1959
In Memory of Grant D. Adams, Class of 1955
Gene P. Adams, Class of 1958
Ray Lefferts in Memory and Honor of My Family and the Brothers at St. James Trade School, Class of 1965
John and Kathy Chepulis in Appreciation of the Brothers at St. James Trade School
Berneice M. Grabowski
Pat and Norma Capranica, Class of 1955

IMAGES
of America

St. James Trade School and Brother James Court

Franciscan Brothers
at Brother James Court

Br. Anthony Joseph, FFSC, author
Phil Shadid, co-author
Br. Christian and Jay Landers, co-editors

ARCADIA
PUBLISHING

ISBN 978-0-7385-7811-8

Published by Arcadia Publishing
Charleston SC, Chicago IL, Portsmouth NH, San Francisco CA

Printed in the United States of America

Library of Congress Control Number: 2009939980

For all general information contact Arcadia Publishing at:
Telephone 843-853-2070
Fax 843-853-0044
E-mail sales@arcadiapublishing.com
For customer service and orders:
Toll-Free 1-888-313-2665

Visit us on the Internet at www.arcadiapublishing.com

This book is dedicated to the men, past and present, who have graced the lives of the Franciscan Brothers of the Holy Cross, and to all those whose lives the Franciscan Brothers have graced. May God, who began these good works, continue to bless those who have been part of our apostolic works these many years. May devotion to Christ and His loved ones always grace our lives as Catholic religious brothers today and in the future.

On the Cover: The 1959 staff and student body stand on the porch of the completed Chapel of St. Joseph the Worker at St. James Trade School in Springfield, Illinois. The chapel building was begun in 1954 and completed in 1959, with all the work done by the students and their instructors. (Courtesy archives of the Franciscan Brothers.)

CONTENTS

Ut in omnibus glorificetur Deus. (That in all things God may be glorified.)

—St. Ignatius Loyola, SJ.

ACKNOWLEDGMENTS

The creation of this book would not have become a reality without the impetus of Jay Landers, development director of Brother James Court, and the untiring assistance of Phil Shadid, a friend of St. James Trade School and currently a member of the Brother James Court Advisory Council. We also need to recognize the great enthusiasm of the alumni and families of St. James Trade School and the families of our current Brother James Court residents who contributed monetary assistance, personal stories, photographs, and priceless memorabilia. All this energy and assistance has made my trips through the community archives and the acquiring of current materials that much more rewarding. Last, but not least, I wish to say thank you to the Franciscan Brothers of the Holy Cross for allowing this project to come forth.

The following individuals have selflessly contributed their time, knowledge, and in some cases memorabilia, or were valuable sources in the making of this book. We are profoundly grateful for their support:

Edward Veseling
Larry Motley
Georgia Wysocki
Dr. Robert L. "Larry" Larison
Albertina McCaffrey
John McCaffrey
Donald McCaffrey
Tony Bauer
Ray Lefferts
Mary Hartman Schmidt
The State Journal-Register
Pete Bono
Laura Rape
Jim Kiesow
Bill Prose
Charlotte Dormal
J. Robert Waters
Ron Wampler
Dawn Blissett
Susan Barrett

All images in this book, unless otherwise noted, are courtesy of the Franciscan Brothers archives.

INTRODUCTION

"The Spirit of Devotion for St. James Trade School Tradesmen and the Men of Brother James Court."

Years will pass and time moves on sometimes before we have a chance to appreciate the beauty that surrounds us on a day-to-day basis where God has planted us. For us, the Franciscan Brothers of the Holy Cross, these past years have been filled with beauty and many achievements that have made it possible for us to found and operate two wonderful apostolates in the Diocese of Springfield in Illinois.

This book is an attempt to look more closely at some of the beauty that has surrounded us these past 82 years when St. James Trade School began and closed, and these 35 years that saw the beginning and continuation of Brother James Court. In pictures and prose, you will get a glimpse of the people and achievements of the day-to-day life of the Franciscan Brothers of the Holy Cross that will elicit memories, we hope, and prayers for the future that will help all of us stand tall and appreciate these accomplishments.

Arriving here in 1928, a small group of Franciscan Brothers took one step at a time to establish their foundation as a religious community in Springfield, and begin their apostolic involvement, to be called St. James Trade School in honor of Br. James Wirth, the founder of their religious congregation. The brothers' lives would give those who would know them and those they would serve a taste for the providence of God, whose loyalty is ever-present and all-powerful.

In the past 35 years, Brother James Court has been the focus on which the Franciscan Brothers have concentrated their efforts to present their religious life and their apostolic witness to others. In previous times they did this through their training and care of those who attended the trade school. At Brother James Court they would continue to care for and train those developmentally challenged adult men who would benefit from their founder's charisma and ideal of service to "the young, the sick, and those in need."

Looking back at these years of success in the vineyard of the Lord hopefully will enhance the reader's appreciation of all that the good Lord has in store for those who love Him. Through economic uncertainty, language difficulties, misunderstood customs, joys and sorrows, these faith-filled followers of St. Francis have shown and continue to show to the American people that their works have benefitted many young men and their families by giving them "respectability, socialization, and a future" in the same spirit with which our founder Brother James began his work in 1862. This legacy from Brother James continues here at Brother James Court and enhances the lives of our men. The spirit is alive and well all these years later.

We invite you to read and enjoy this small book. May these pictures and the accompanying script give you cause to smile and time to reflect. Please remember the Franciscan Brothers of the Holy Cross in your prayers and pray, too, for their apostolic works.

As this project comes to an end, I find myself contemplating the wealth of information revealed. Before beginning this project, it would have been impossible to imagine how extensive the research, how detailed the writing, how in depth the copy work, or how intense the collaborating would be. I must admit that it had to become a labor of love or it would have been overwhelming.

My research brought to clearer light these facts about St. James Trade School: opened in 1930, closed in 1972, first graduating class in 1932 (one apprentice), largest graduating class in 1969 (29), last graduating class in 1972 (16). The sports teams' mascot was the Tradesmen, and the school colors were blue and gold. Our teams belonged to the Catholic High School Athletic Association, the Illinois High School Association, and the Macoupin-Sangamon-Morgan (MSM) Conference. Baseball was played from 1930 to 1971, football from 1934 to 1956, and basketball from 1941 to 1971.

For economic and other reasons, such as small enrollment, increasing costs, and fewer Franciscan Brothers available as instructors, the school had to cut costs where it could. Football was eliminated as the Brothers concluded that the school could no longer compete with neighboring schools in size, talent, or number of players. In some years, the football squad was composed of fewer than 18 boys. Another factor contributing to the decision to close the school in 1972 was the loss of contracts to supply milk, bread, and meat to local institutions.

This is the first history of our community written in a very long time and many of the histories we do have are translations from the original German publications that have come to us from Europe. Many sources, past and present, have become my heartfelt "companions on the journey" and have enhanced, by the grace of God, all these pages.

I will end with the Latin quote found earlier in this book: *Ut in omnibus glorificetur Deus*," which means, "That in all things God may be glorified." God bless you all!

In Jesus' name,

Brother Anthony Joseph, FFSC
Franciscan Brothers of the Holy Cross

One

The German Beginnings of the Franciscan Brothers of the Holy Cross

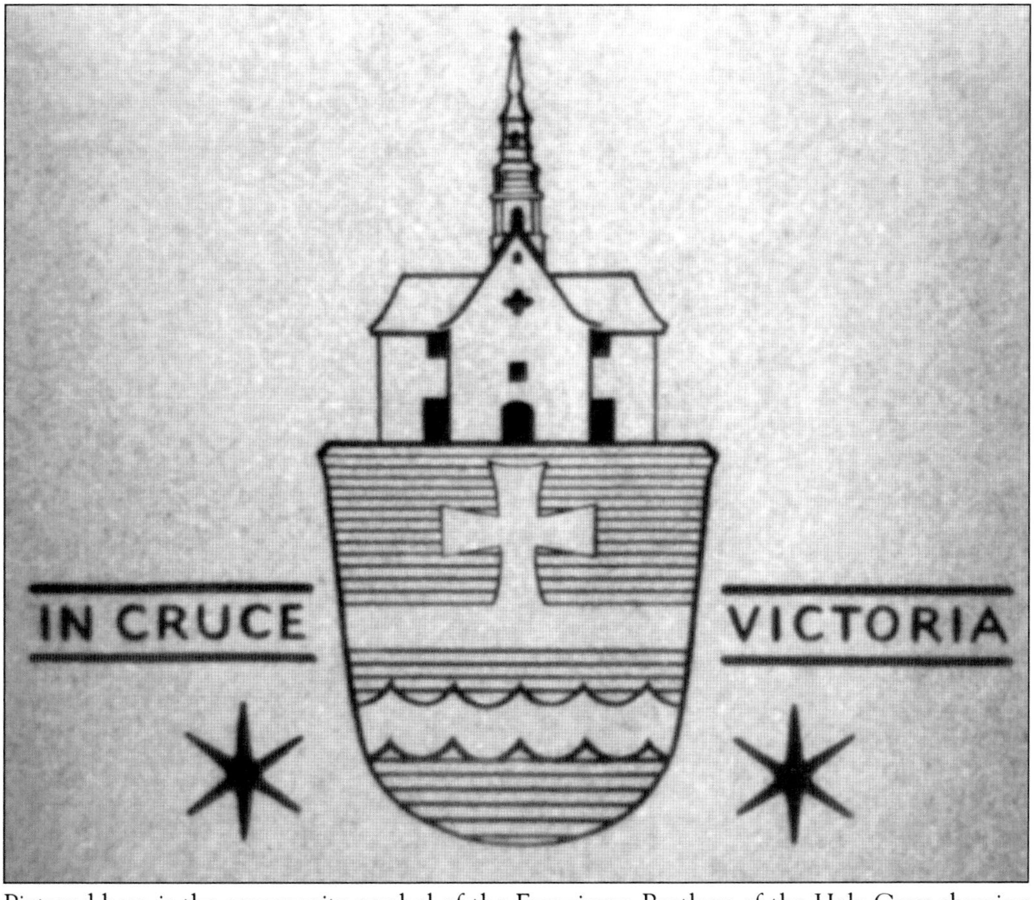

Pictured here is the community symbol of the Franciscan Brothers of the Holy Cross showing the Foundation Chapel and the community motto *In Cruce Victoria*, which means, "In the cross is victory."

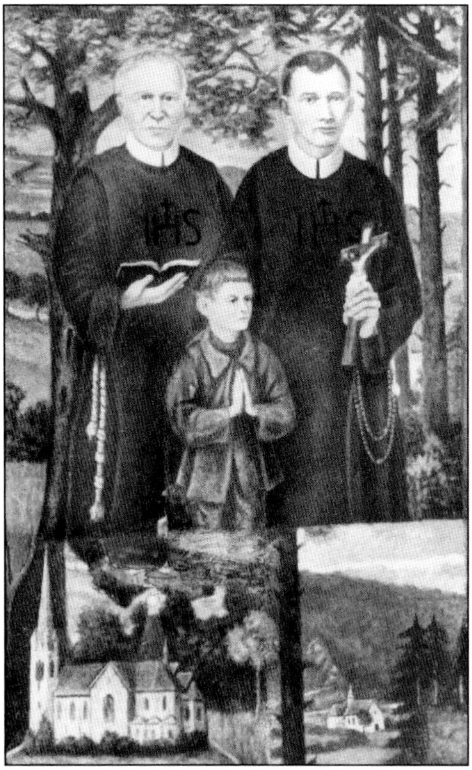

Pictured in this mural, from left to right, are Br. Anthony Weber, an unidentified orphan, and Br. James Wirth. The bottom portion shows the Motherhouse Church (left) and Chapel of the Cross (right), both located in the Wied River Valley in Hausen, Germany.

In the footsteps of St. Francis, the founders humbly began the community in the Chapel of the Cross. This chapel was built in 1694 to house the cross that had been in a shrine on the near mountainside. The cross was once lost due to the actions of a disturbed man. Its location was seen in a dream and found by searchers led by a bright light to the spot in the Wied River where it had been thrown. Because of this event, the cross was venerated as "miraculous." The chapel has been in possession of the Franciscan Brothers of the Holy Cross since 1925.

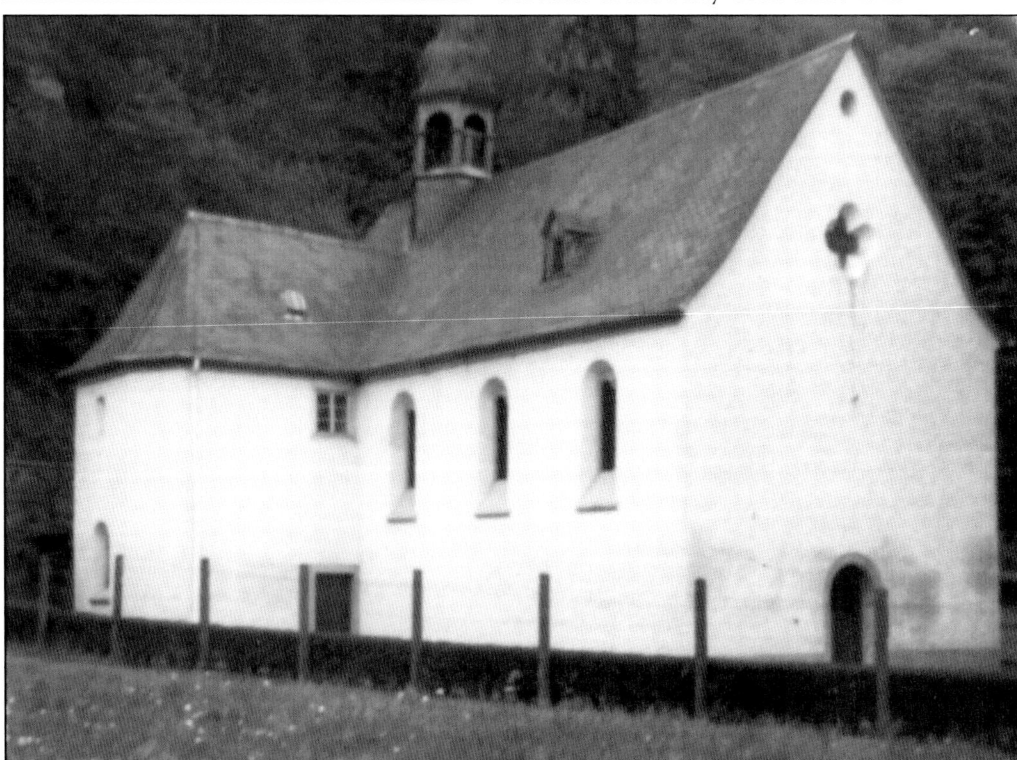

The congregation is still in possession of the cross and stewardship of the chapel is shared with the Franciscan Sisters, whose foundresses also inhabited the chapel before Brothers James and Anthony lived there. The Franciscan Brothers have an affection for and a filial relationship with this congregation of Franciscan Sisters due to the fact that the founders of both congregations had been Third Order Franciscan Tertiaries long before the community was founded. Seen at right is a section of the Motherhouse Church, and below is St. Josefhaus in Hausen, Germany.

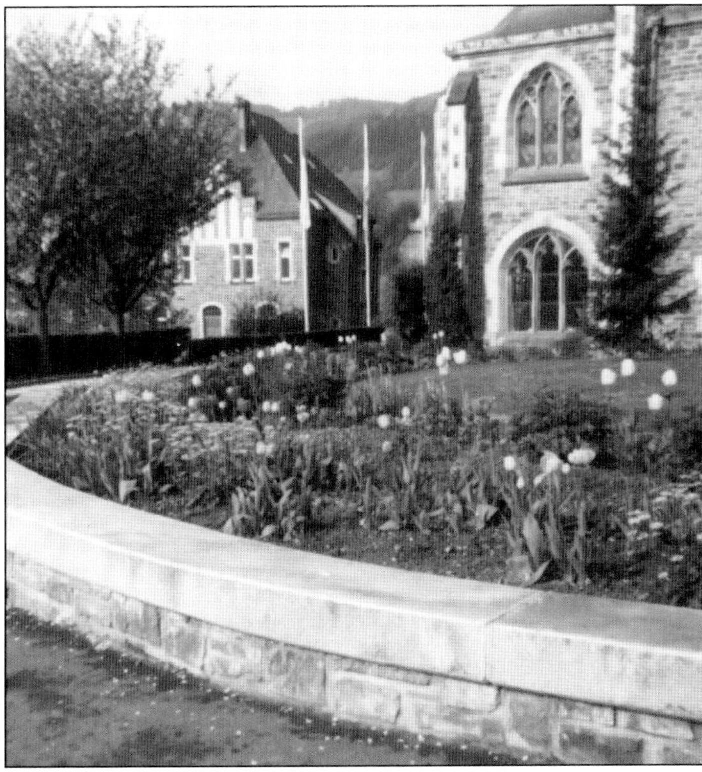

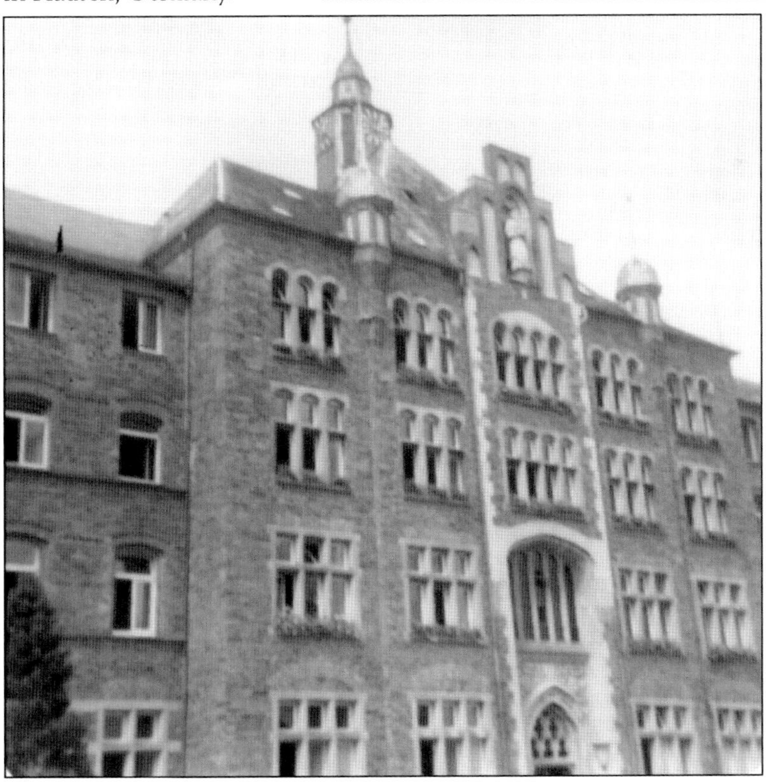

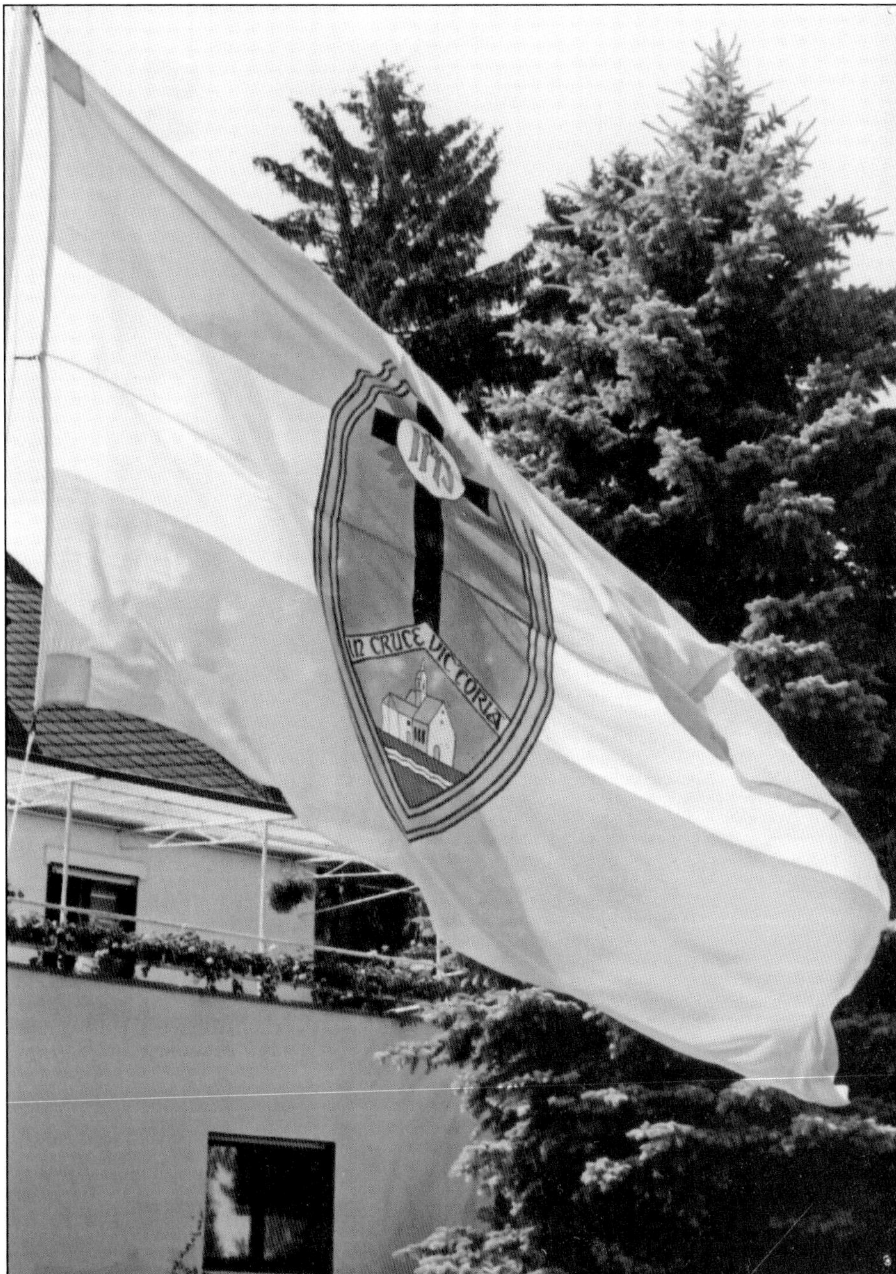

Each year on June 12, Foundation Day fondly recalls the day on which the founder and cofounder dedicated themselves to following Jesus in the spirit of St. Francis. The celebration of investiture and profession of vows took place in the Chapel of the Holy Cross on June 12, 1862. That day the chapel was decorated with green boughs, flowers, and wreaths. In more recent years, colorful flags decorate the Motherhouse Church, the yard of St. Josefhaus, and the 1962 monument (opposite page) to Brothers James and Anthony. Flags are a wonderful way for the brothers to celebrate and can be seen decorating all the little towns in the vicinity, even private homes, for all types of holidays and holy days. This flag shows the congregation's earliest community crest.

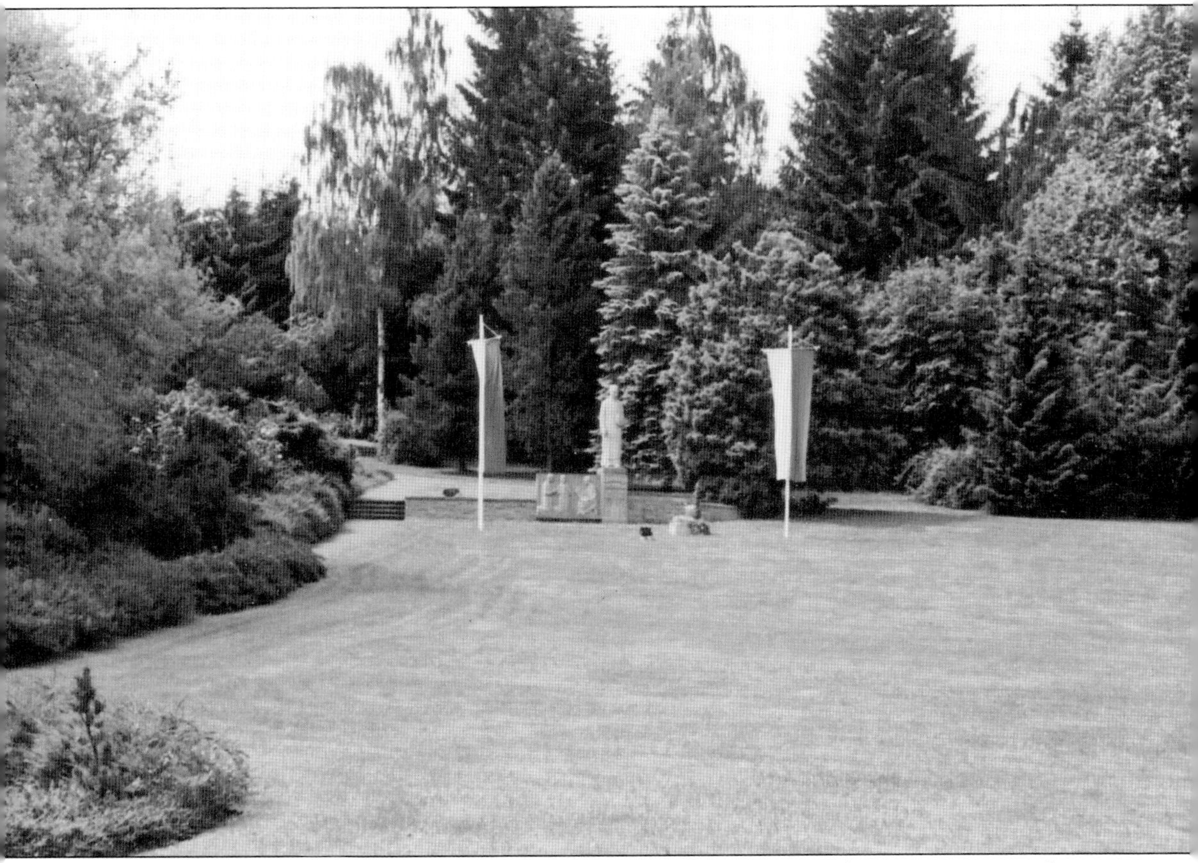

On Foundation Day, as depicted in the statue, both brothers knelt at the communion railing, where Father Gomm, the bishop's delegate, gave them the newly blessed religious habits and the new names they would have as religious men. At the communion of the mass, Father Gomm permitted the two brothers to profess the vows of voluntary poverty, perfect chastity, and perfect obedience for a period of five years. While the brothers had lived the Franciscan rule for lay people, they now followed the Rule of the Third Order Regulars for brothers and sisters in religious congregations, as approved by Pope Leo X in 1521. The statue, which stands in the park behind St. Josefhaus, was erected in 1962 to celebrate 100 years of community.

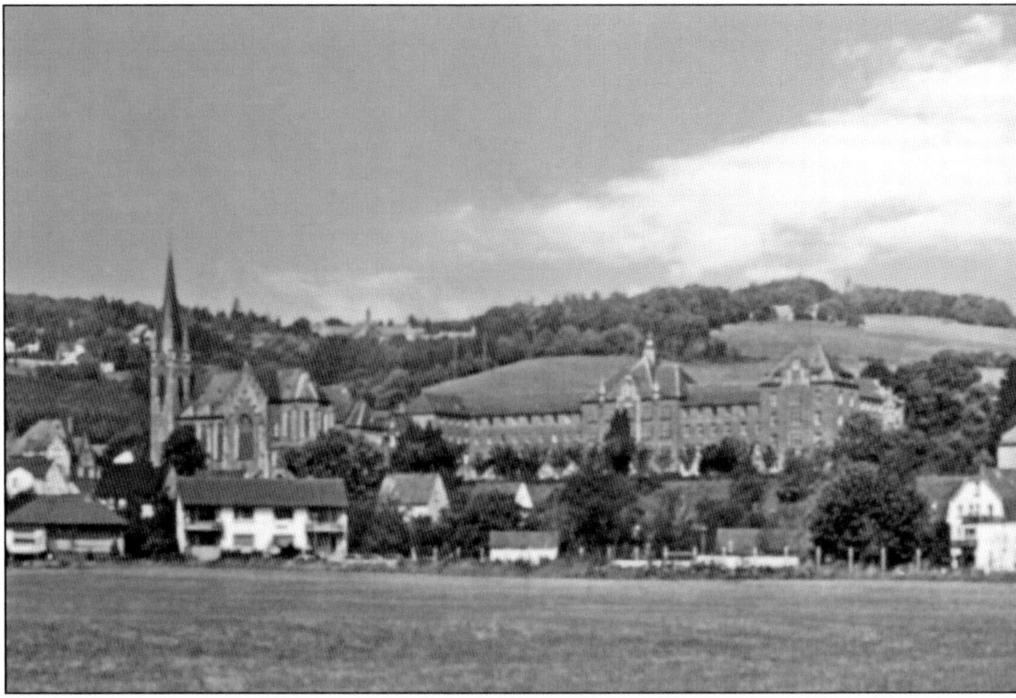

Nestled in the lusciously green, forested hills in the heart of Germany is the Motherhouse of the Franciscan Brothers of the Holy Cross. In the small town of Hausen, St. Josefhaus sits above the Wied River, where the Chapel of the Cross is a well-known shrine and place of prayer.

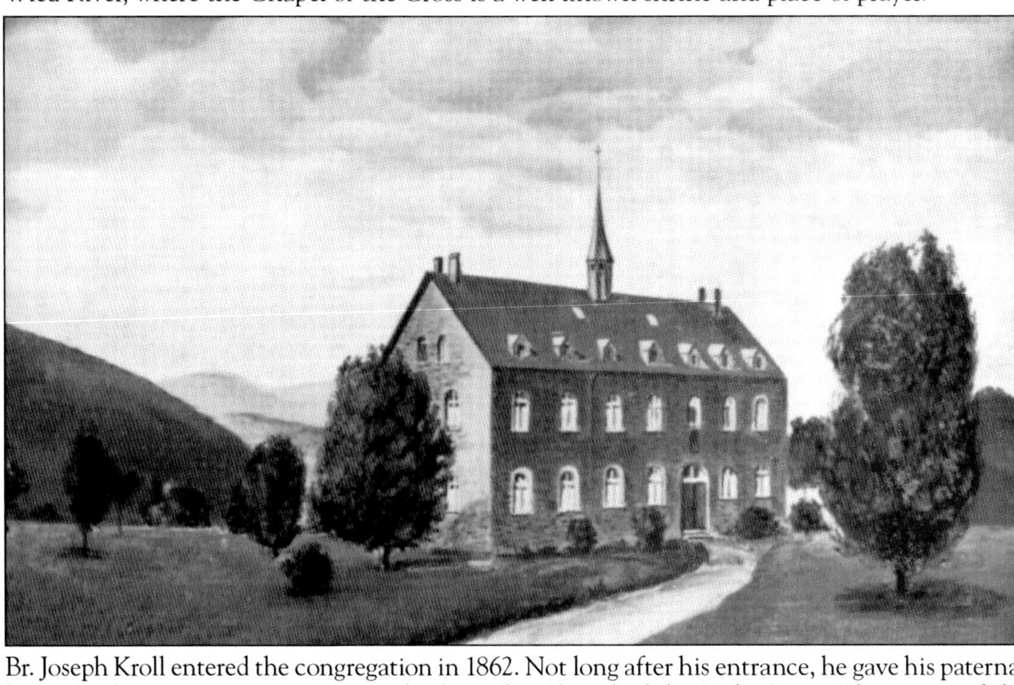

Br. Joseph Kroll entered the congregation in 1862. Not long after his entrance, he gave his paternal home to the community. It was not far from the Chapel of the Holy Cross. The rooms of the chapel continued to be used for sleeping and a simple building was constructed near the Kroll house. A chapel in the main house was the beginning of the present Motherhouse.

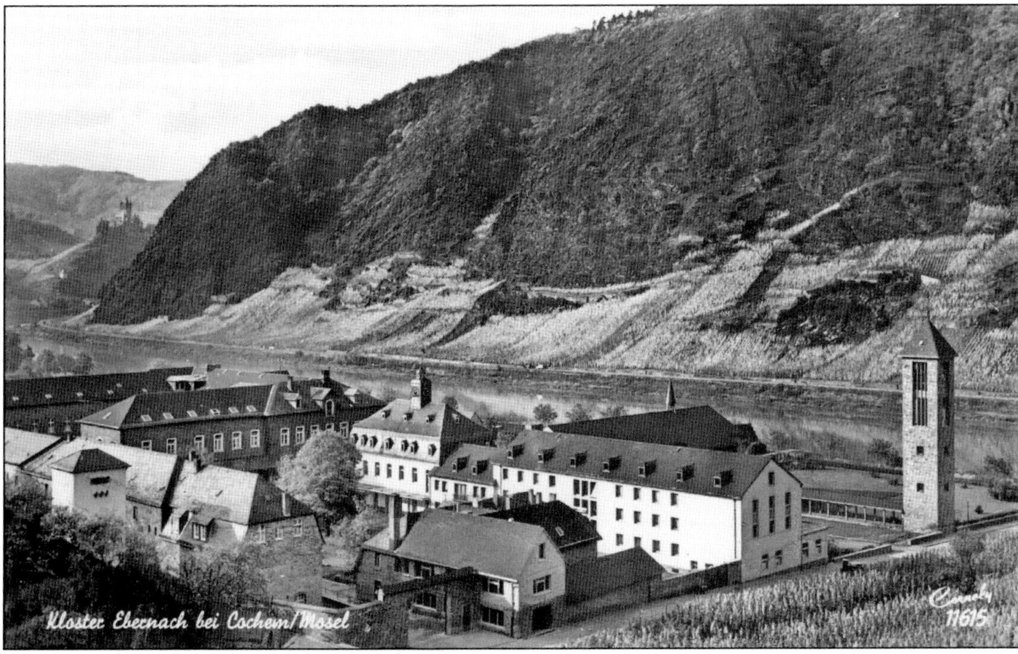

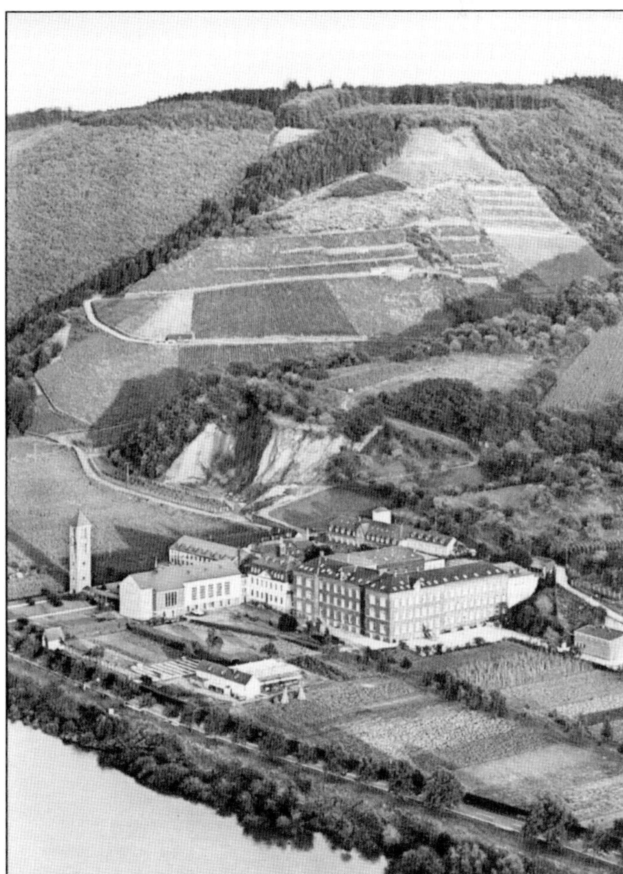

At the Chapel of the Cross, Brother James taught the cobbler trade to some of the orphans who also lived there, and Brother Anthony taught some of them to be tailors. Shortly after the beginning of the congregation, however, the brothers were no longer able to teach the trades. In 1870, the government of Germany instituted the laws of the Kulturkampf (culture struggle), wherein teaching, especially religious teaching, was outlawed for religious orders, but nursing and custodial care were still allowed. The residential home for the developmentally disabled, called Ebernach, pictured above and below, was founded in 1887 and remains to this day in the town of Cochem, Germany. This work for the poorest of the poor flourished, and according to the 1924 community calendar, 38 brothers were stationed at Ebernach.

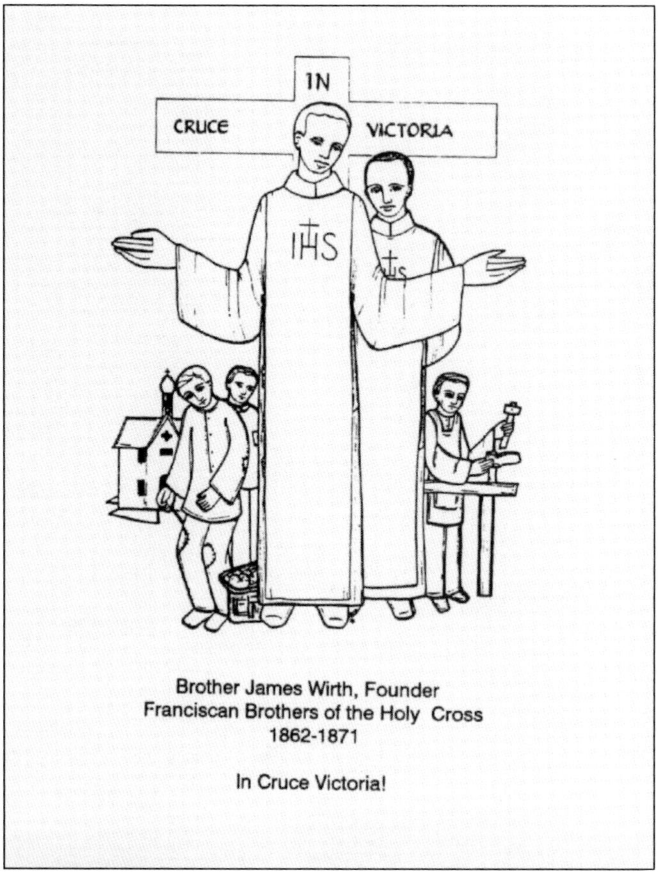

This holy card shows Br. James Wirth and orphans learning the trades from the Franciscan Brothers of the Holy Cross.

During the community's growth years before World War II, from 1920 to 1939, both the bishops and superiors predicted a rich future. This gave the bishops the courage to suggest new works for the brothers, and the brothers—like Brother Felix, standing third from right in this photograph—the courage to respond to those requests.

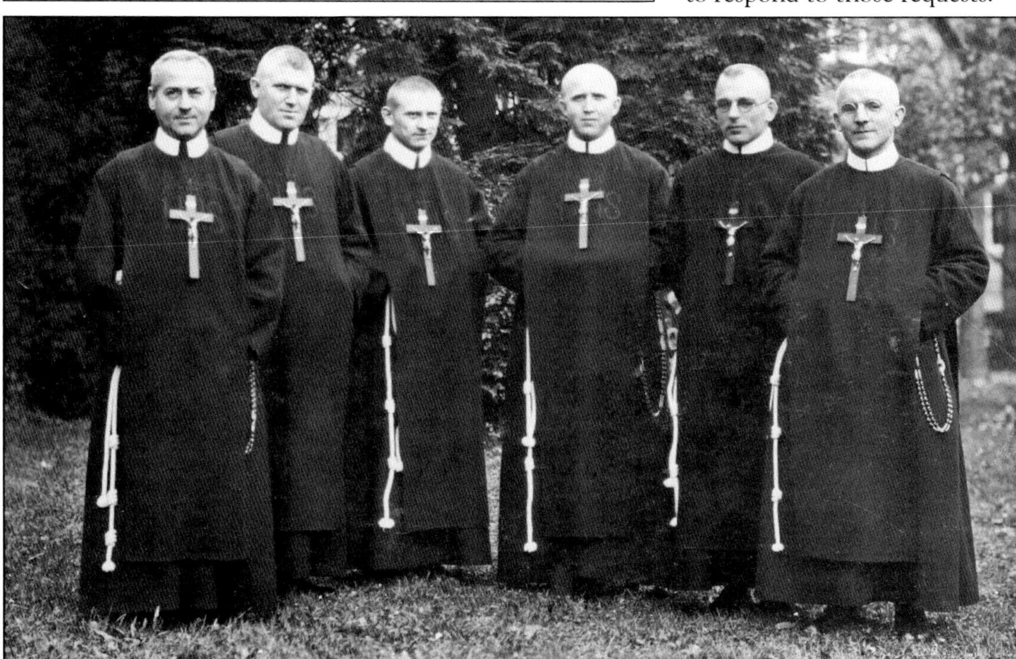

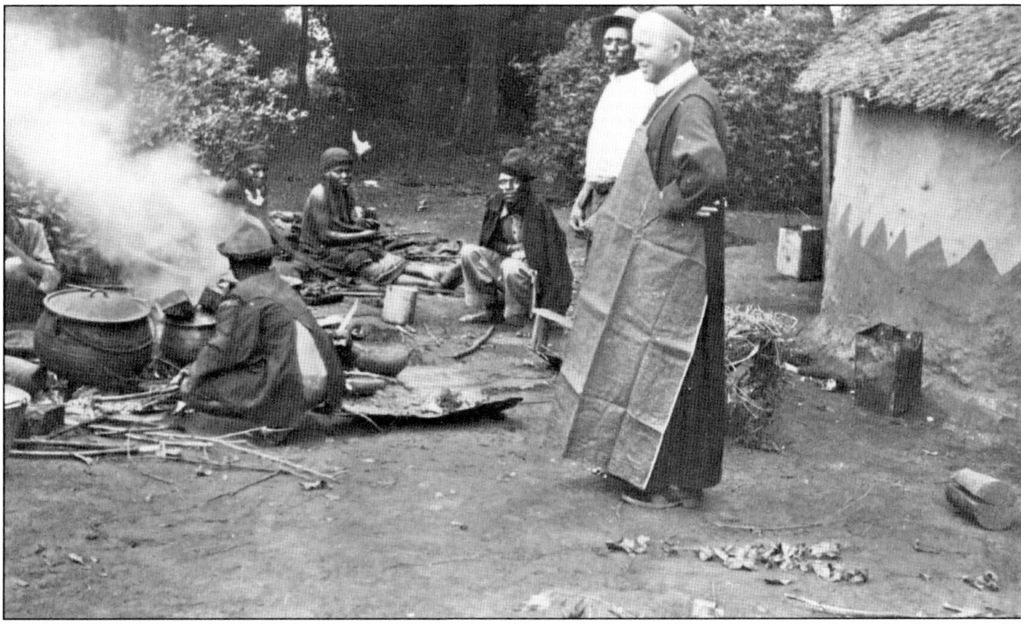

One of the most courageous efforts was to go to Africa to start a congregation of native men. This photograph shows Brother Felix hard at work in Africa, Christmas 1936. Called the Brothers of St. Joseph, that new diocesan congregation still serves the church in Africa today.

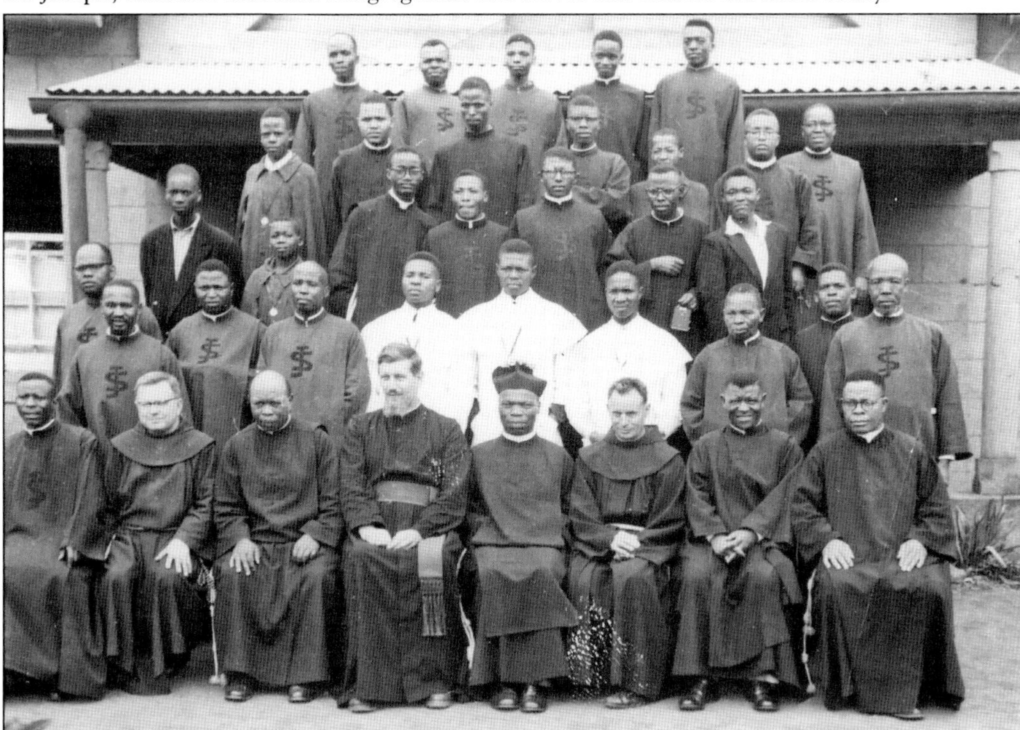

The last two German brothers were added to the Springfield community from Africa in 1948. Brothers Felix and Nicodemus joined that year and did not leave after three years as they were told to do—they are buried here.

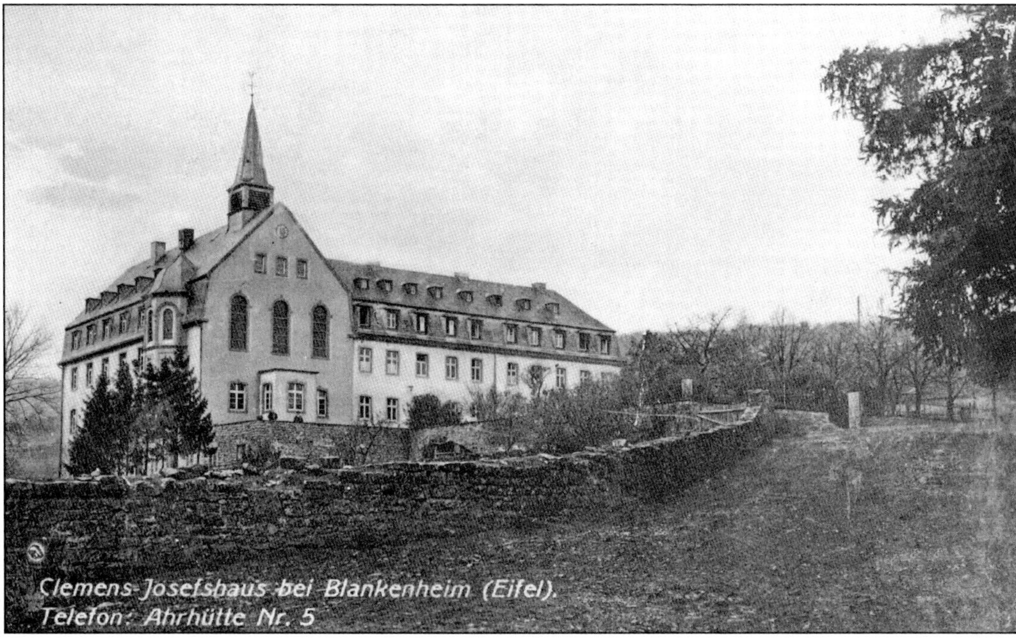

The 1938 community calendar does not name the brothers stationed at each house—like those pictured in these old postcards—but does have addresses for 27 houses. There were 15 in Germany, 3 in Italy, 2 in Switzerland, 1 in Ireland, 2 in Africa, 1 in Palestine, 1 in Holland, and 2 in the United States. There are 346 names on the calendar listing brothers' name days (saints' anniversaries), celebrated like birthdays in religious communities.

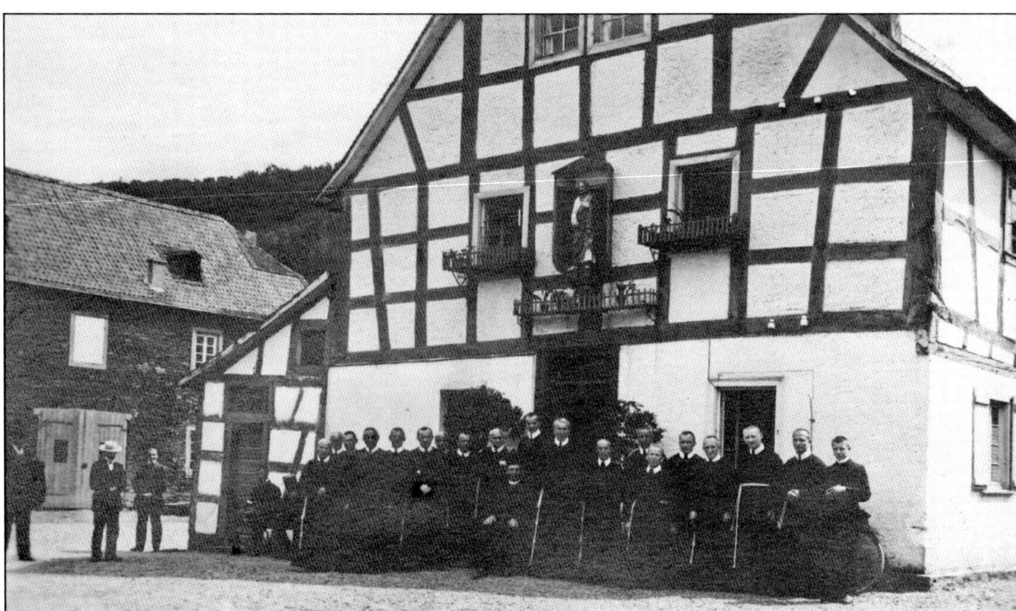

Other opportunities for expansion came to the community from Rome. From 1926 to 1975, the community had between one and three houses in Rome. During the years 1926 to 1933, the brothers were chosen to be the domestic staff to run the household of Pope Pius XI, who is pictured here.

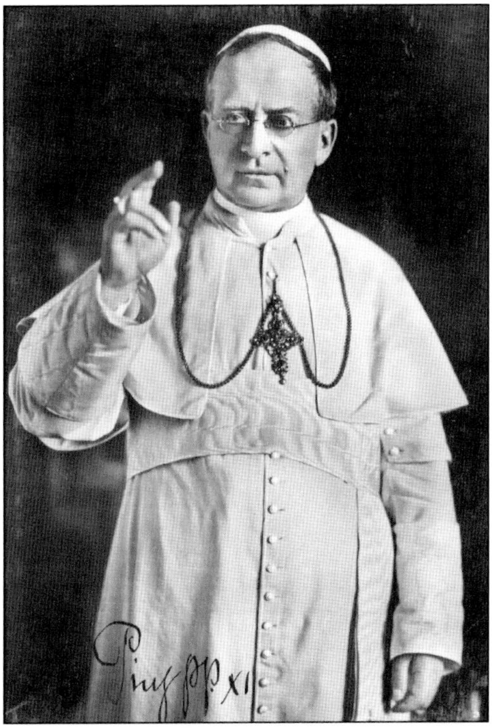

Here is a picture of Pope Pius XI's vesture, preserved to this day at the St. James archives in Springfield. The brothers managed the Pope's household needs, and one of the brothers stationed there was even charged with tasting the food the Pope was to eat to eliminate the possibility of food poisoning or attempt on his life. This brother later served the community by being superior general for many years.

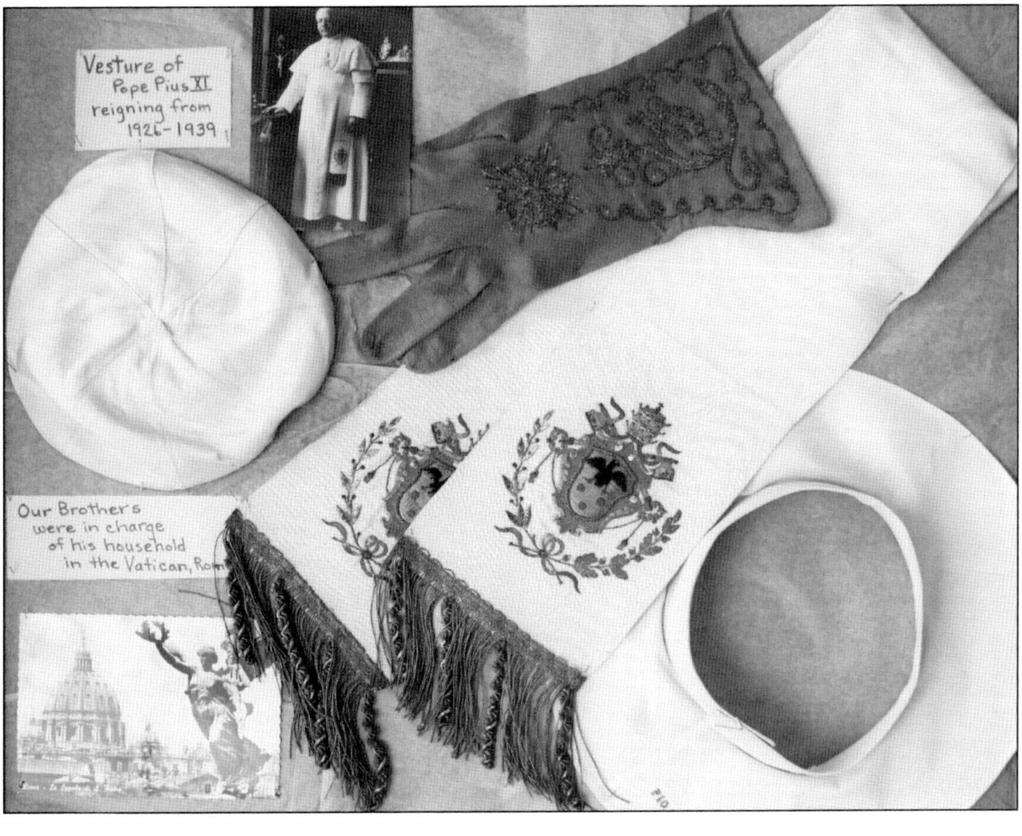

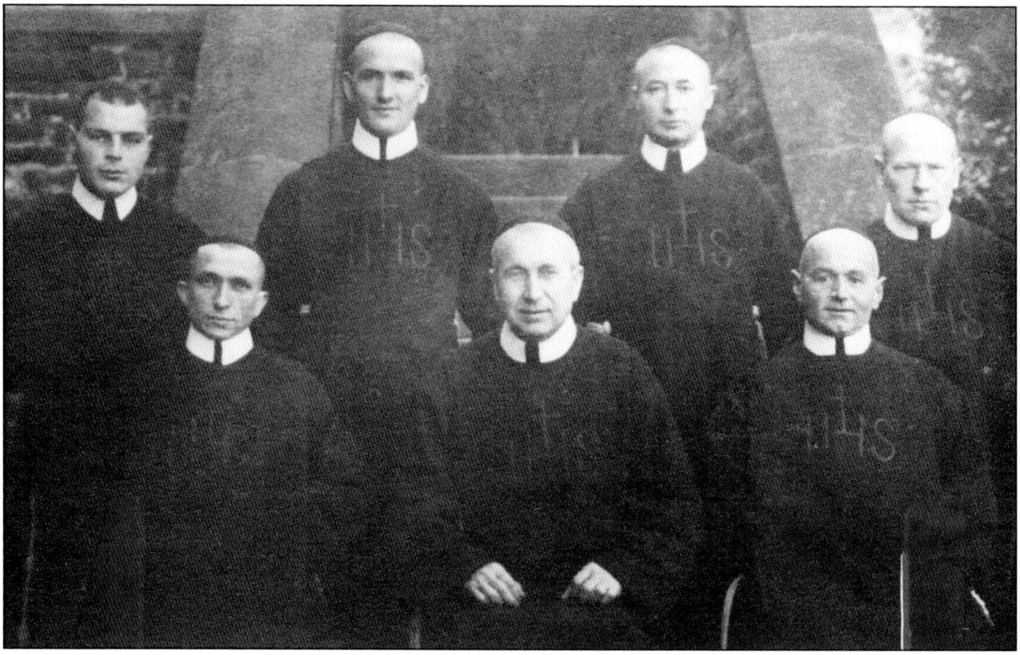

In 1924, the Franciscan Brothers from Hausen, Germany, were invited by the Archdiocese of New Orleans to staff an orphanage. Pictured here, from left to right, are (first row) Brothers Placidus, Camillus (superior general), and Hildolph; (second row) Brothers Fabian, Justus, Wiho, and Marcellinus. Brother Camillus was not one of the six sent but chose those who would go and accompanied them on their journey. Five of these original six later moved to Springfield to begin St. James Trade School—only Brother Marcellinus would return to Germany.

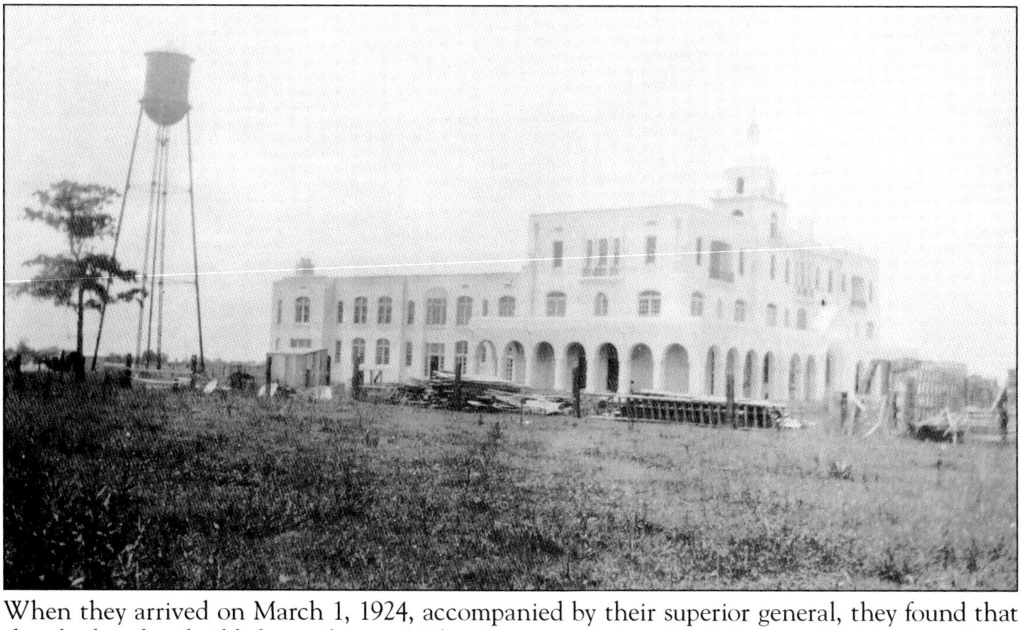

When they arrived on March 1, 1924, accompanied by their superior general, they found that they had to first build the orphanage. The six were missioned to Marrero, Louisiana, and the buildings were ready by September 16, 1924. This institution was called Hope Haven, and it still serves the archdiocese as Hope Haven-Madonna House.

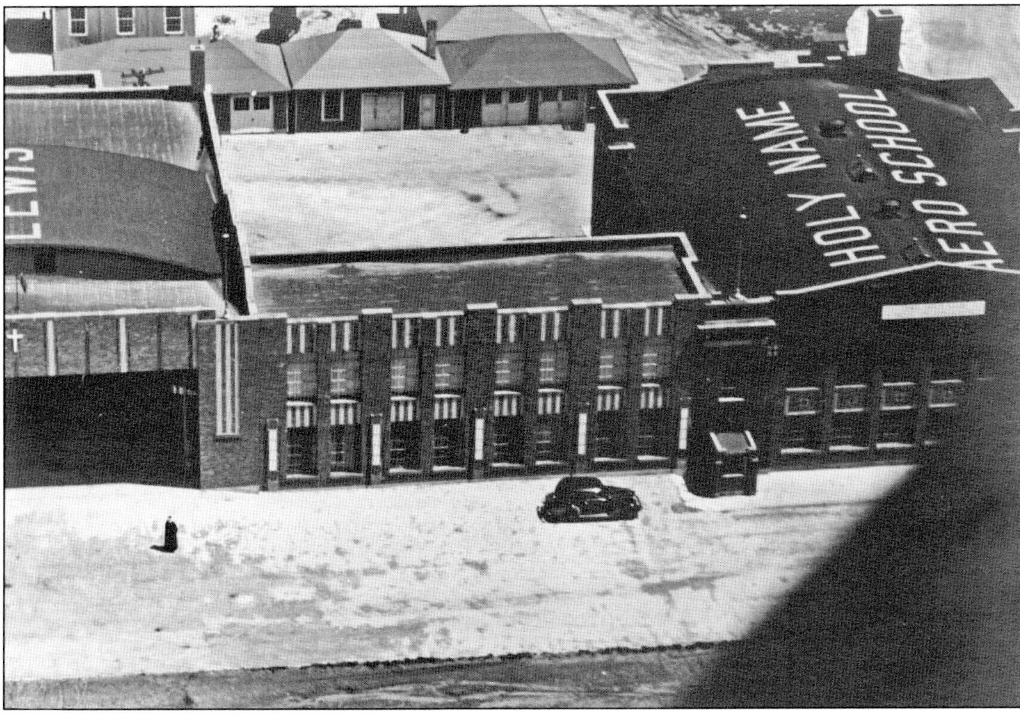

In 1931, the brothers from Springfield took on the foundation of Holy Name Technical Institute in Lockport, Illinois, again as builders. This was an alternative educational possibility for teenage boys, which the Archdiocese of Chicago saw as a need in their educational programs. Aeronautics was taught there, and the brothers also took on raising guide dogs. The community was there until 1938, when these brothers returned to Springfield as talk of war became stronger.

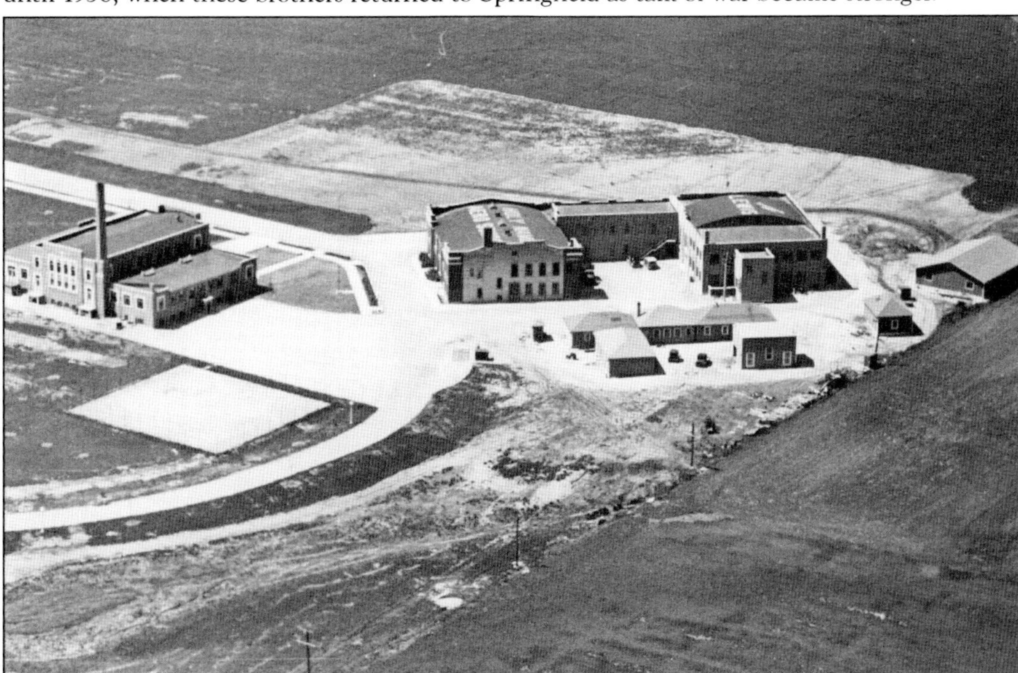

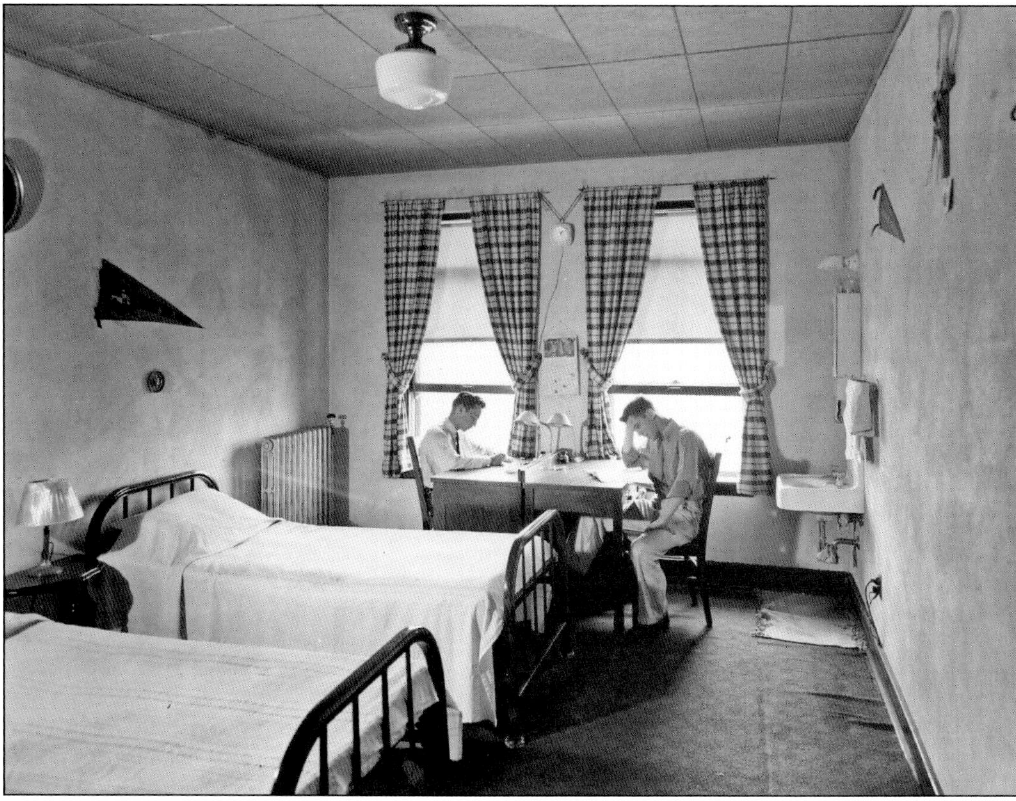

From humble beginnings in 1931, Holy Name Technical Institute would grow into the educational institution known today as Lewis University, a Lasallian school in Romeoville, Illinois. In 2003, Brother Hildolph was recognized as one of the four principal founders of the university. When there, the brothers were administrators, librarians, teachers, farm workers, and disciplinarians. Brother Hildolph was the first superior of the community of eight brothers assigned to Lewis.

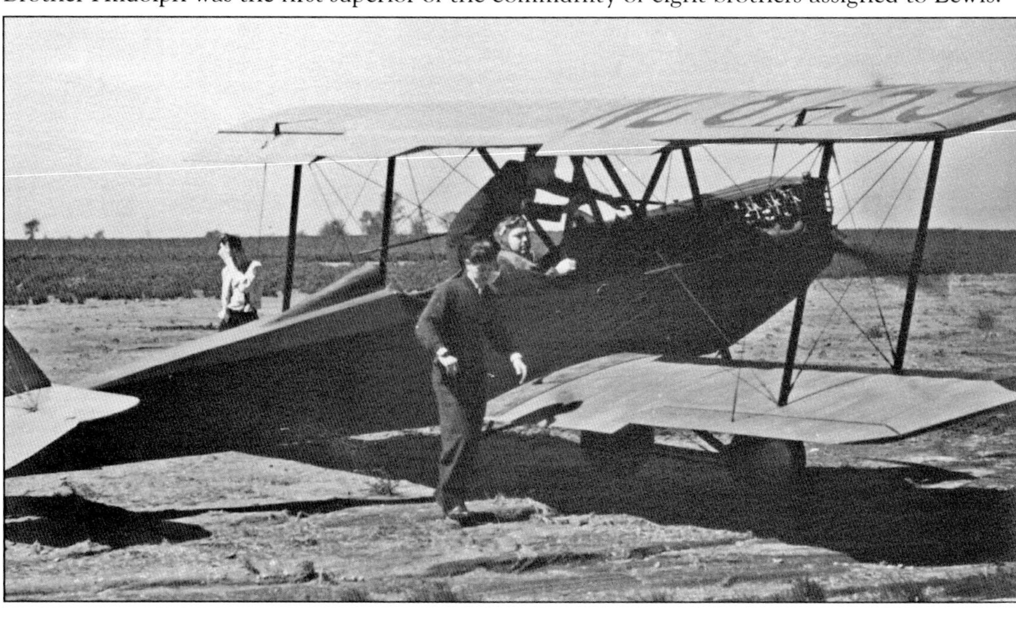

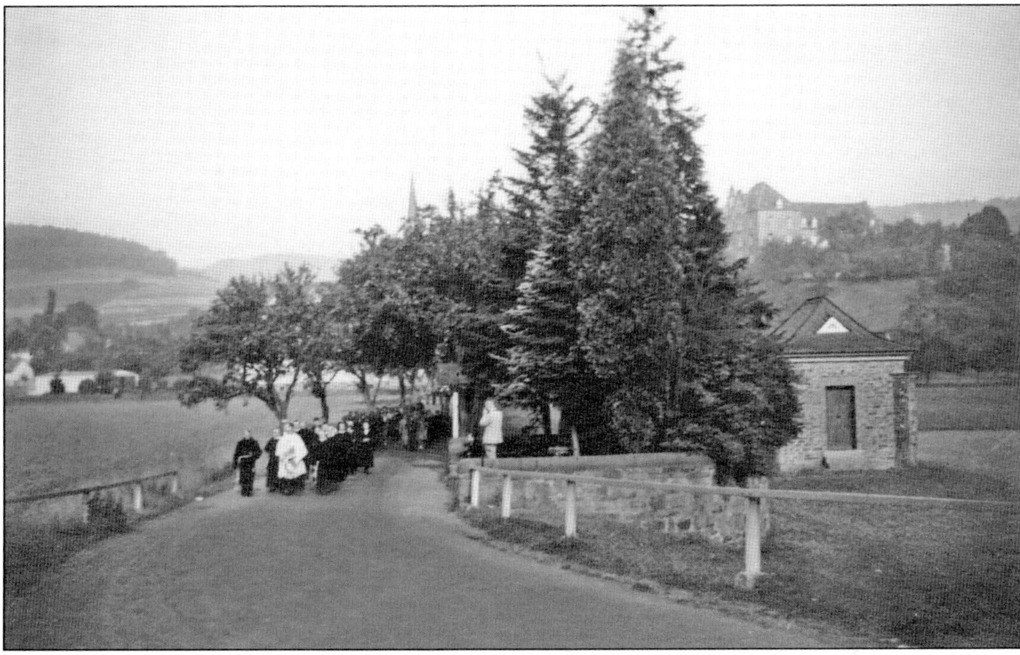

In 1936, persecution of the congregation led to the expulsion of the brothers from the Motherhouse in Germany. The elderly were allowed to seek shelter with the Franciscan Sisters on the hill.

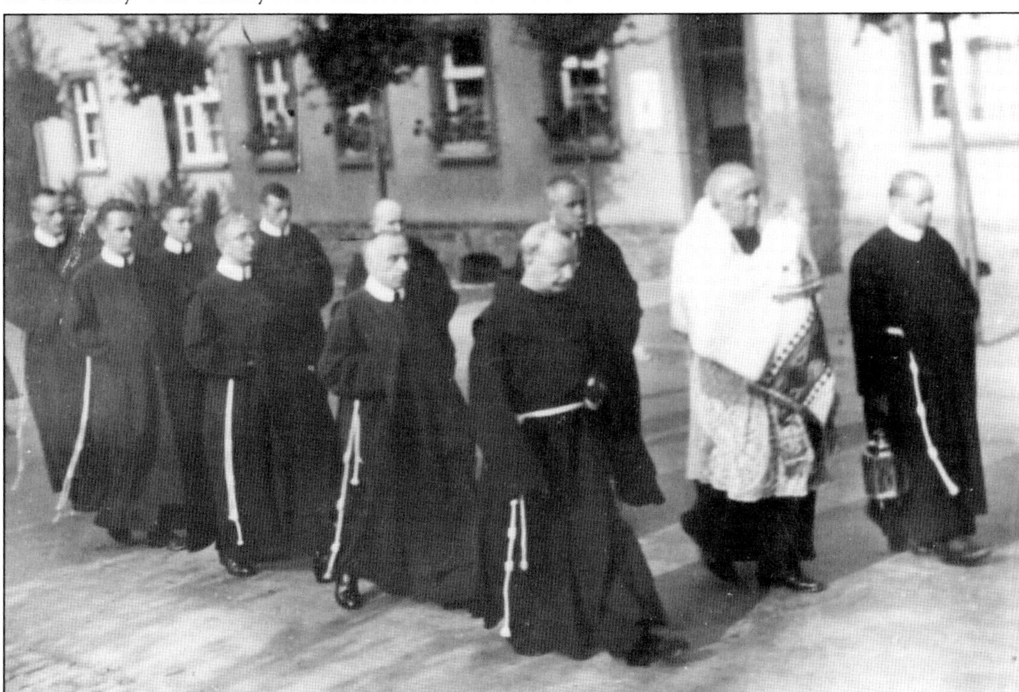

The Blessed Sacrament was taken in procession to the parish church. It is said that Hitler thought he could harm the Pope in Rome by hurting a papal community. The brothers were not able to return to the Motherhouse until 1946, at which time they had to pay the German government to have it returned to their possession.

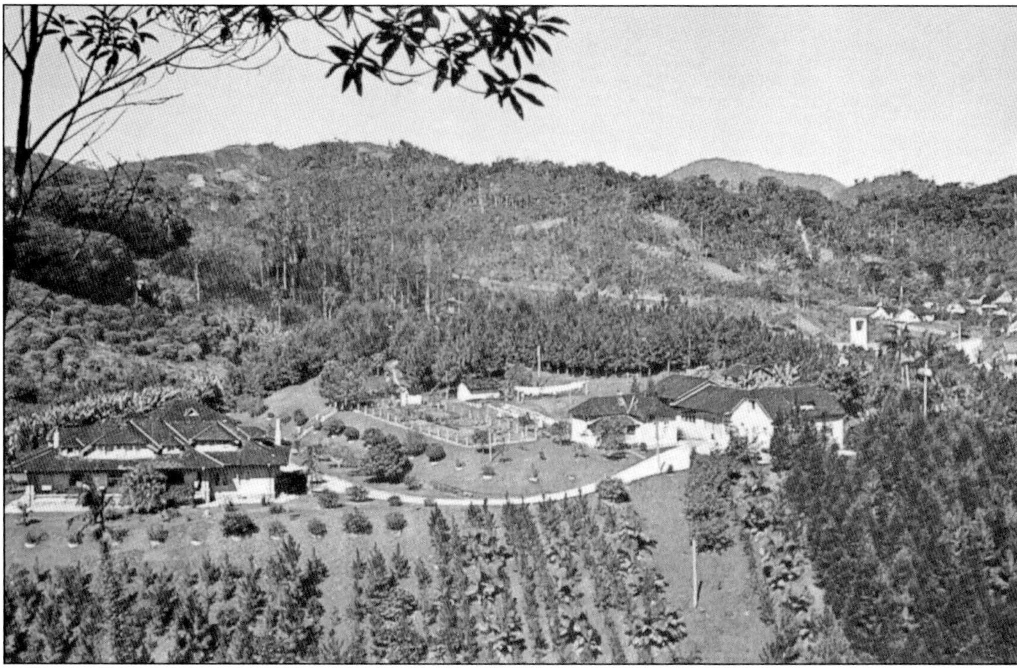

Another important outreach for the community came in 1963 when the brothers began a new foundation in Blumenau, Brazil. There the Franciscan Brothers of the Holy Cross continued their health care endeavors by providing physical therapy to a largely German population. Two American brothers were also sent there in 1965 to build up the religious community. They stayed on for one-and-a-half years, and the mission closed in 1988.

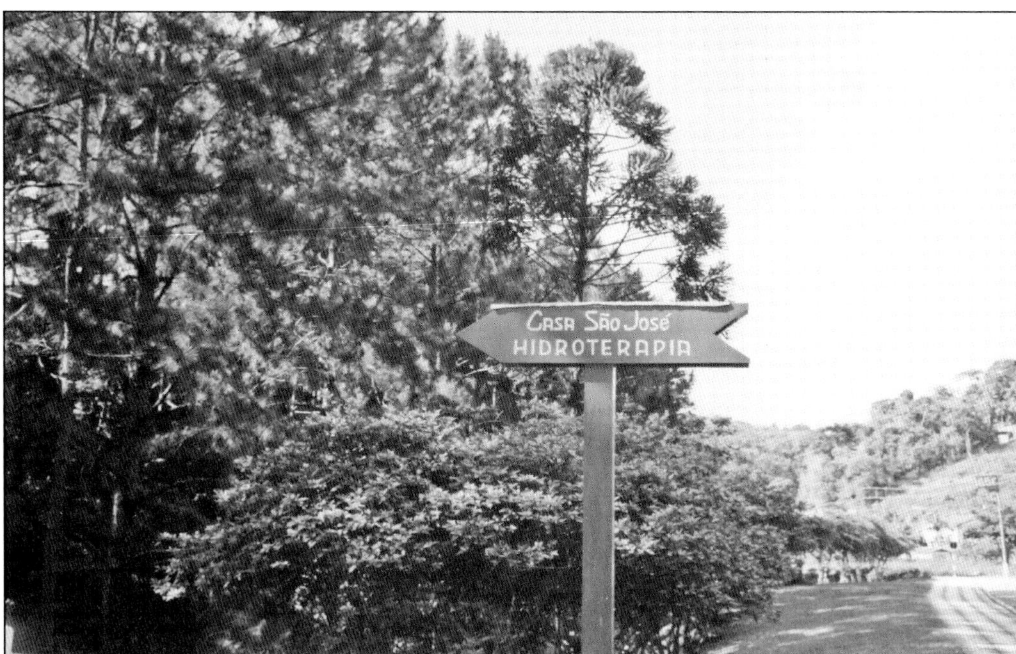

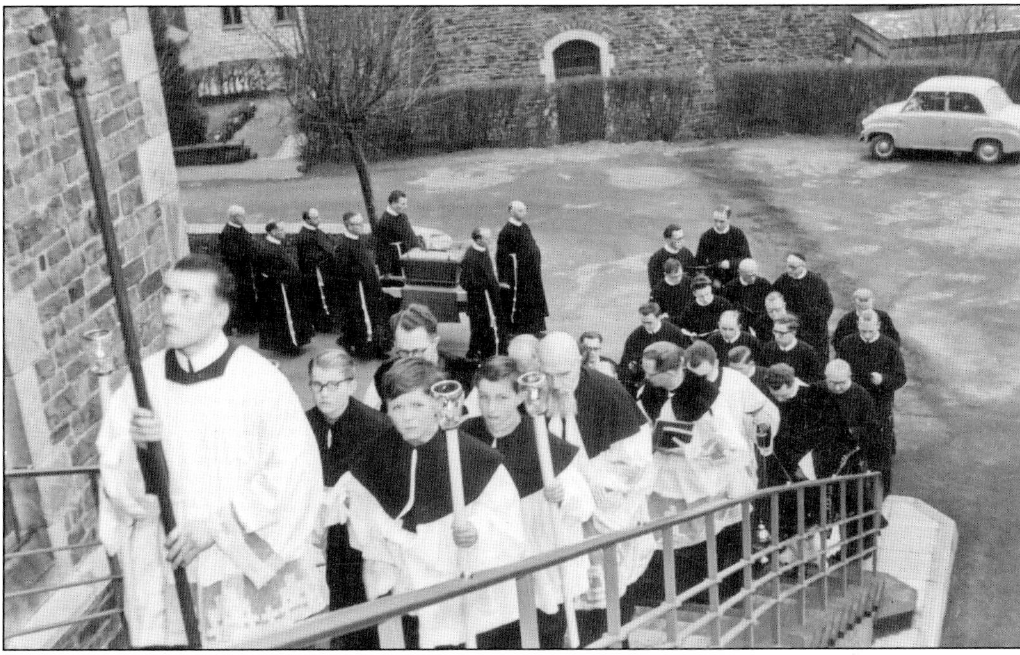

Brother James died at the age of 40 on March 28, 1871, nine years after founding the congregation. He was elected first superior general in 1869, and the community numbered 37 brothers at the time of his death. In 1957, the mortal remains of Brother James, pictured here, were moved from their resting place in the cemetery crypt to the recently made shrine in the church.

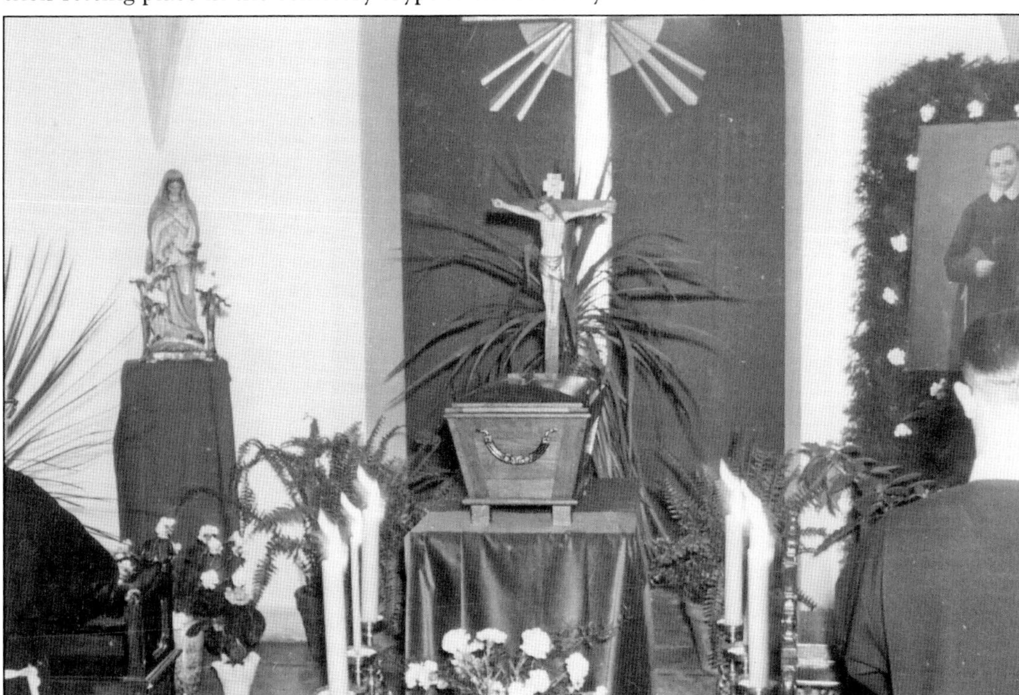

A beautiful shrine was created in the back of the Motherhouse church, which made devotional visits more convenient for community members and visitors.

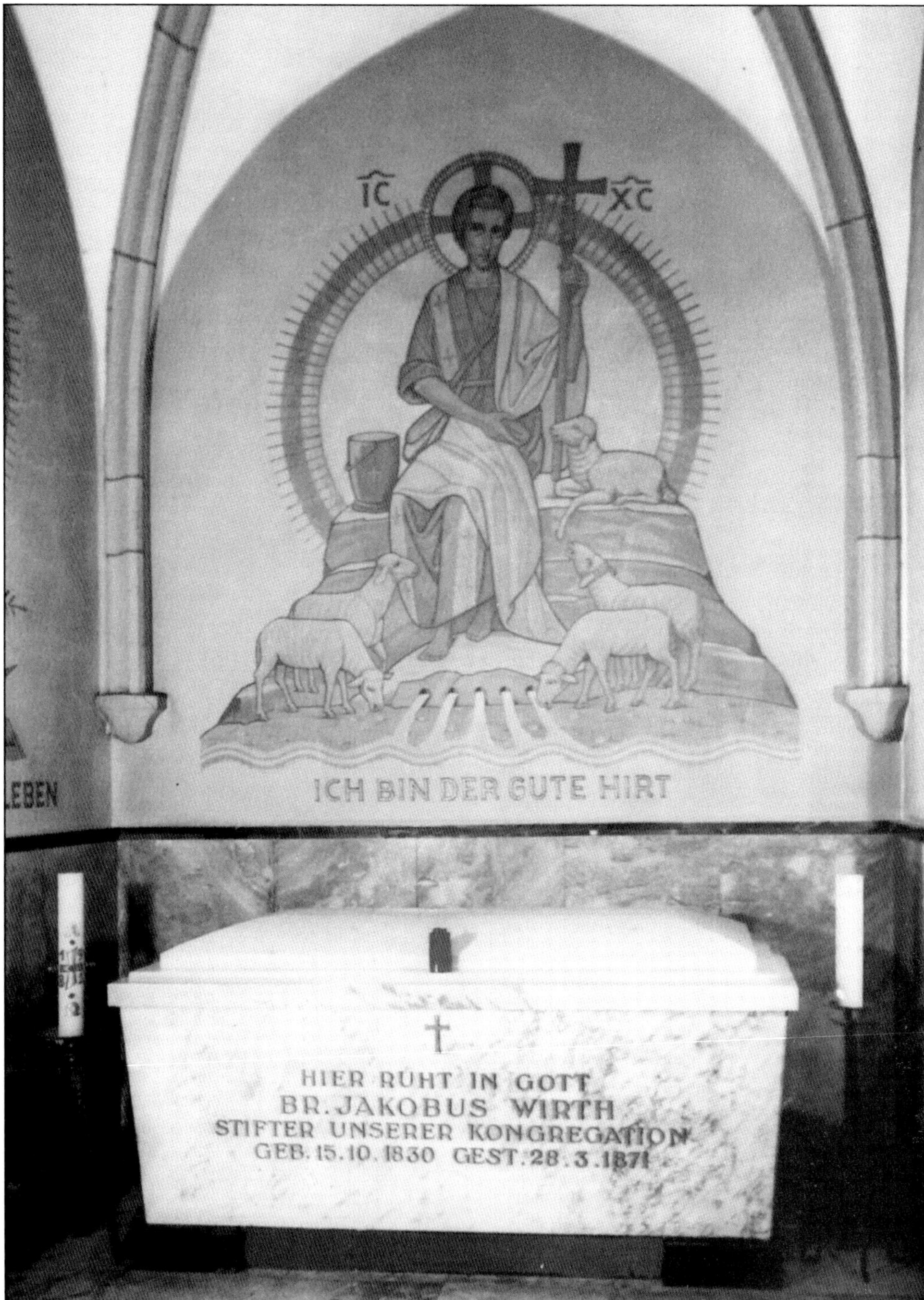

Though these remains have turned to dust except for a few bones, they are a treasure to those who feel a strength that comes from such holy relics. The guest book in the shrine shows that visitors from near and far recognized the holiness of this place. One story has surfaced that the remains of Brother Anthony, who died in 1910, have also been put with those of his companion. This story remains unverified, but it would seem a fitting way to honor Brother Anthony, who is considered the congregation's cofounder.

Two

American Beginnings, St. James Trade School

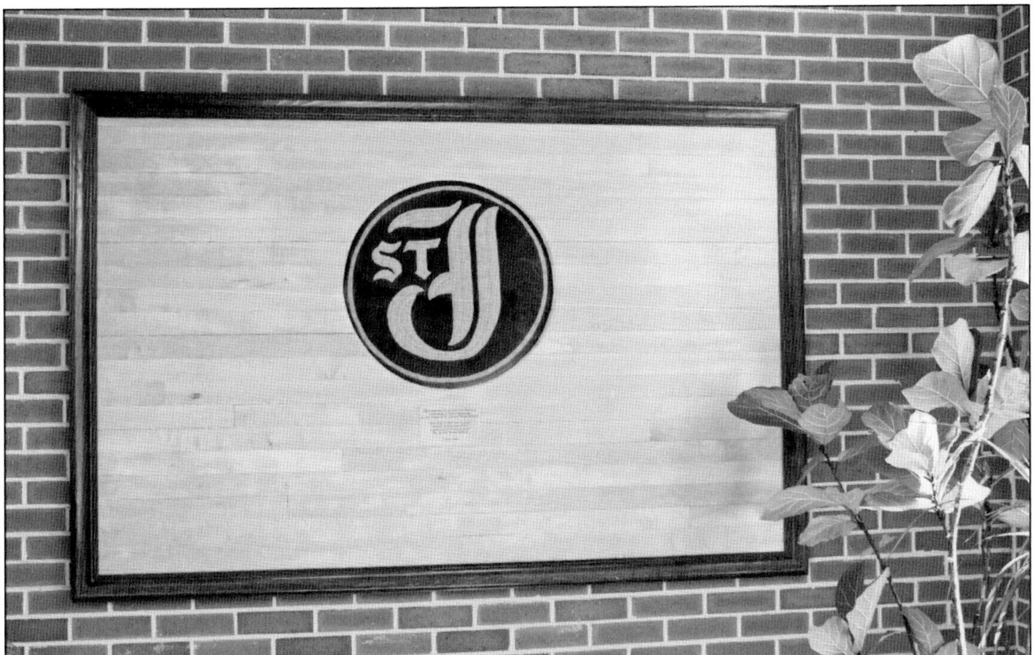

The trade school symbol seen here is from a portion of the original floor of the gymnasium. The school song was "Good Old St. James," as sung to the tune of the University of Notre Dame fight song: "Come on and cheer for good old St. James/ The boys of the trade school playing their games/ Fighting hard and winning too/ Blocking and passing and running through/ They are the boys with will to win/ They will stick through thick and thin/ So they'll fight life's battles long/ With courage and bravery." (Courtesy of Bill Prose.)

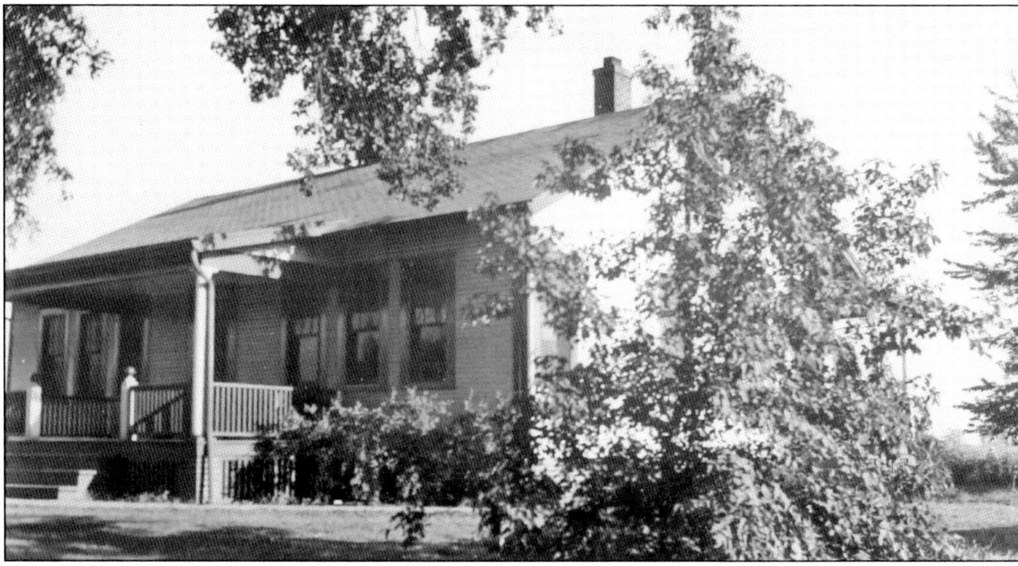

In January 1928, the first four brothers arrived to take over the farm and dairy from the hospital sisters. The brothers lived at St. John's Sanitarium while building a home for themselves on the farm property. These brothers assumed control of the farm and dairy immediately and fulfilled their religious obligations with the sisters. They were joined by six other brothers from New Orleans in June. A chronicler who was able to identify many earlier photographs said: "In these two houses on the road to the sanitarium, the brothers found their first shelter." They were used until a suitable structure could be built to house all 10 of the brothers. It became the first St. James Monastery and is still in use today by the community.

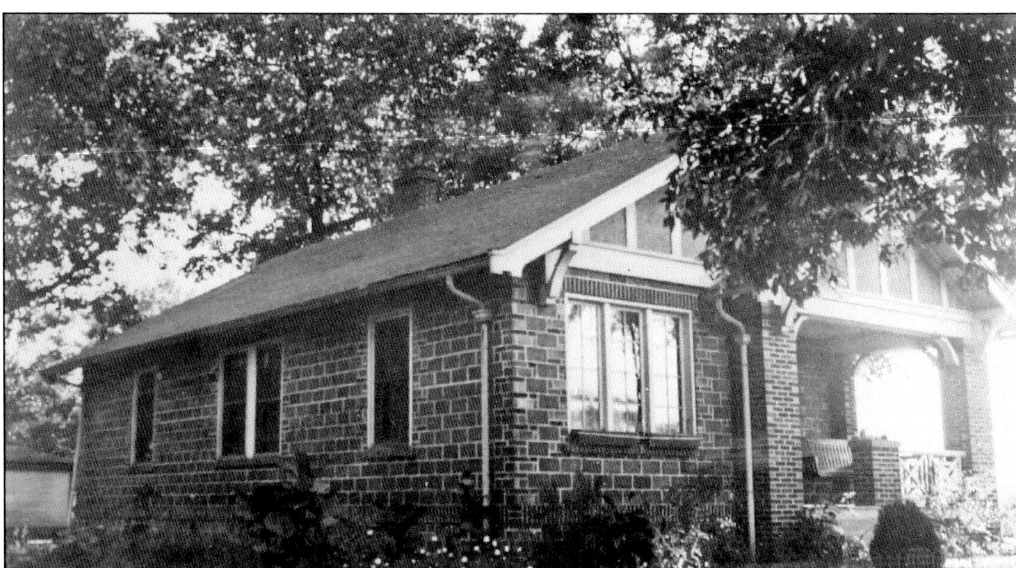

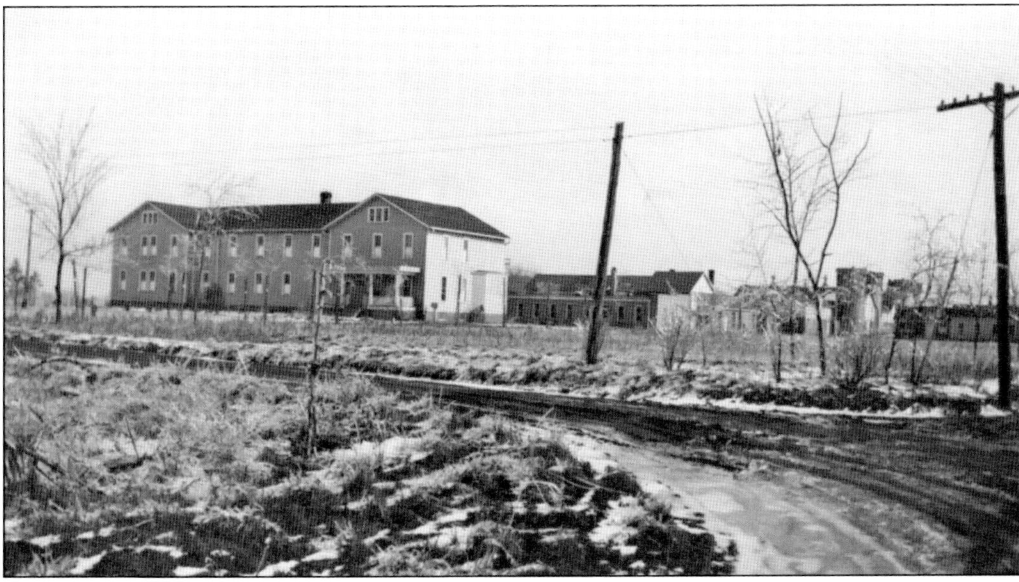

The old adage that big things happen one step at a time certainly applies to the beginnings of what came to be known as St. James Trade School. After the completion of the monastery (above), the brothers began living their common life as religious men. During this time, more buildings were constructed to enhance the farm that would later be the resource for those who would become boarders two years later. The first students came in 1930 from the Alton Children's Home as a group of 10 teenagers. Some of the public thought St. James was a reform school, but the brothers emphasized that it was established to help orphaned and disadvantaged boys get a chance at a better life. The aerial photograph below is of the completed farm buildings and most of the other buildings of the trade school.

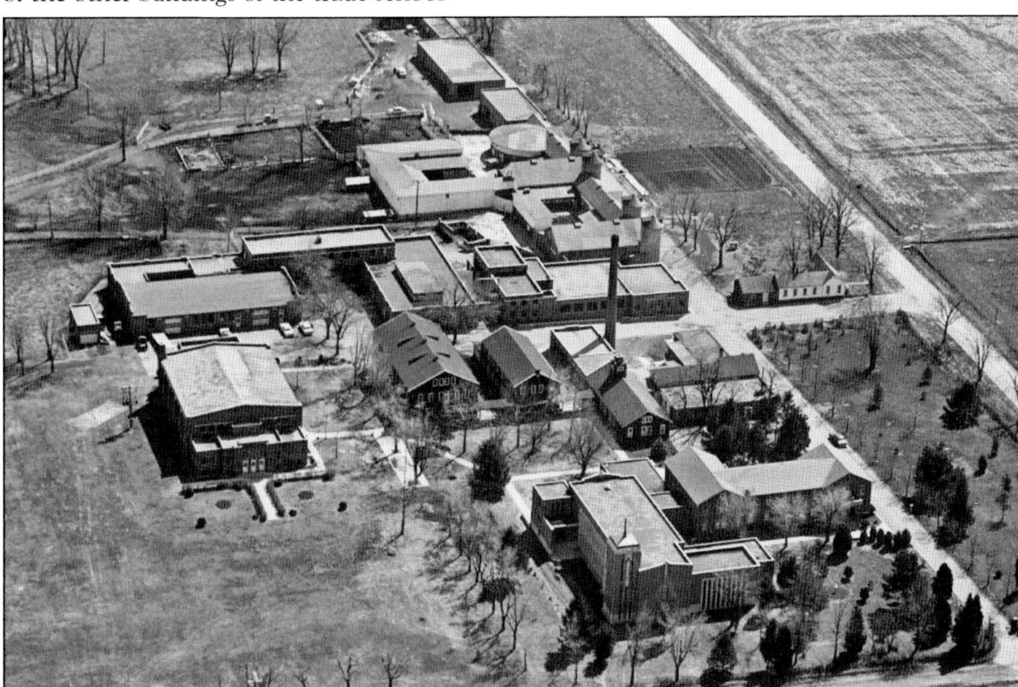

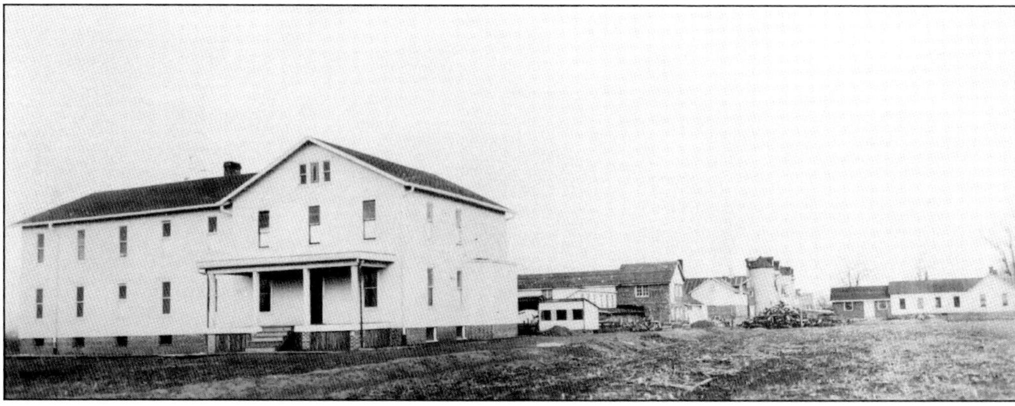

The first monastery was built with wood donated by the Springfield bishop, who was dismantling two houses to create a playground for the cathedral school. Barns and farm buildings in this picture were part of the landscape until 2008. The main barn was still used by the farmer who rented from the brothers until that time. (He still rents the fields for his cattle and crops.)

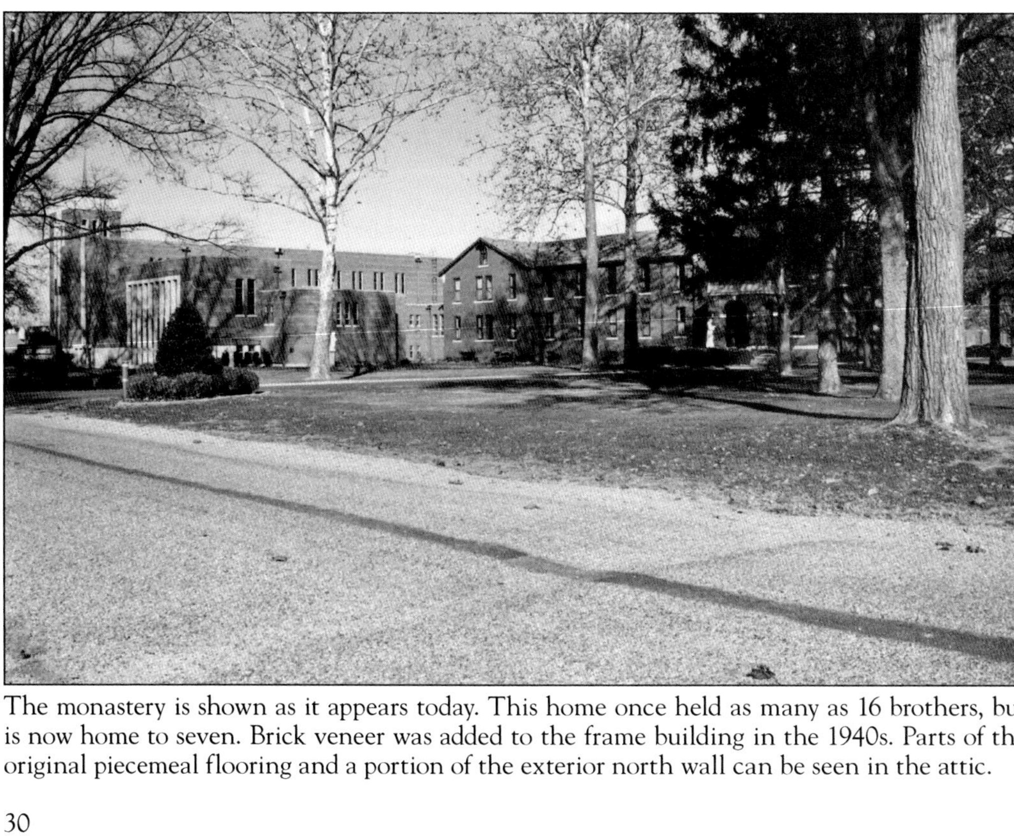

The monastery is shown as it appears today. This home once held as many as 16 brothers, but is now home to seven. Brick veneer was added to the frame building in the 1940s. Parts of the original piecemeal flooring and a portion of the exterior north wall can be seen in the attic.

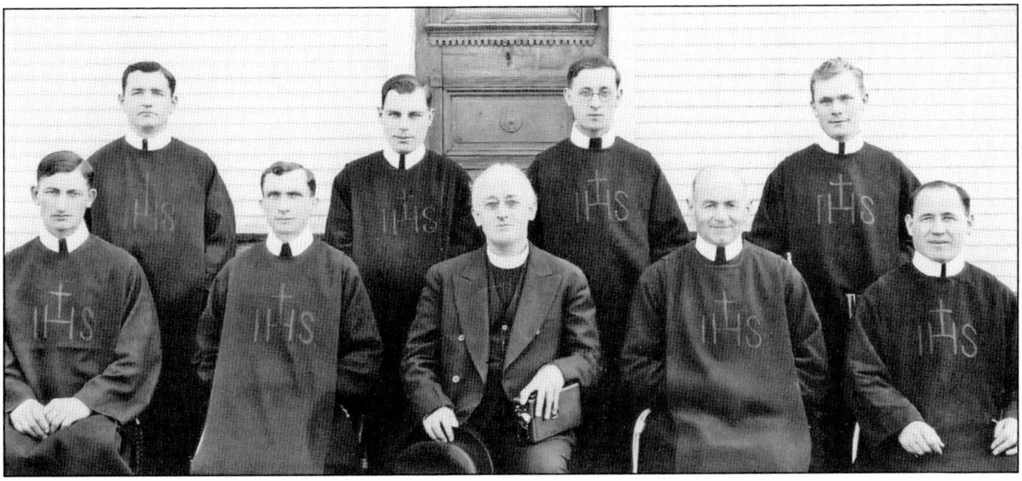

In the above photograph, most of the original community members are shown with a priest friend from St. John's Sanitarium, which was next door to the Franciscan Sisters Motherhouse. By June 1928, the brothers had moved north from Hope Haven Orphanage in the Archdiocese of New Orleans to start the Springfield community. From left to right are (first row) Brothers Theodosius, Placidus, Father Philip, Hidolph, and Egbert; (second row) Brothers Wigbert, Fabian, Aegidius, and Louis. The picture below shows the full community gathered in front of their new home with the superior general, Brother Pancratius, who visited during his term of office, 1929–1934.

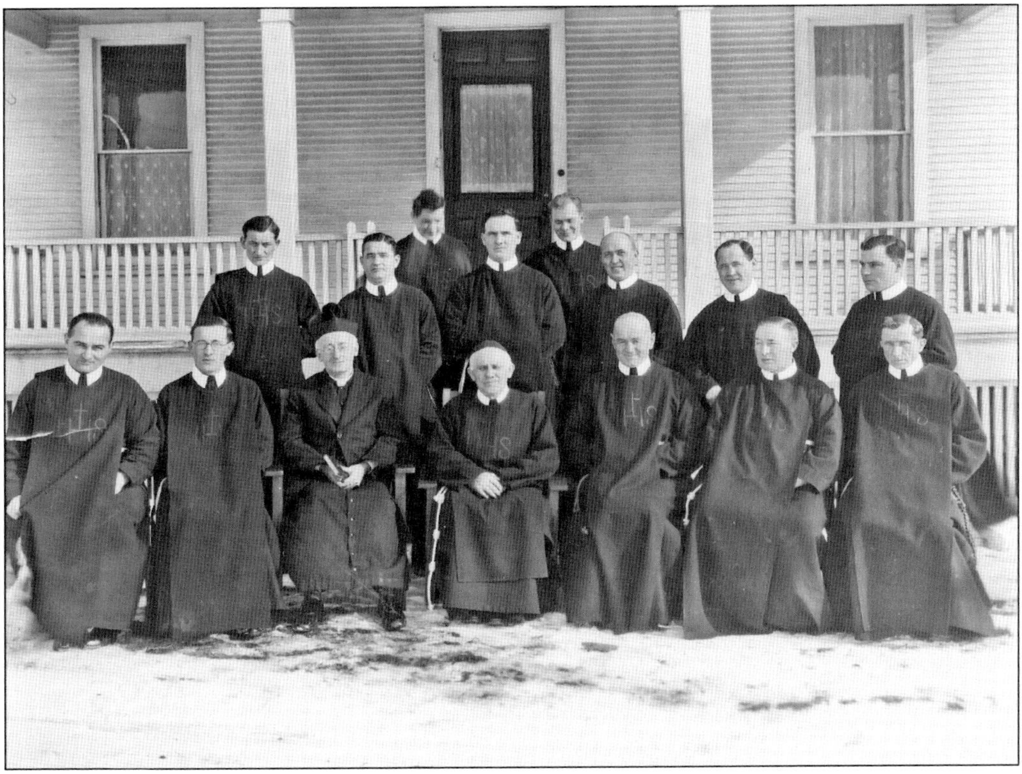

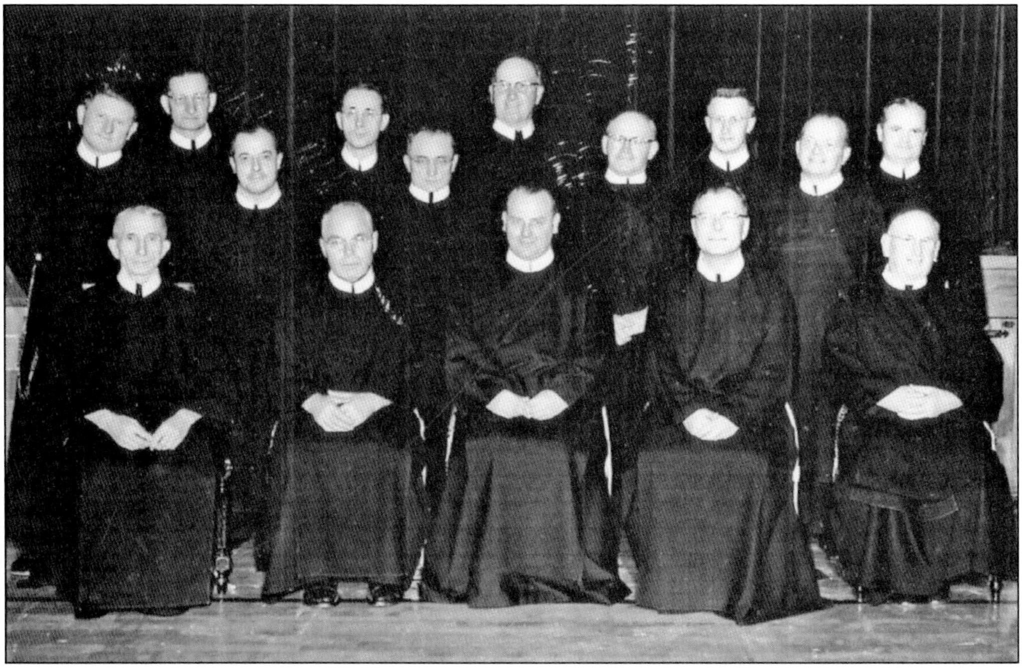

The brother community is pictured with their superior general, Brother Berardus, during an official visit in the late 1950s. The brothers are listed with their trades, from left to right: (first row) Rembert, carpenter; Michael, teacher; Berardus, superior general; Fabian, mechanic; and Placidus, butcher; (second row) Nicetius, carpenter; Demetrius, shoemaker; Viktorinus, tailor; Sergius, farm manager; Justus, farmer; Onuphrius, baker; Aegidius, registrar; Nestor, tailor; Theodosius, painter; and Elpidius, bricklayer.

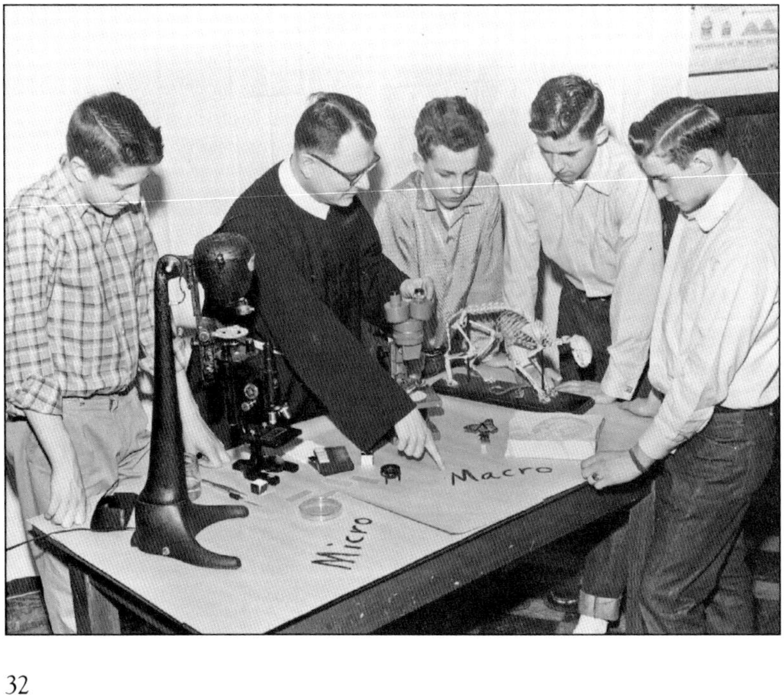

Using his aptitude for the sciences and the nurse's training he received prior to becoming a brother, Brother Michael taught in the academic portion of the trade school and gave the pupils a good foundation for future college studies.

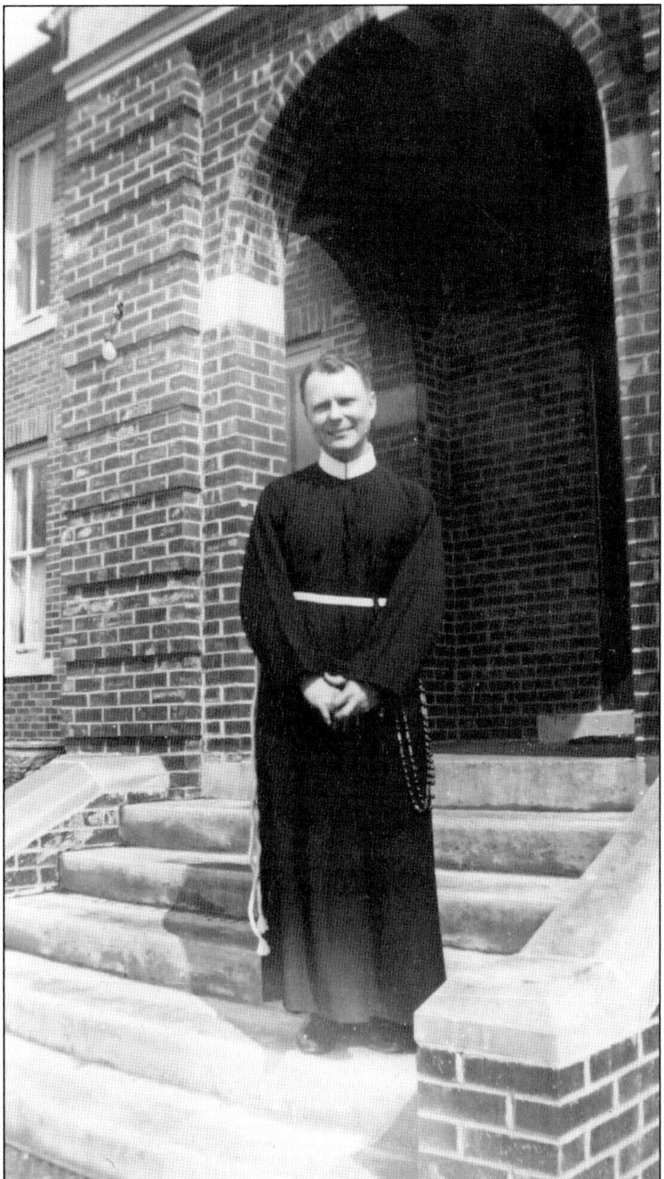

Br. Michael Groesch, who grew up on North Sixth Street in Springfield, walked to SS. Peter and Paul Grade School (the parish is now gone). The school was fondly known as the "Dutch Penitentiary" because of the number of German students and the no-nonsense Ursuline nuns who taught there. He graduated from Springfield High School in 1931. After being employed by the Bunn Capitol Company for seven years and receiving nurse's training from the Alexian Brothers of Chicago, he entered the Franciscan Brothers in 1946 as the first American to enter the congregation in the United States. His profession of vows was held at the Sisters' Motherhouse in their St. Francis Church, as St. Joseph the Worker Chapel had not yet been built, and the brothers' small house chapel was not big enough to hold guests. Other young men joined Brother Michael and the German brothers from time to time, but none of them persevered. Hence, he actually was alone for 11 years with the German confreres.

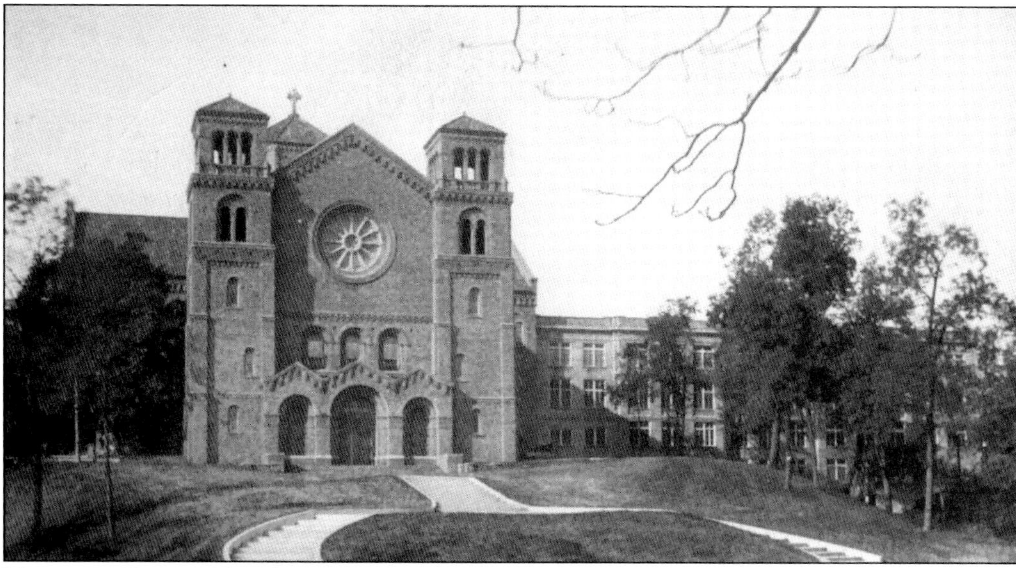

Here is St. Francis Church, Hospital Sisters of St. Francis, Springfield, Illinois.

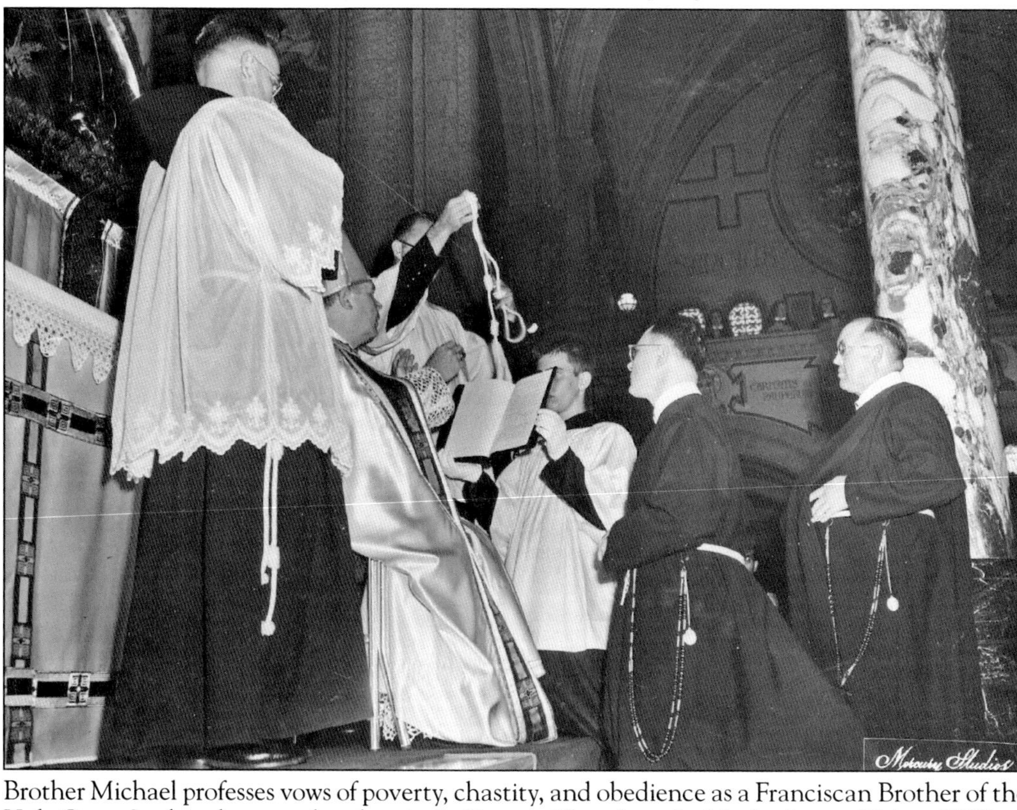

Brother Michael professes vows of poverty, chastity, and obedience as a Franciscan Brother of the Holy Cross. In this photograph, taken in St. Francis Church at the Motherhouse, Bishop William O'Connor blesses and hands the Franciscan cord with three knots to Brother Michael, who exchanges his novice cord (without knots) with the help of the superior, Brother Felix. Fr. Roger Niemeyer, OFM, stands on the bishop's right. Father Roger was the chaplain for the brothers, the trade school, and Brother James Court for over 26 years, before retiring at the age of 89.

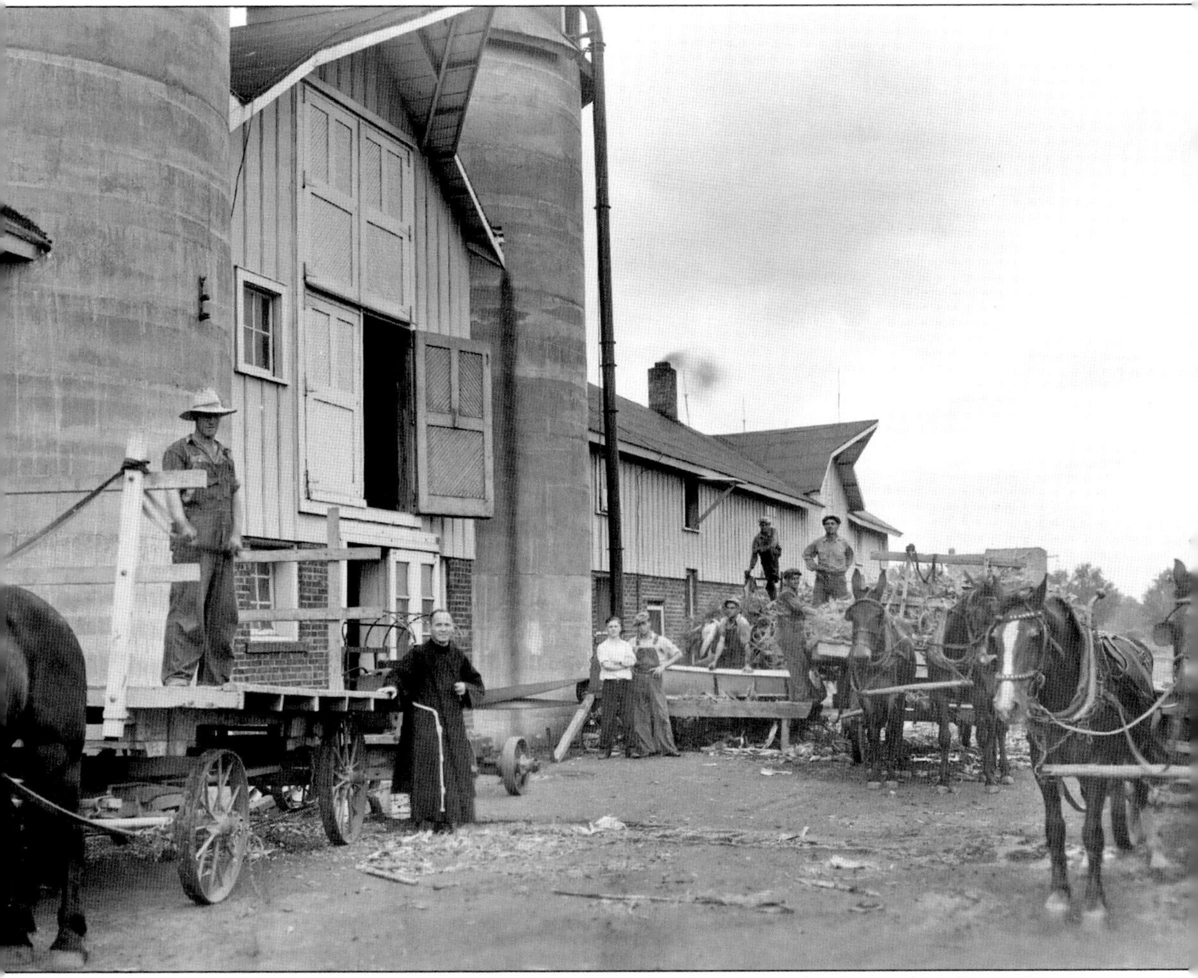

Harvest time at St. James is pictured here around 1938, in front of the barns. Brother Egbertus is in the foreground next to the wagon while students and other workers pause to look at the camera. In 1928, the Franciscan Brothers owned 209 acres, 3 buildings, 12 horses and mules, 50 cattle, and 1,500 chickens, with an estimated value of $90,000. By 1948, they had abandoned horses, mules, and chickens, and their property amounted to 227 acres, 12 buildings, and 100 cattle, all valued at $446,000.

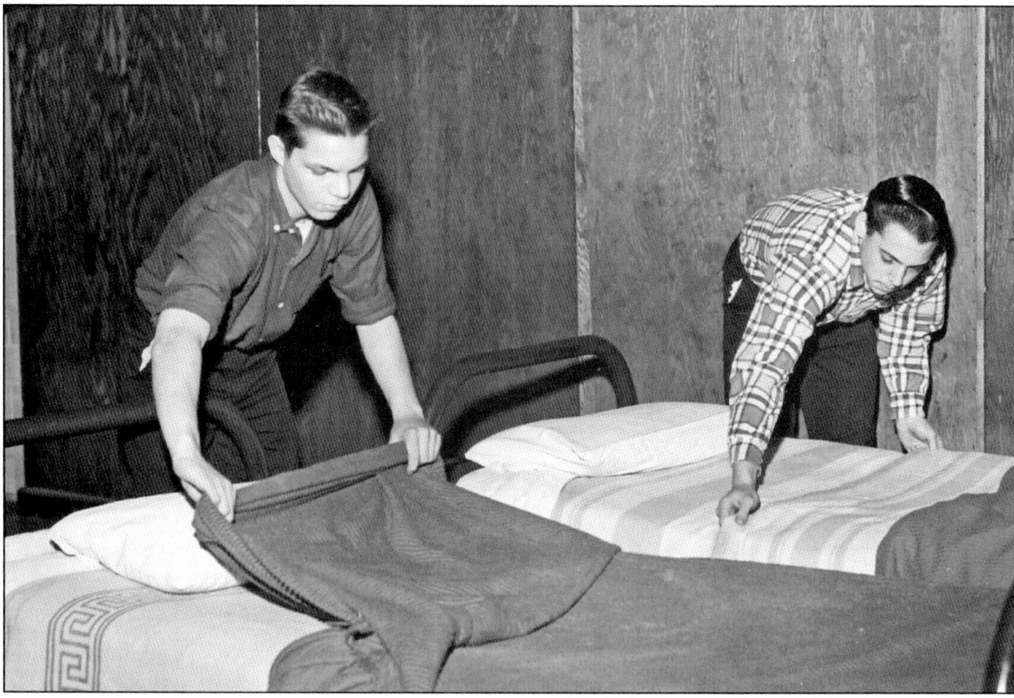

Part of a boy's life at St. James was making sure the dormitory beds were made each day. Dormitories held up to 50 students. In the 1959 photograph above, Robert Waitkus (left) and Kenneth Runkles complete their task before heading to the shop or classroom. Below, a group of students are in the recreation room on the third floor of the Boys House. Card games, pool, radio, and music were favorite pastimes (television came in the 1950s).

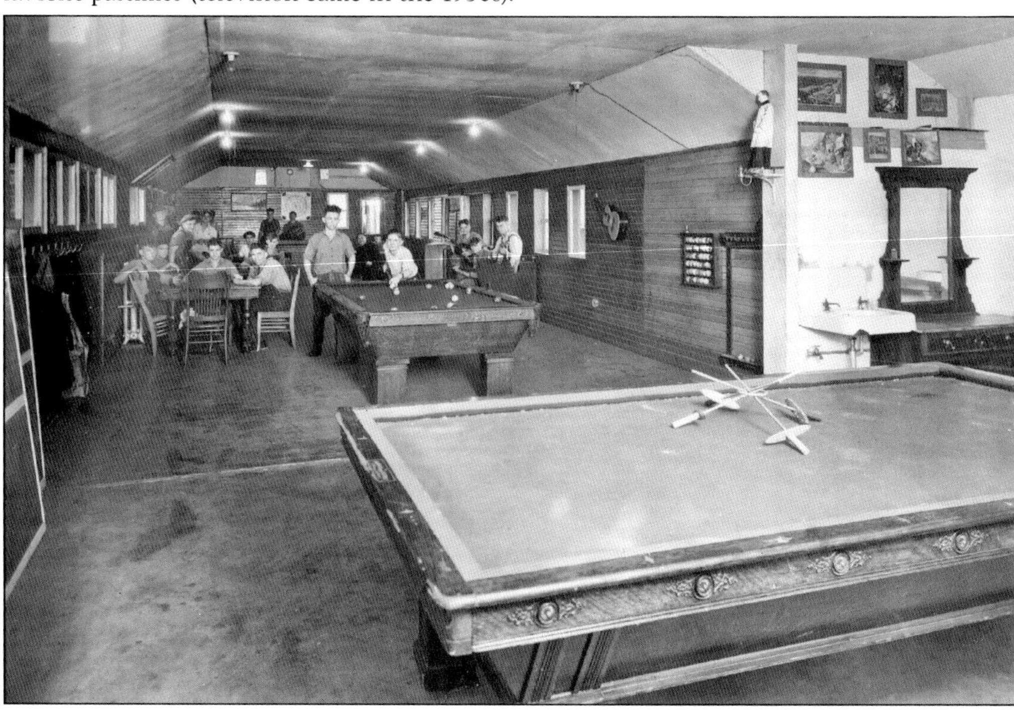

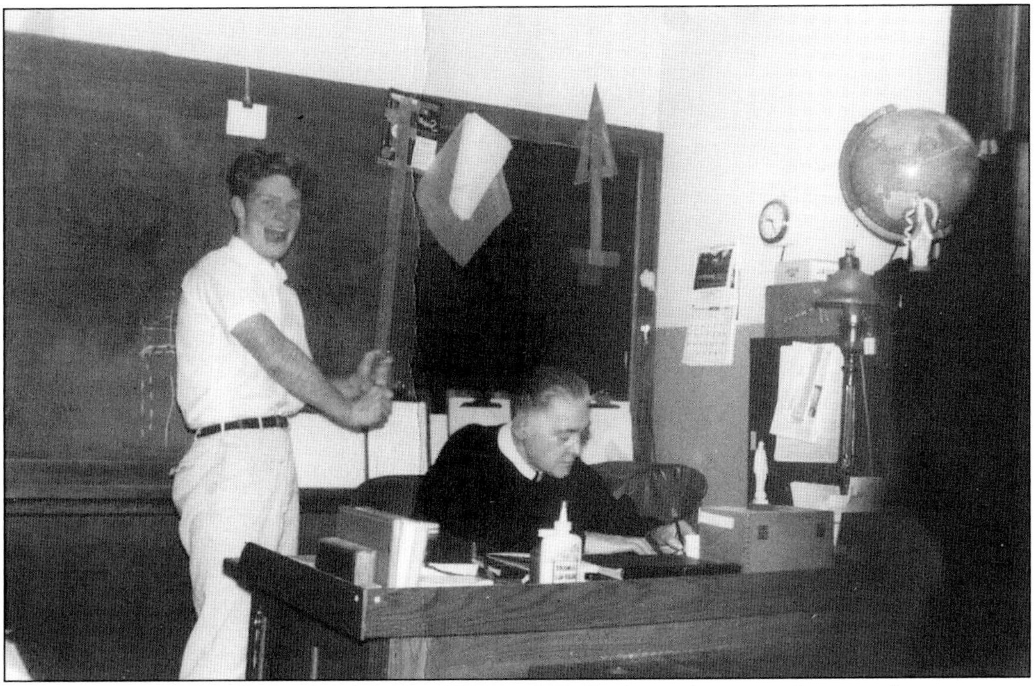

St. James was a boarding school from 1930 until 1963. As with any gathering of young men, energy spills over into "creative" entertainment, which happens at times to spill over into the classroom. In the above photograph, Jack "Red" Leonard is "crowning" Brother Lubentius in the mechanical drawing classroom. Most of the young men on this page and the next are from the class of 1962. (Photographs courtesy of Jack "Red" Leonard.)

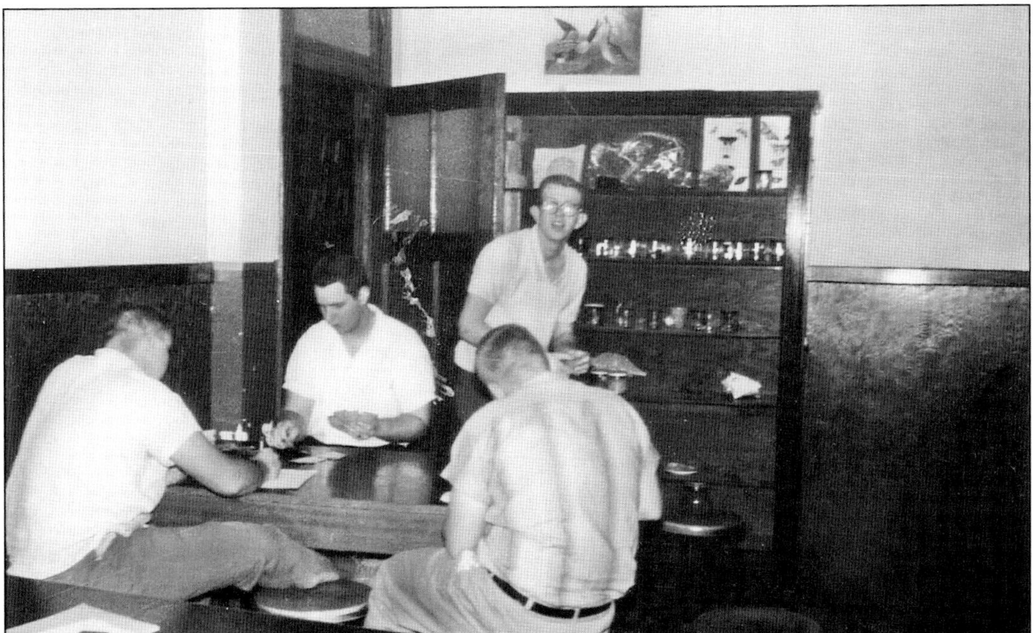

Some class of 1962 members, from left to right, are Mike Schubert, Tom Vogel, Charlie Hetzel (wearing glasses), and Mike Rheinecker (seated).

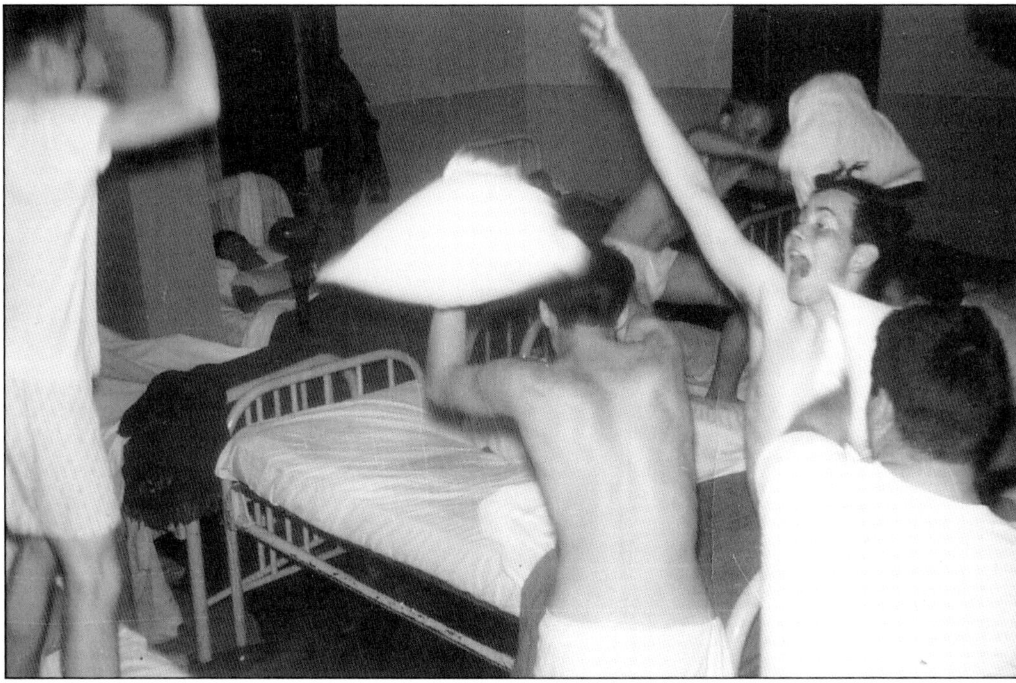

This pillow fight occurred at the senior quarters in June 1962. (Courtesy of Jack "Red" Leonard.)

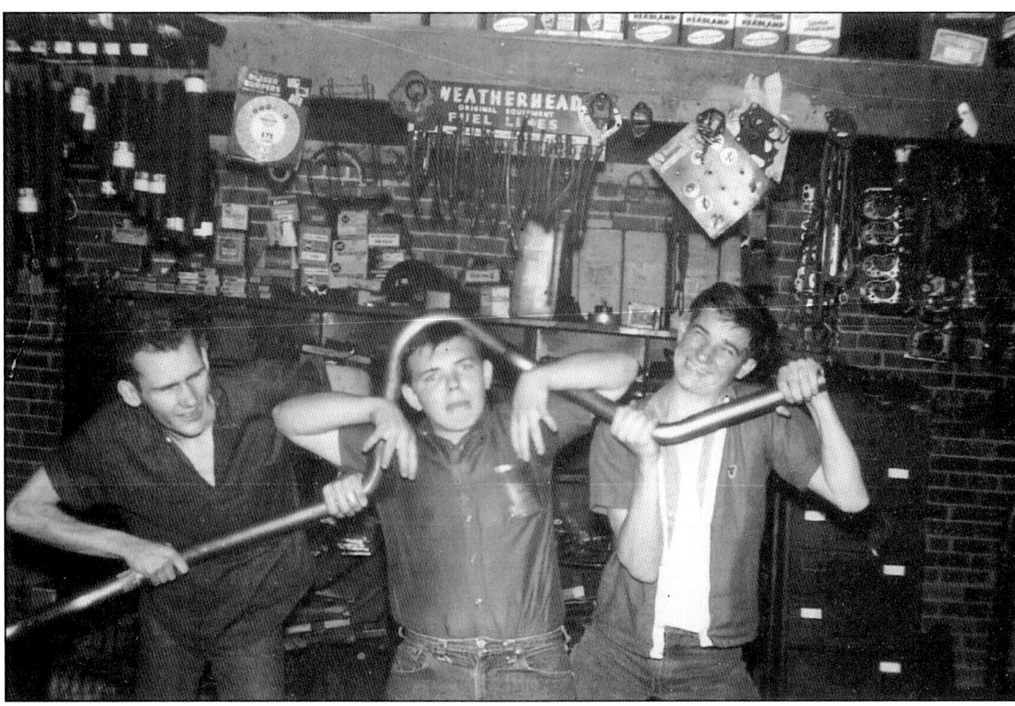

Paul Pasqualli (left) and Bill Edwards (right), of the class of 1963, are pictured in this June 1962 photograph in the auto mechanics shop with Jim Gray, class of 1962. (Courtesy of Jack "Red" Leonard.)

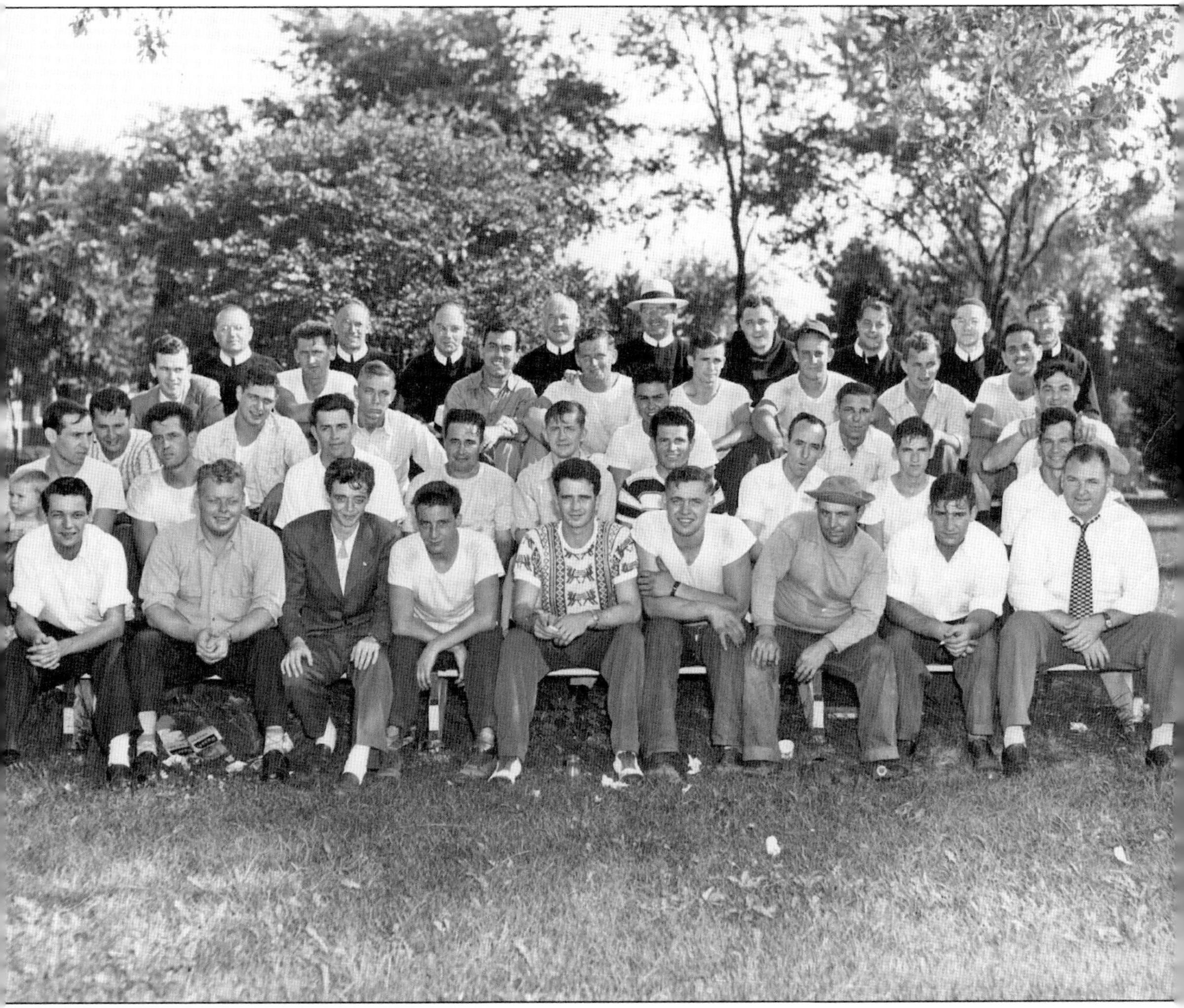

St. James alumni have reunions on a frequent basis. This group of alumni and brothers got together in the early 1950s on the school grounds to renew friendships and to reminisce about their time at the trade school.

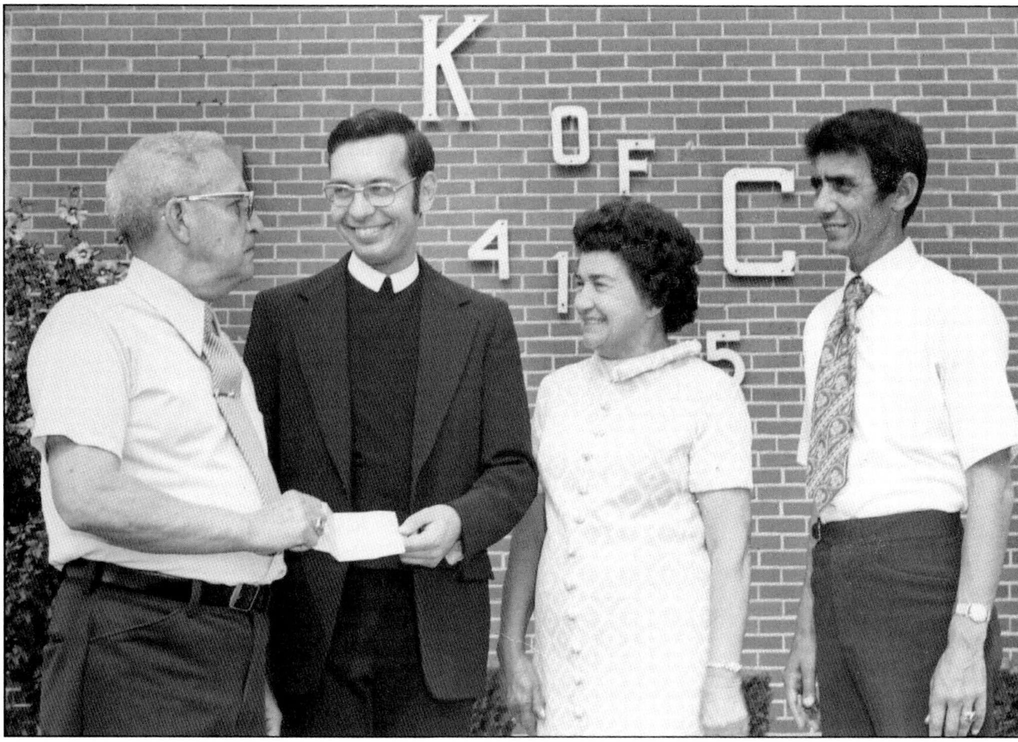

Fund raising to help support the school was a vital part of St. James' existence. Many councils of the Knights of Columbus (K of C) regularly awarded funds to the school. In the above photograph Br. David Sarnecki (principal, 1966–1972) accepts a check from James Wolf, Anne Mehlick, and Leonard Seman of the K of C Devereaux Council. Pictured below around 1970 is Br. Michael Groesch (at the school from 1946 to 1972), superior of St. James, receiving a monetary contribution from August Morosi and Edward Carter of the K of C Father Burtle Council.

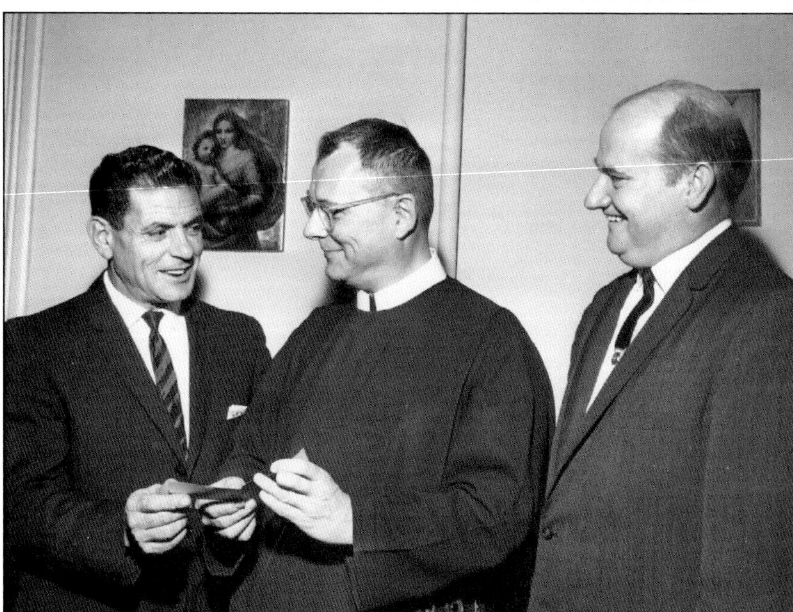

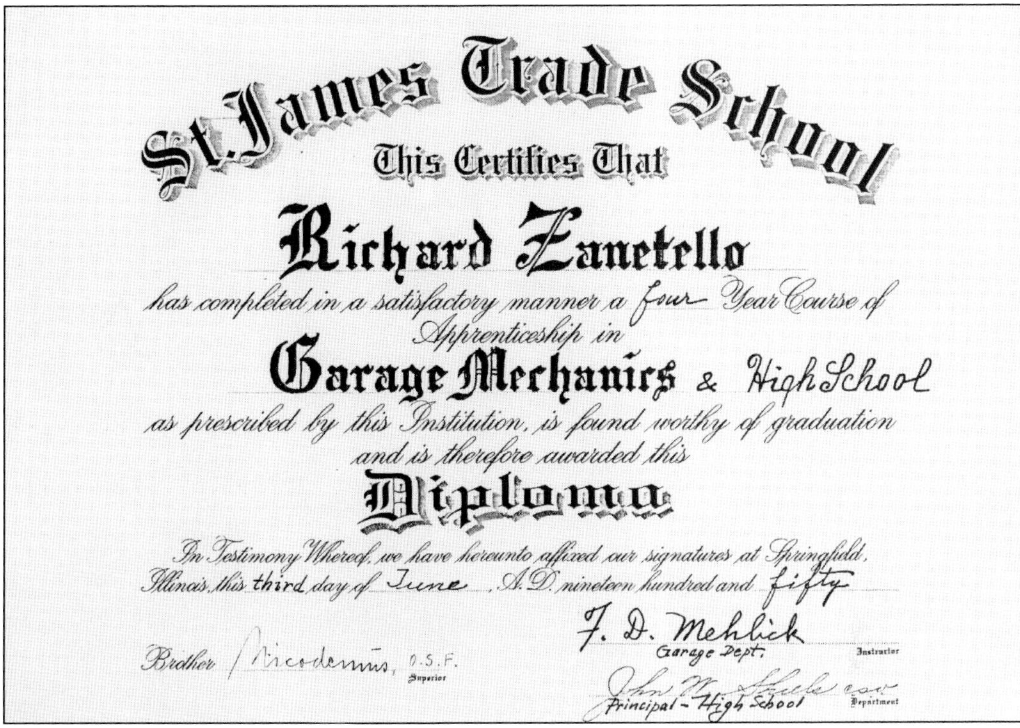

St. James Trade School

This Certifies That

Richard Zanetello

has completed in a satisfactory manner a four Year Course of Apprenticeship in

Garage Mechanics & High School

as prescribed by this Institution, is found worthy of graduation and is therefore awarded this

Diploma

In Testimony Whereof, we have hereunto affixed our signatures at Springfield, Illinois, this third day of June, A.D. nineteen hundred and fifty

Brother Nicodemus, O.S.F.
Superior

F. D. Mehlick
Garage Dept.
Instructor

John M. Steele [illegible]
Principal - High School
Department

Pictured here is the high school diploma and certificate of coursework from the auto mechanics shop issued June 3, 1950, to Richard Zanetello.

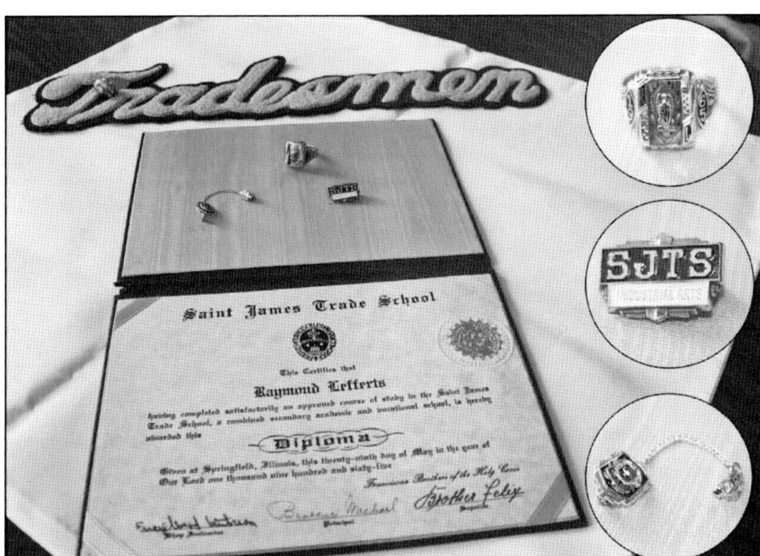

This photograph shows the diploma of 1965 graduate Ray Lefferts and some of his pins and class ring. At the top of the photograph is the insignia from a school jacket in the school colors of blue and gold. (Courtesy of Bill Prose.)

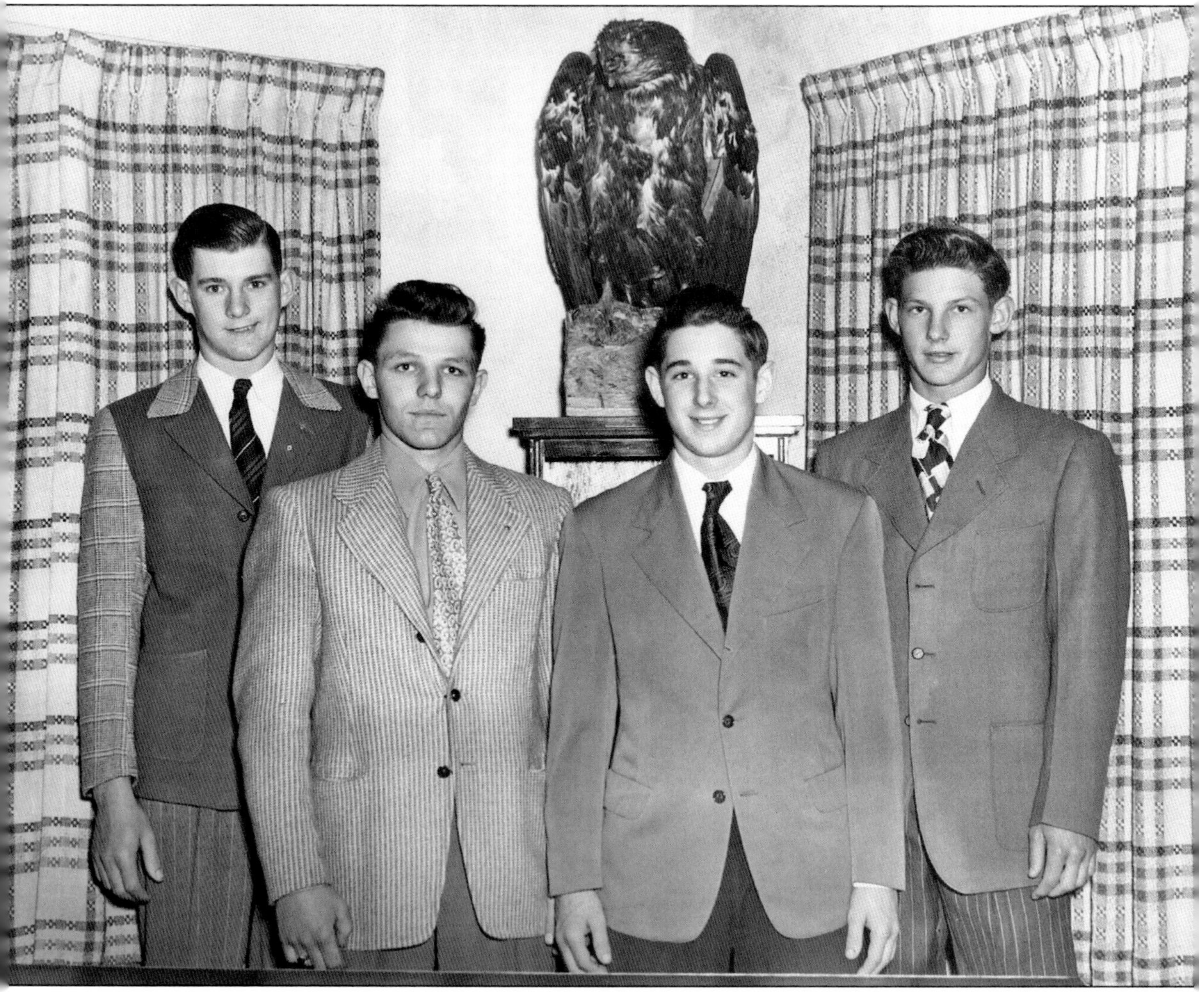

From an initial student body of 10 boys from the Alton Children's Home in 1930, the Tradesmen grew to an enrollment of 80 by 1972. The above photograph is of the 1948 graduating class, the first to receive a high school diploma as well as a certificate in their trade. From left to right are Dwight "Slim" Butterfield, John "Johnny" Nagy, James "Jim" Rabus, and William "Casey" Graham.

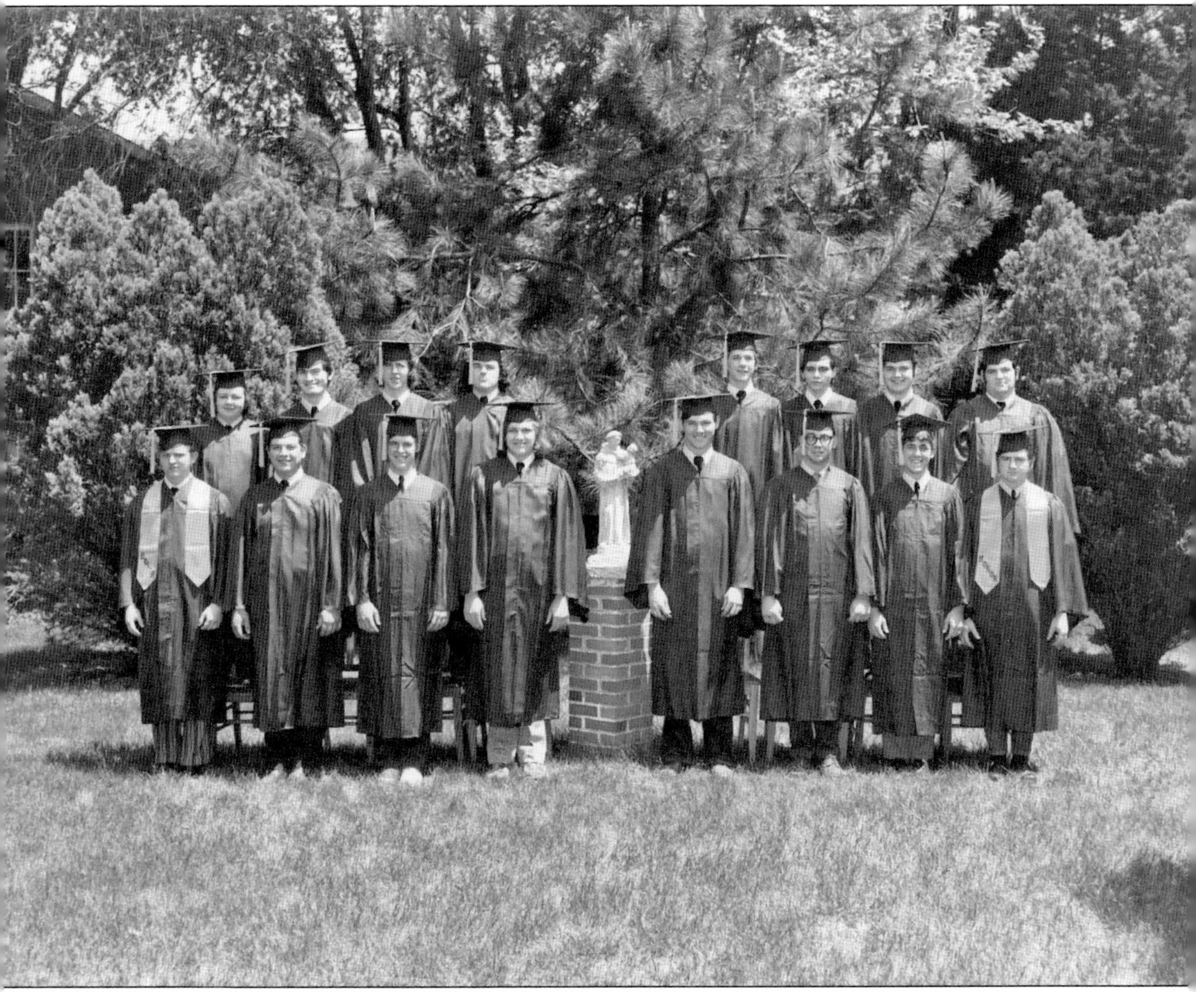

Here is the class of 1972 on graduation day. From left to right are (first row) Ken Hughes, Joe Henton, Bob Reside, Jim Gasparin, Bill Tucker, Steve Delay, Terry Rapps, and Larry Roth; (second row) Chris Reed, Bill Forgas, Hugh Rachford, Terry Valenti, Mike Morrow, Ron LeMasters, Mike Voges, and Tom Reeves. These men were the members of the last St. James Trade School graduating class. The wearing of caps and gowns came to be the norm in the 1960s.

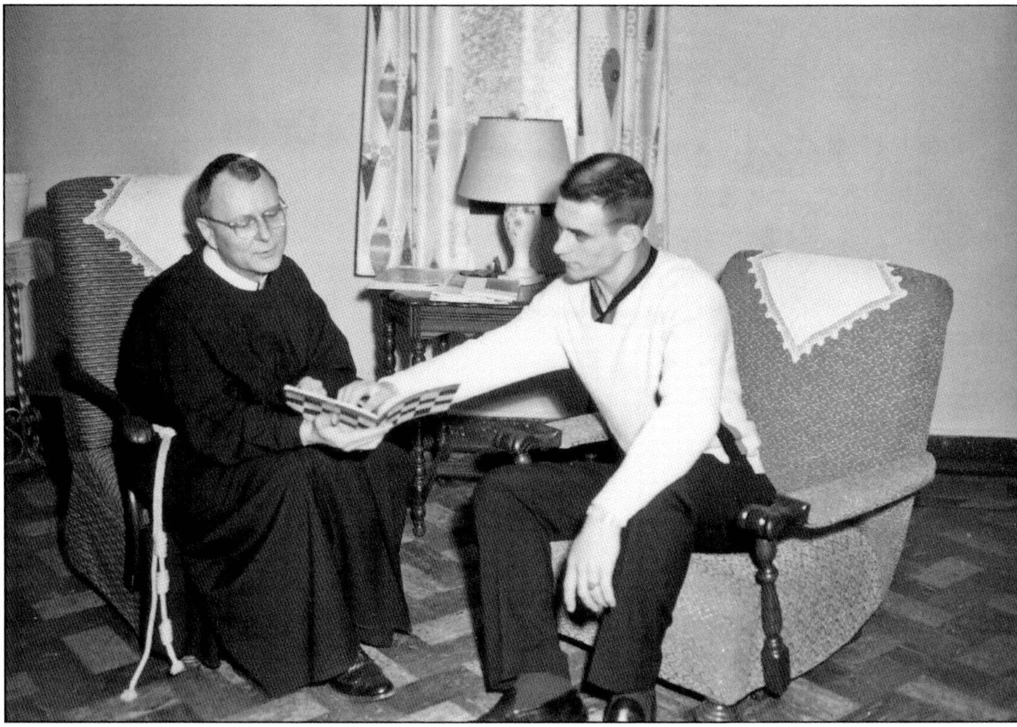

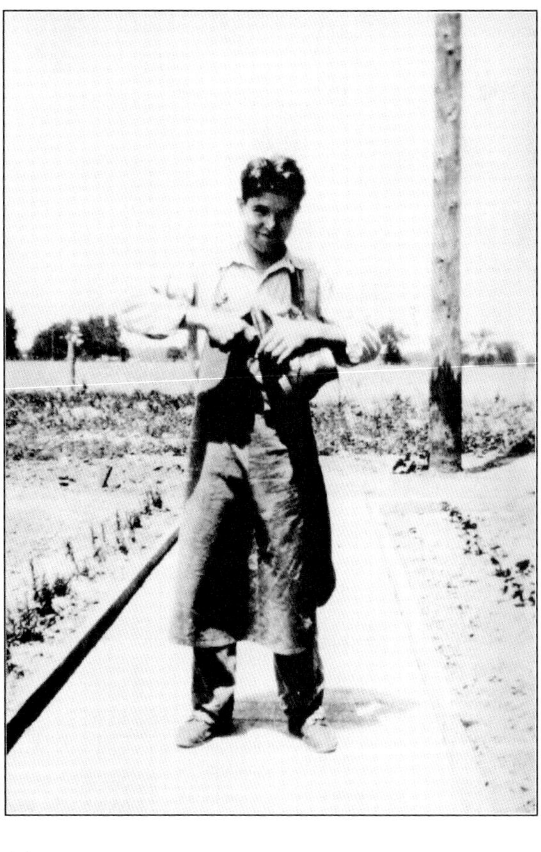

School principal Brother Michael is shown giving student David Twellman (class of 1964) advice about future plans for education beyond high school. Twellman was preparing to enter college.

This photograph shows Mario "Sammy" Caruso, the recipient of the first certificate of completion in a trade before the implementation of the academic program at St. James. Caruso, who received his certificate as a shoemaker in 1932, came from the Alton Children's Home as part of the first group of apprentices in 1930. After graduation he returned to the home and remained there for more than 30 years, making and repairing shoes for the children and staff.

In 1938, Brother Lubentius, a self-taught librarian, came to the trade school from the community of brothers who had been stationed at Holy Name Technical (Aeronautics) School in Lockport, Illinois. Here he uses his knowledge to teach mechanical drawing to his students. The academic portion of the school began in 1944.

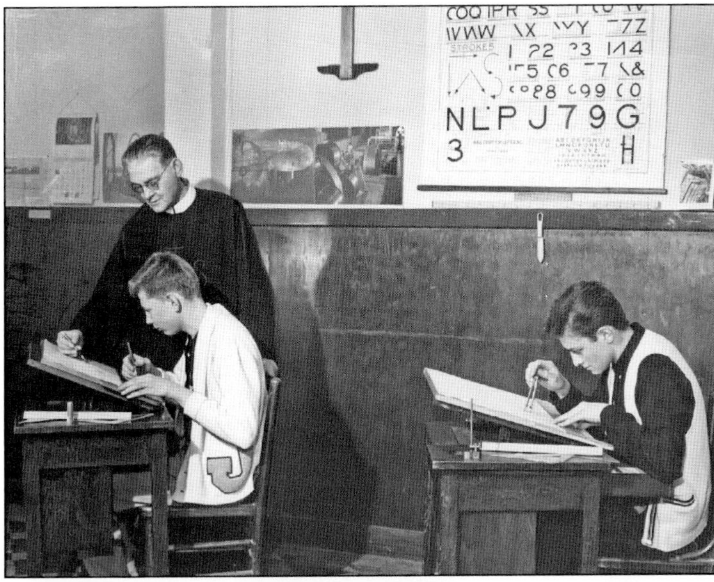

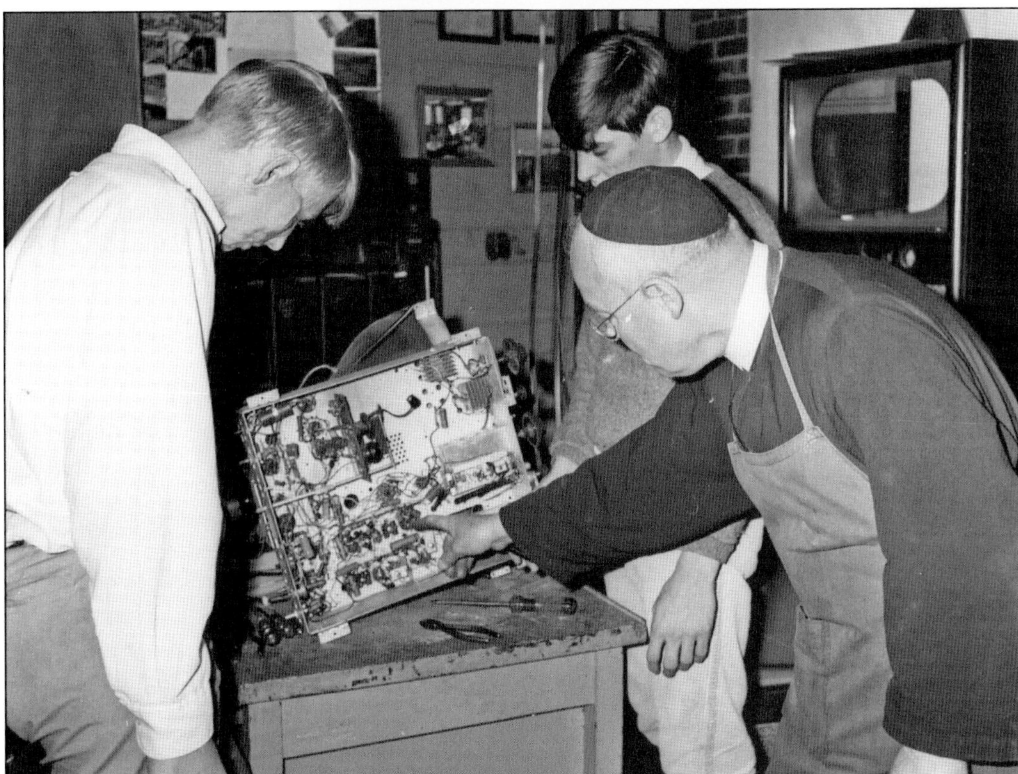

A portion of the school day was spent in the academic program leading to a high school diploma, and the other half of the day was spent in a chosen trade. With television becoming common in the country, electronics was added to the curriculum. Students were trained in the practice of safely installing wiring and repairing various electrical equipment. In 1952, St. James issued an apprentice certificate to its first electrician. Brother Fabian, who was at the school for its entire existence (1930–1972), is shown above.

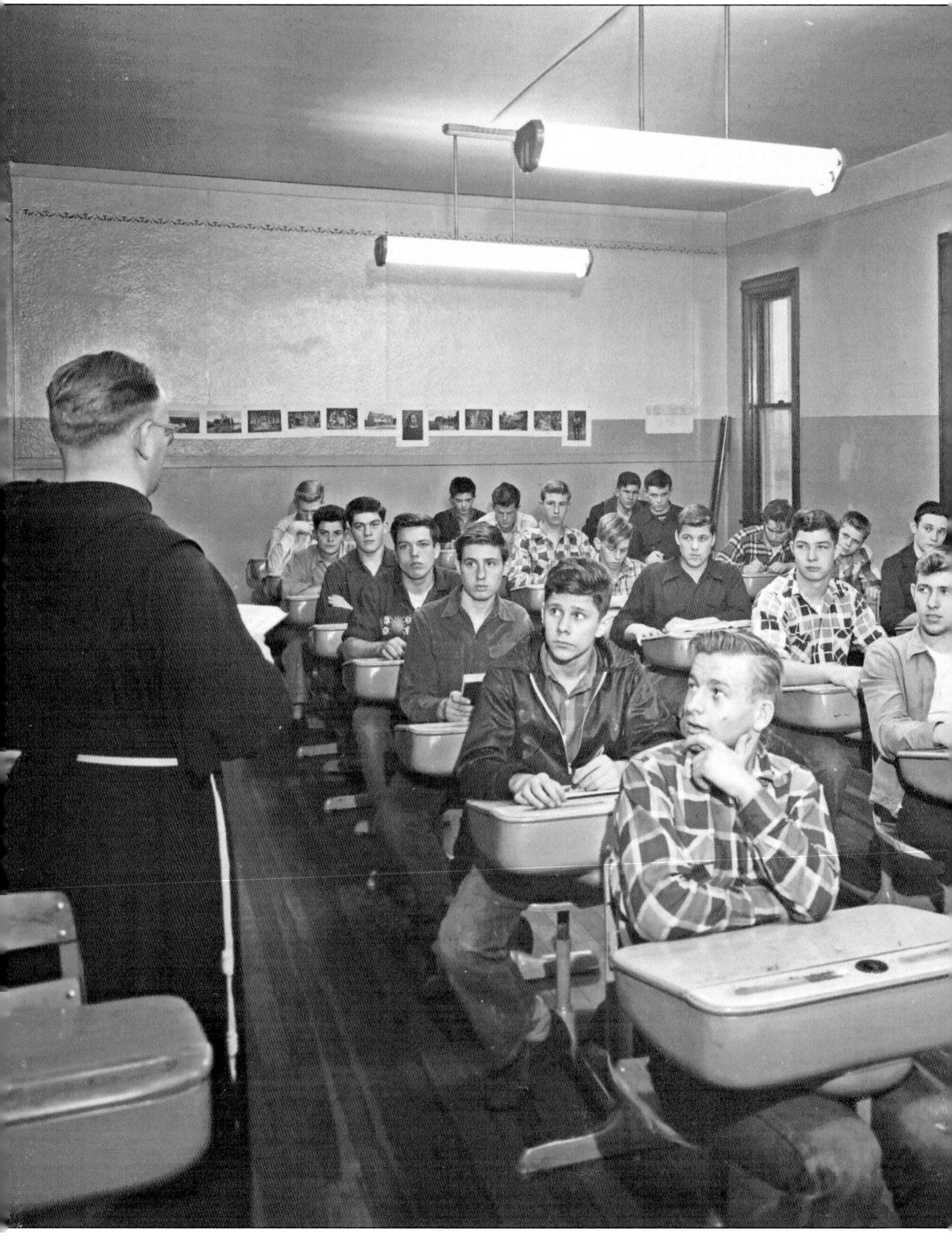

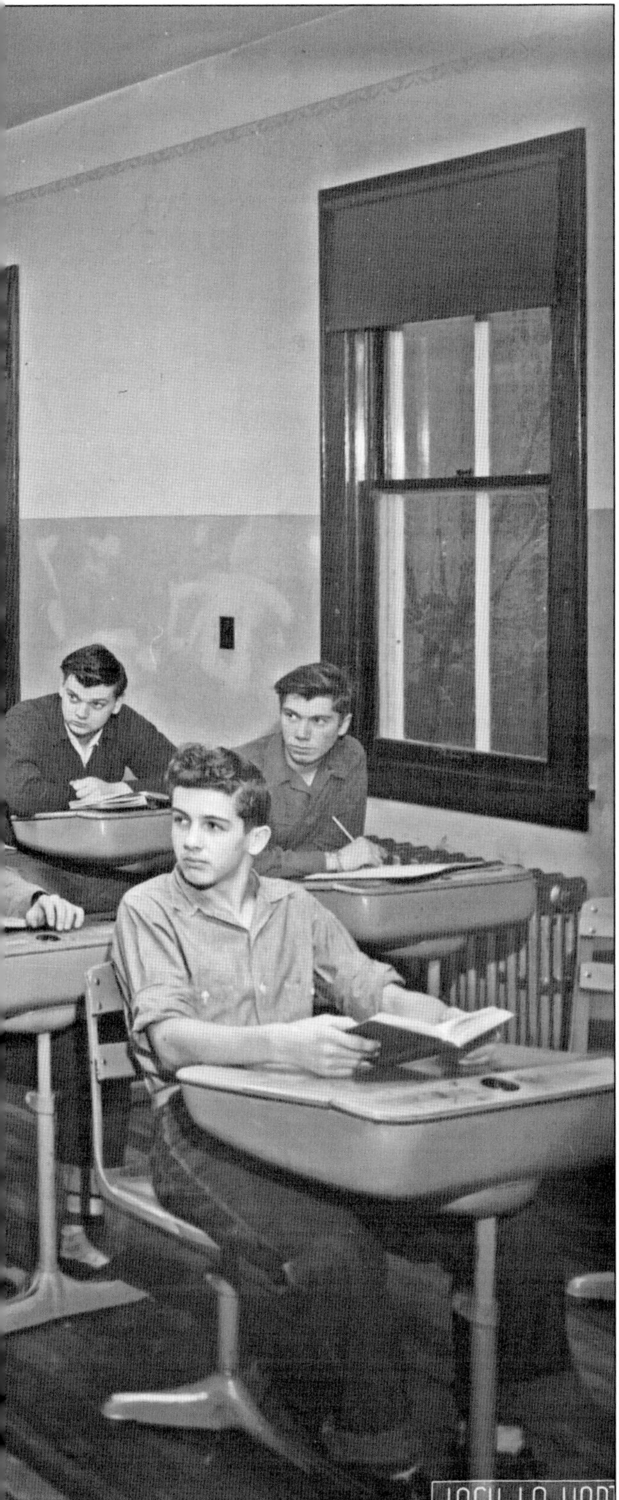

Religion classes were often taught by priests from the Viatorian community (Cathedral or Griffin High School) or the Franciscans of the Sacred Heart Province, who were frequently chaplains for the brothers. In this 1954 photograph, the teacher is Father Roger, who spent almost 30 years as a chaplain to the brothers.

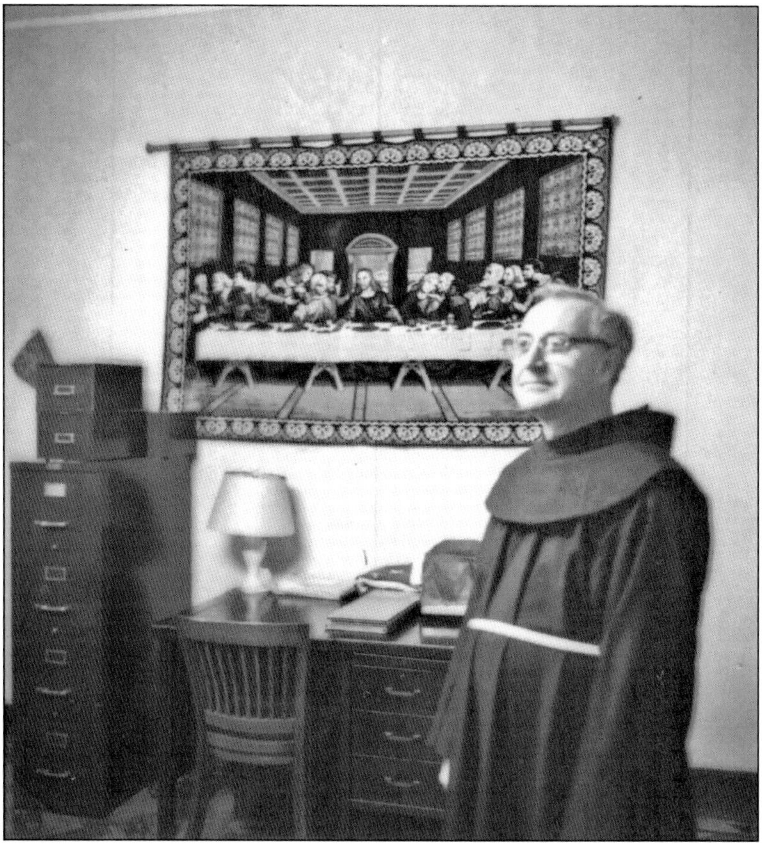

To the left is Father Fabian, OFM, also a chaplain at St. James. In the photograph below from 1946 or 1947 are three Franciscans sitting among the brother instructors. Sitting third from left are an unidentified man, Father Evarist (OFM), and Father Fabian.

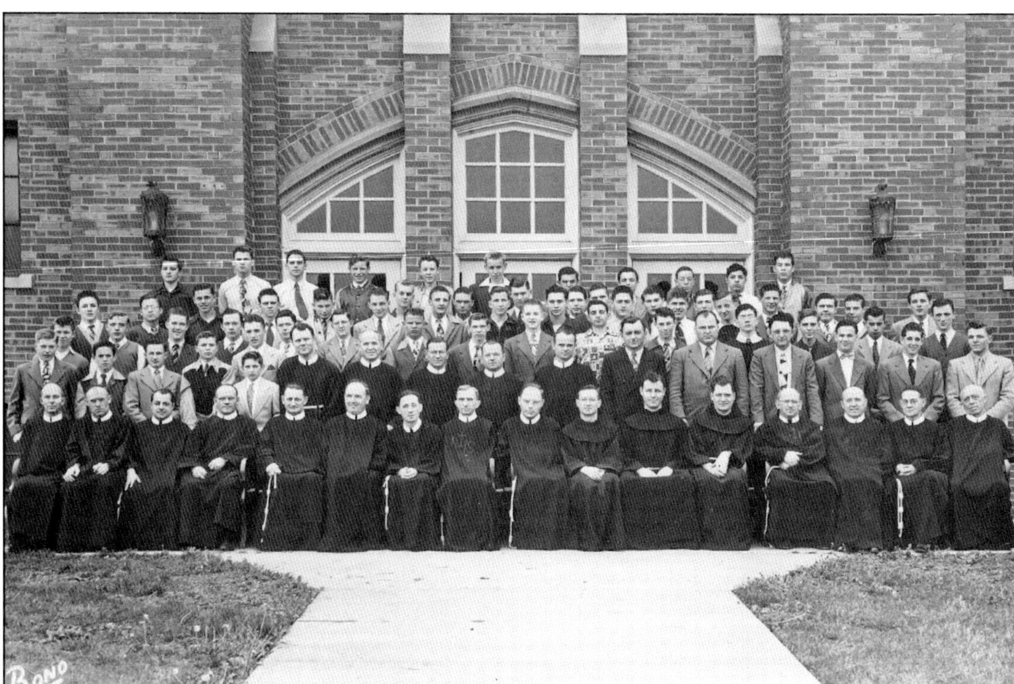

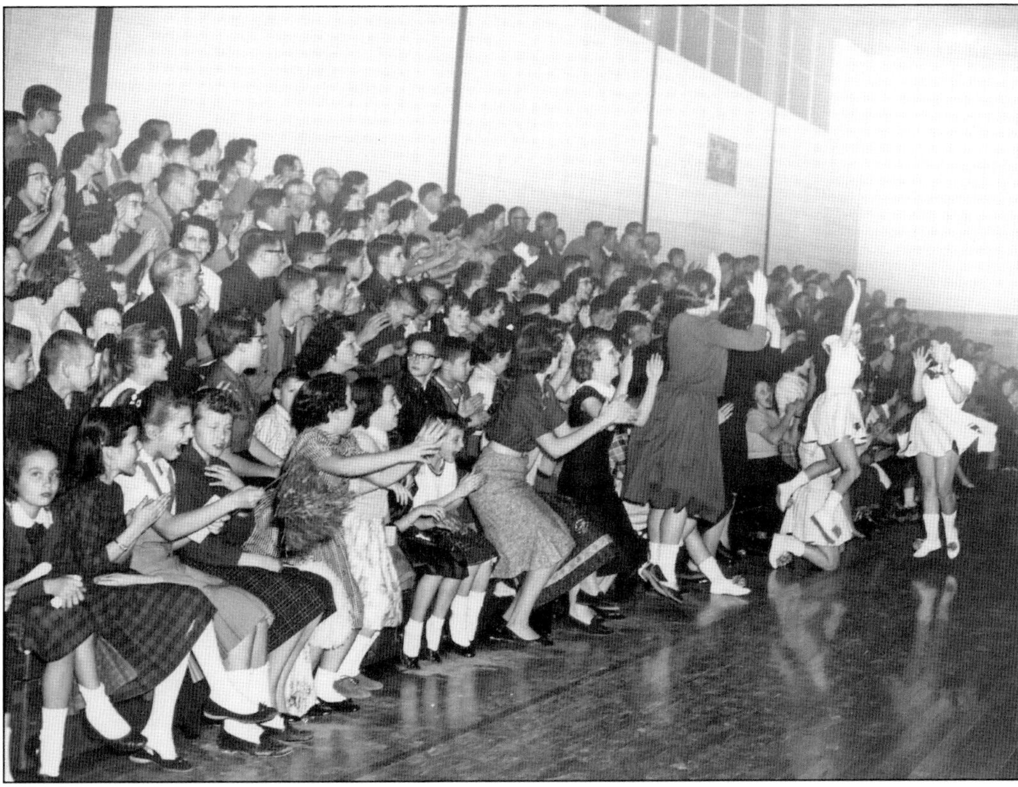

The Tradesmen not only enjoyed Ursuline Academy's activities, they also had girls as their cheerleaders, ensemble accompanists, and even prom dates. The Ursuline nuns, fine, forward-thinking educators, allowed this fraternization long before Ursuline Academy became coed. The above photograph, about 1959, shows a packed house for the Farmersville High School game. Below is a dance held in Ursuline's gym. In the lower right corner is St. James student Larry Motley, class of 1959, who later became an instructor in the trade school's butcher shop.

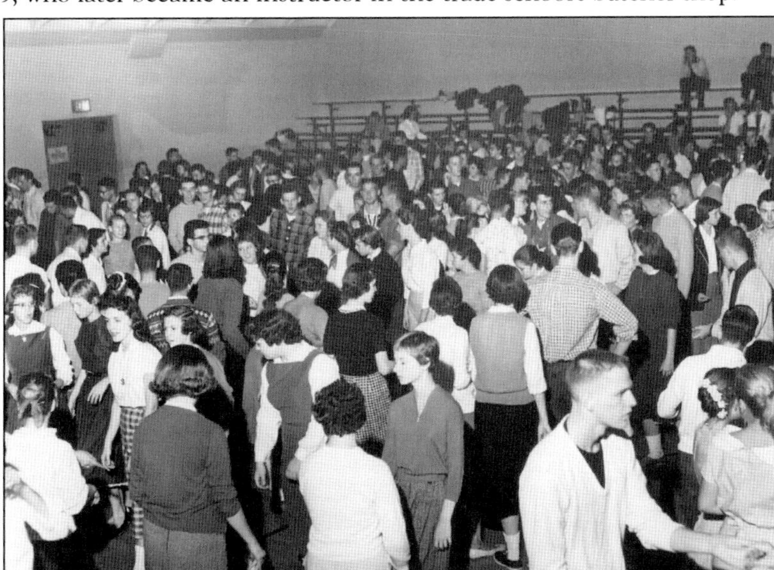

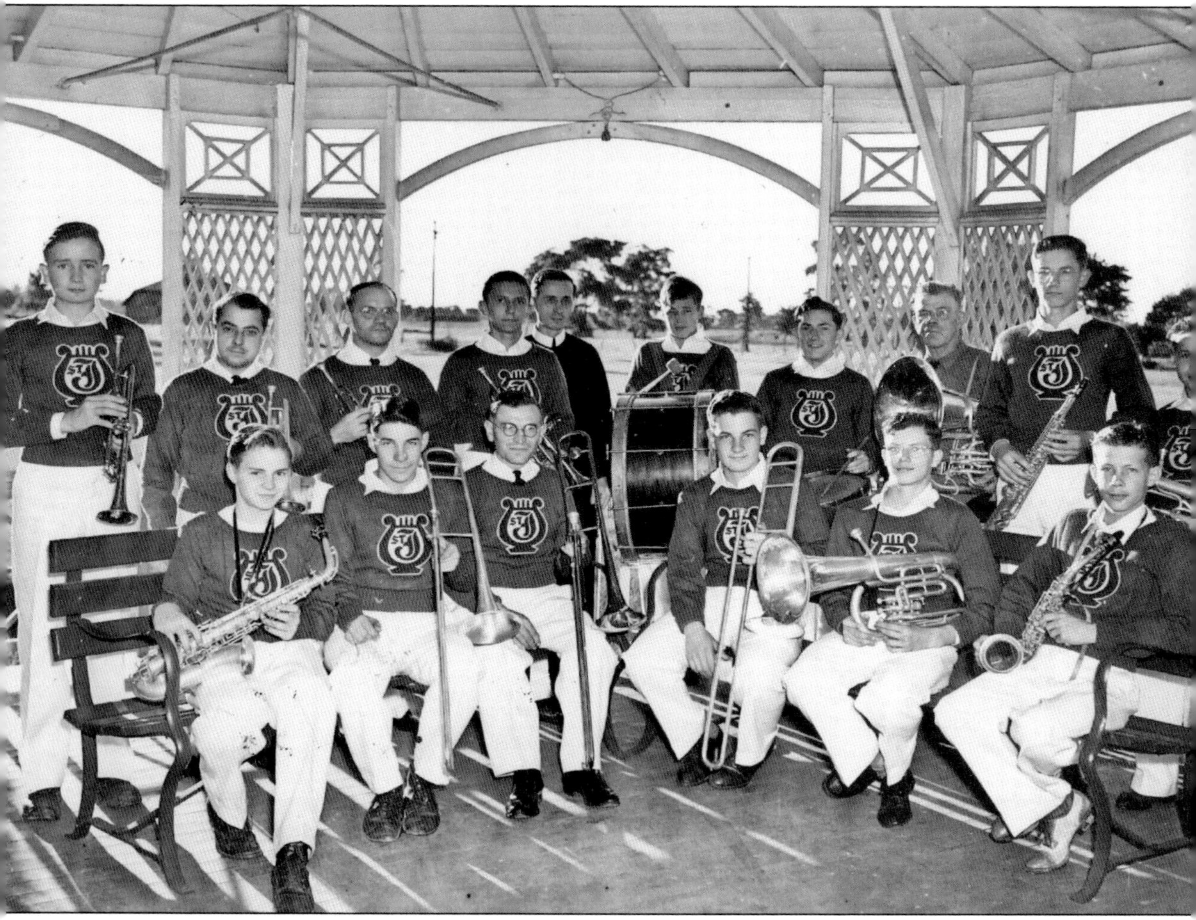

Besides learning a trade and playing sports, the boys could also become musicians. This is the 1943 band at the band shell, which was originally in front of the monastery. Three brothers joined the group, and are seen here in the back row: Brother Nestor (second from left), Brother Sergius (third from left) and the director, Brother Aegidius (fifth from left). Anthony "Mickey" Wysocki (class of 1939), interviewing Brother Aegidius for the school's newspaper, *The Tradesmen*, once asked why the band didn't play for football games. Brother Aegidius replied, "If you can call a long time out we can get the band together. Half the band members are on the field."

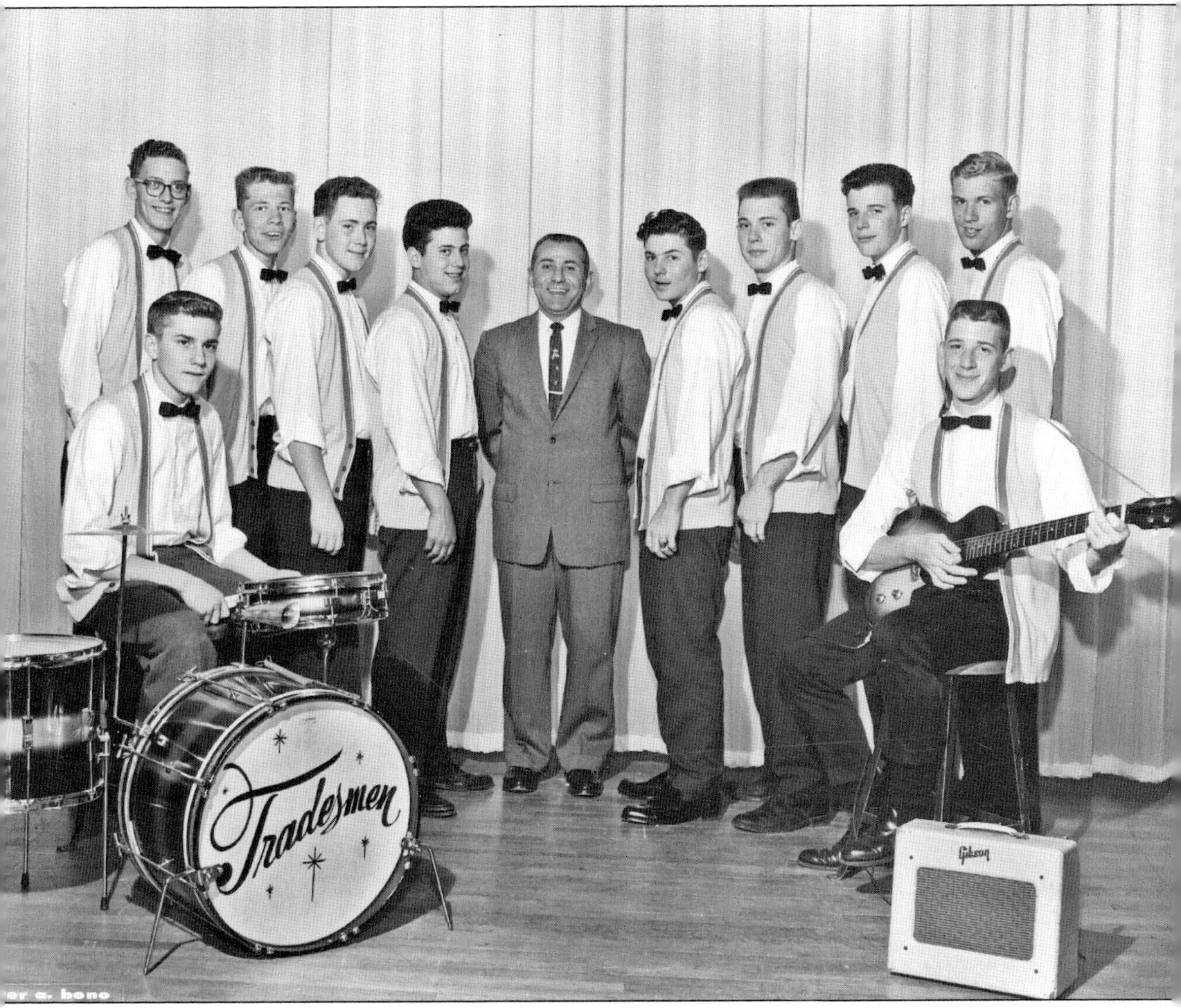

Budding vocalists could find their skill with the St. James Choristers, under the direction of William Croutcher, who was also an English teacher at the trade school. This photograph was taken around 1964.

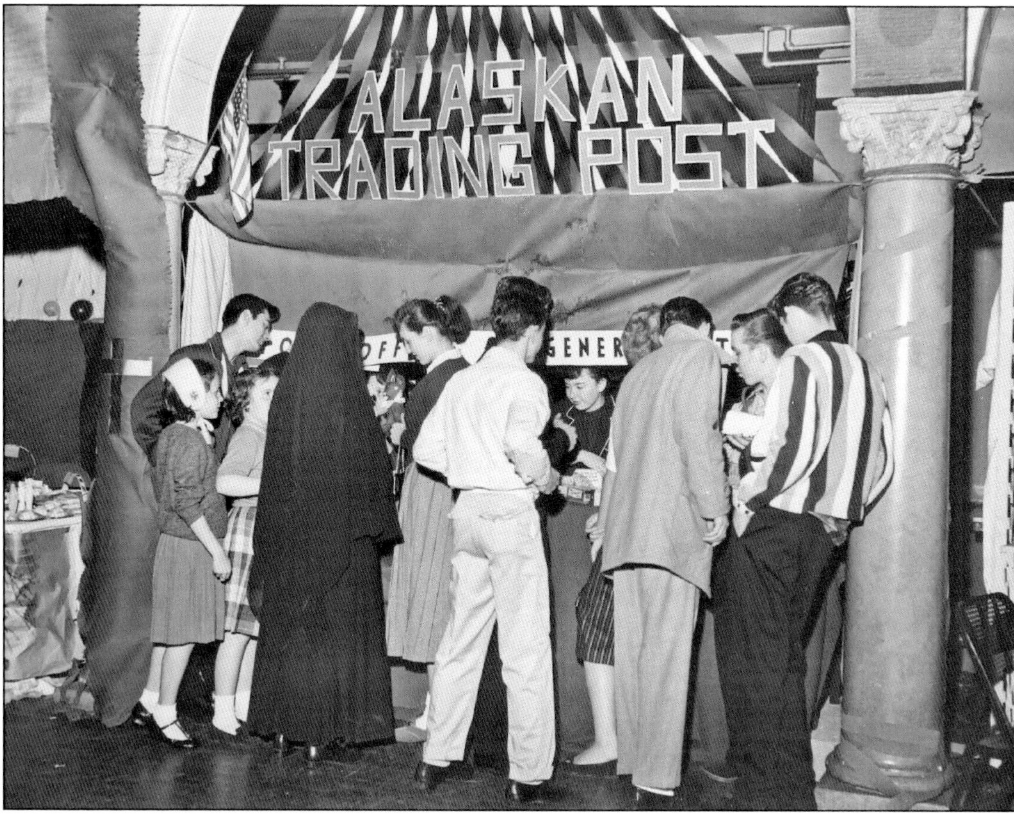

Two photographs of the 1959–1960 Mission Fair at Ursuline Academy are shown here. Although they went to a single-sex high school, the Tradesmen did not lack female companionship. The boys often met with the girls of the other northeast Springfield private school. Sadly, Ursuline closed its doors forever in 2008 after 151 years of educating students. Above, from left to right, are John Tafari, Tom Benedict, Arthur Grant, Ken Novum, and Denver Hoelscher.

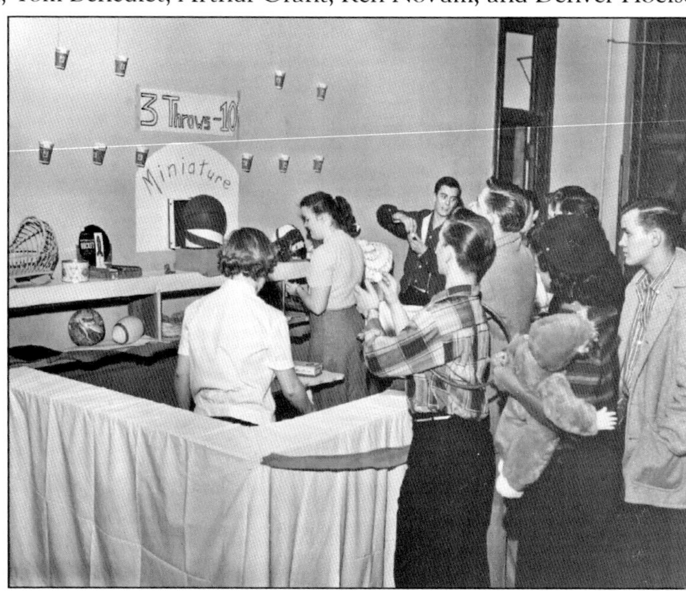

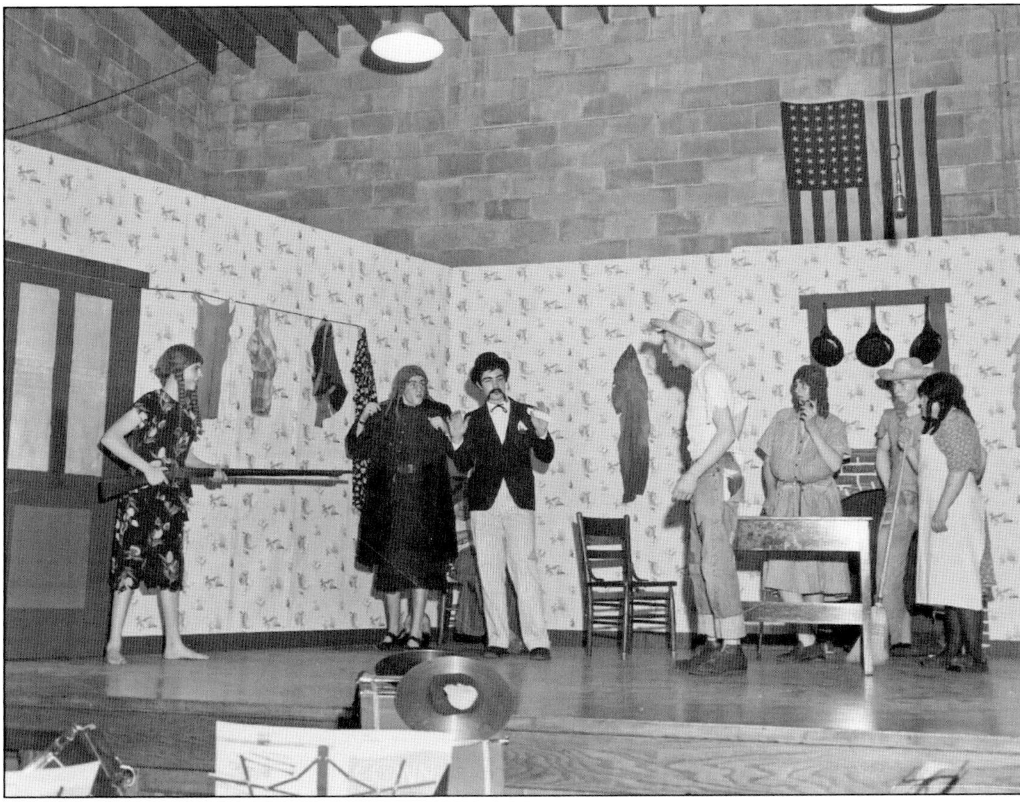

Attending an all-boys school was no problem for these budding thespians when female characters were needed in a play. Thespians pictured above are, from left to right, Rudy Caselli, Joseph Moran, John Steiner, George Savage, William Evanik, Art Evans, and Don Reiser. An enthusiastic crowd filled the gymnasium for the show below, staged around 1954.

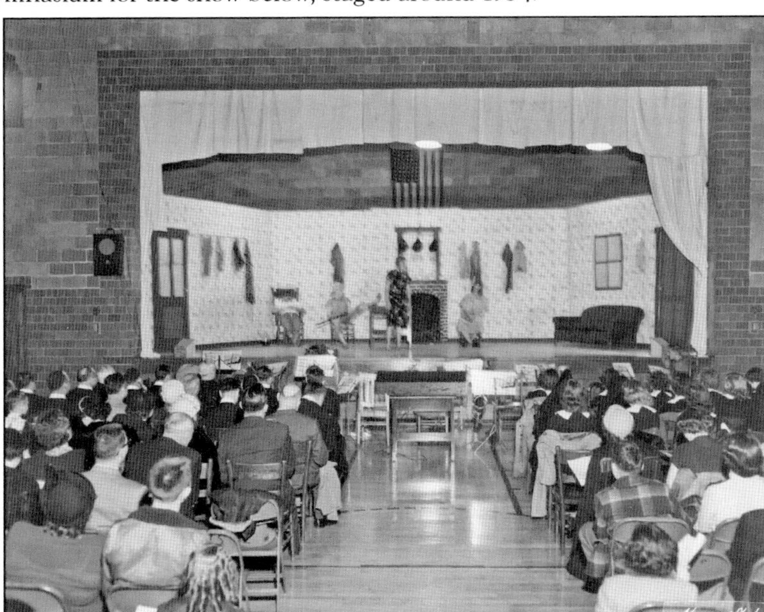

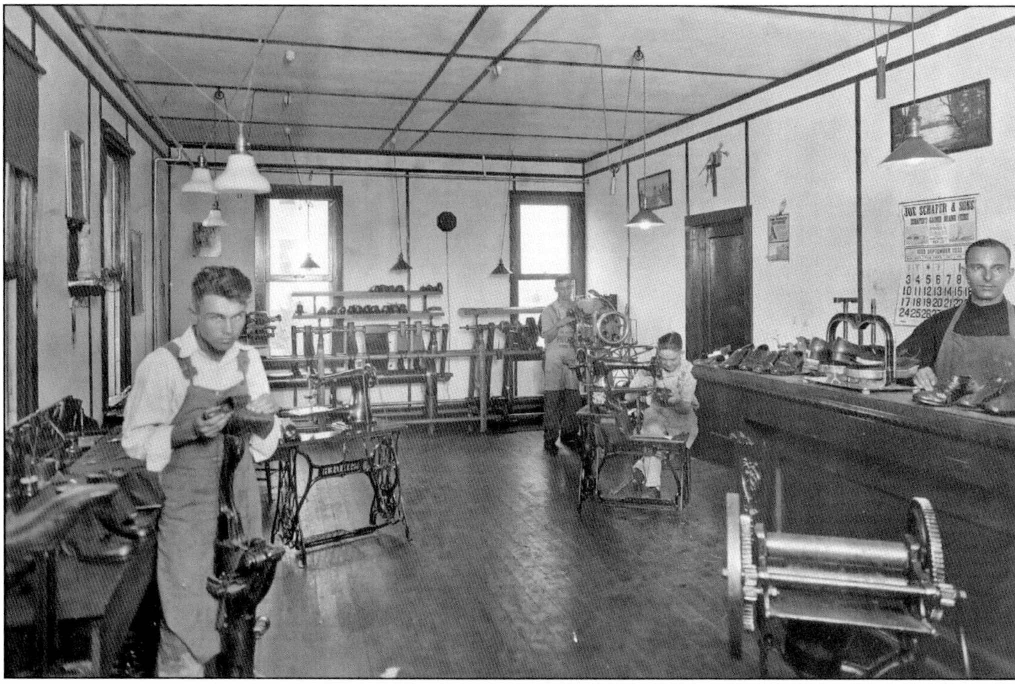

One of the earliest trades taught was shoemaking. In addition to repairing shoes, the apprentices learned how to make a shoe from a foot mold, something that has become a lost art. Brother Adam, teacher at the school from 1931 to 1966, is shown above with three of his students in 1933. Brother Demetrius also taught the craft for 15 years. In the 1952 picture below, he is instructing William Evanik, the last graduate (in 1955) to receive a certificate as a shoemaker.

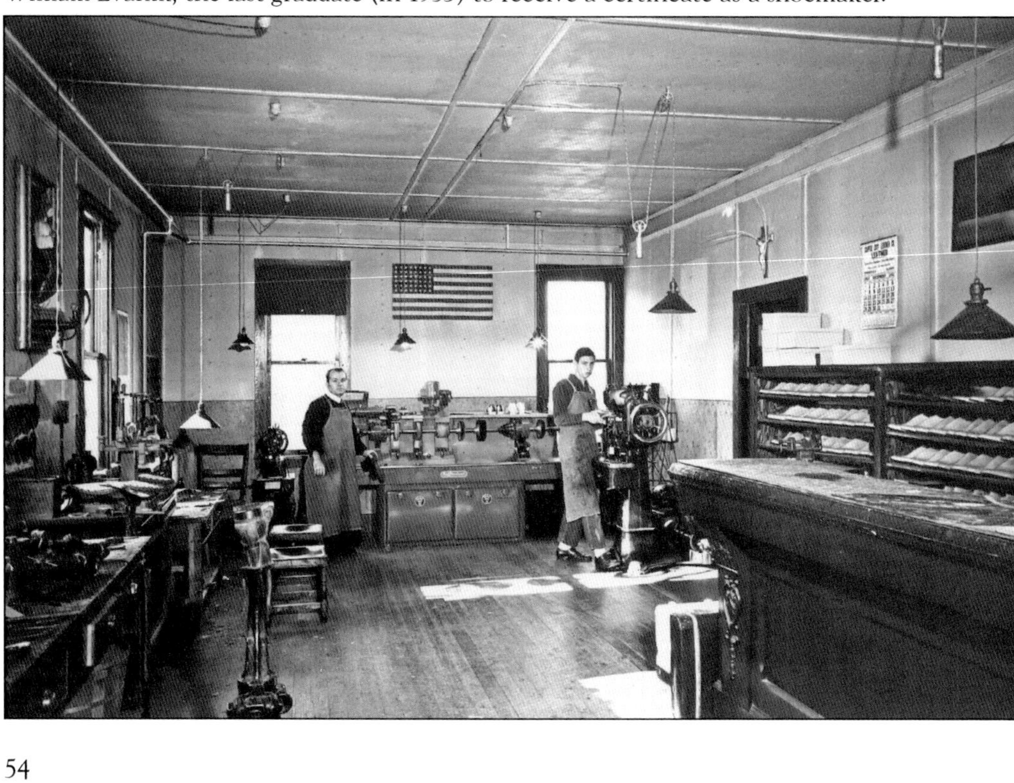

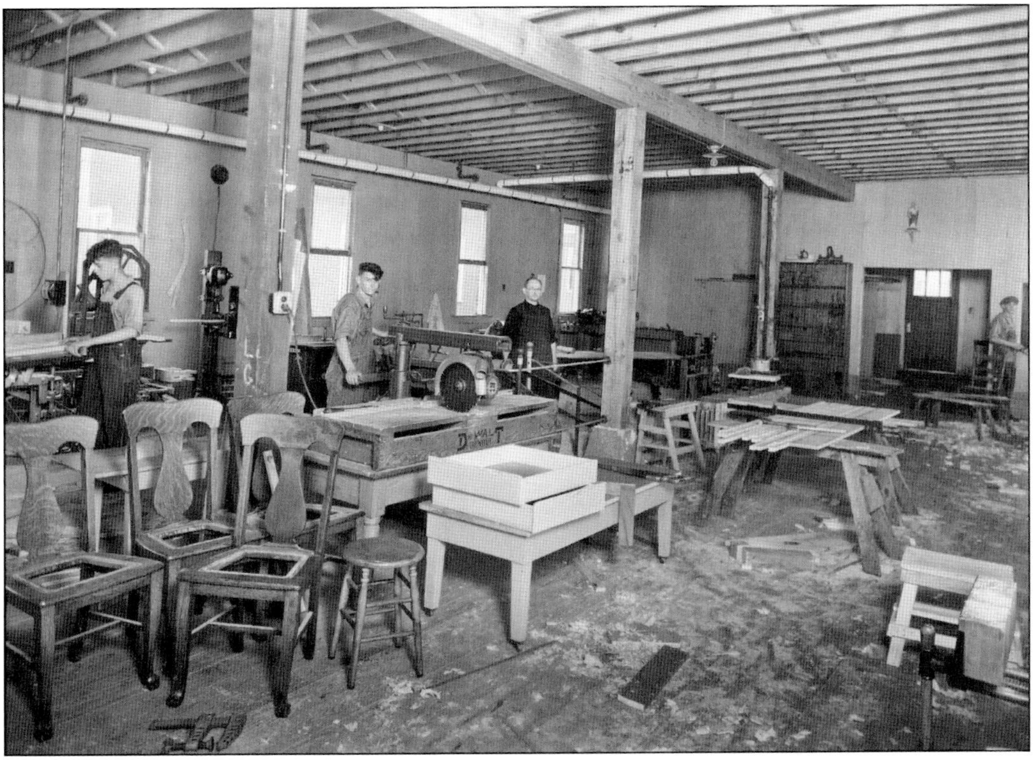

Carpentry was a craft eagerly sought by many students. Brothers Wiho and Rembert were experts in the field. Brother Wiho, who was at the school from 1928 to 1937, was also an architect. He designed and helped build the bandstand. Brother Rembert (instructor 1931–1967) is shown in the 1935 photograph above with Andrew Chism (left) and Robert Herron. A new carpentry shop was completed in 1954 under the direction of Brother Rembert, and more modern equipment was procured. Student bricklayers, electricians, and carpenters all contributed to the construction of the new facility.

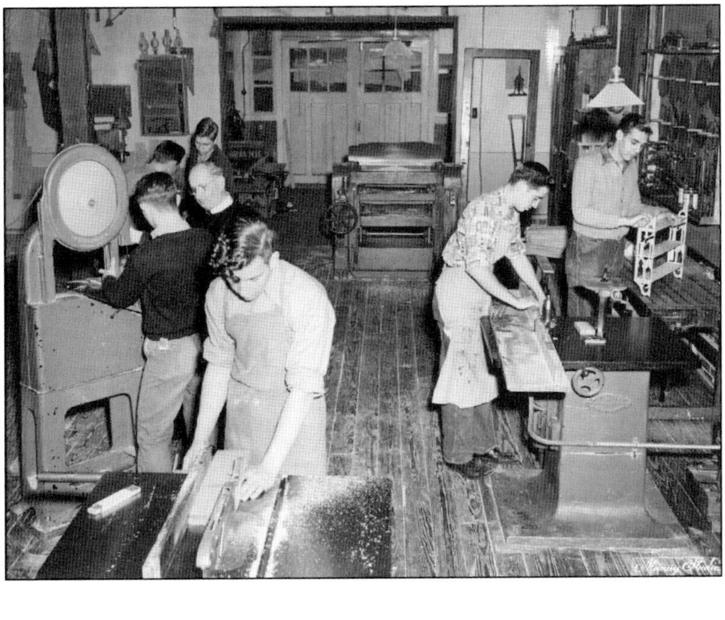

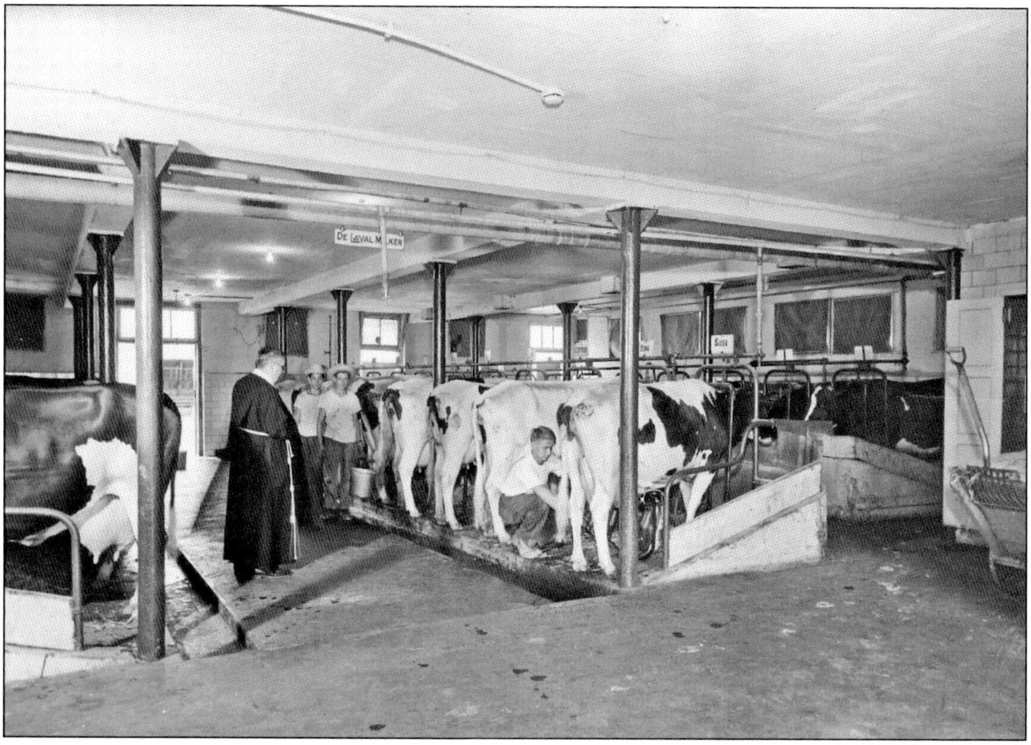

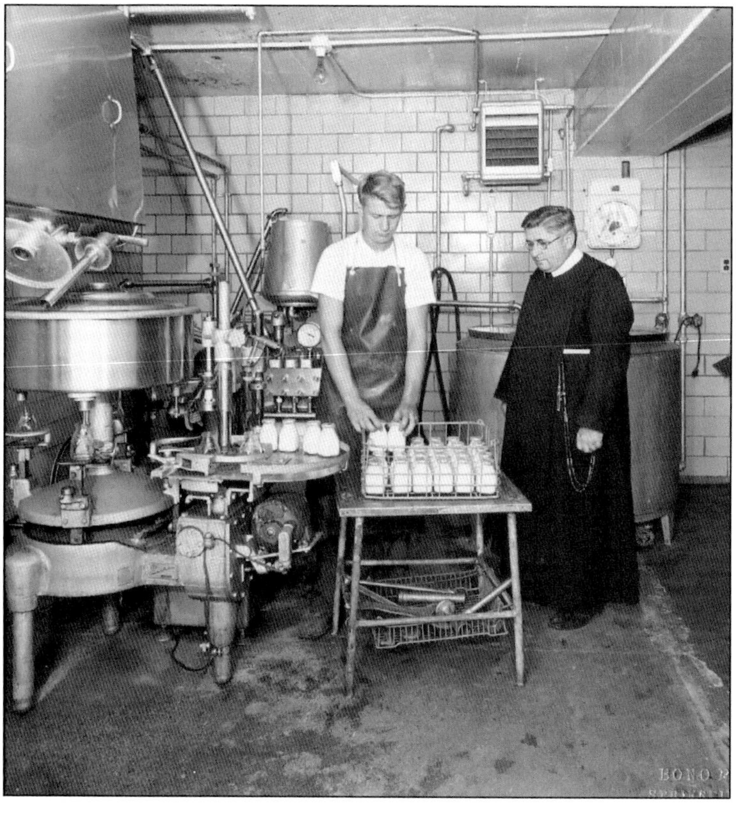

Inside the dairy barn around 1952, Brother Nicodemus (instructor 1948–1972) watches as students set up the milking machines for "Shorty," Louise, Gertrude, and others. The dairy installed a pasteurization-bottling machine to meet health standards and requests from customers for bottled milk. The boys also bottled orangeade and chocolate milk. Eventually, 3,000 bottles were produced on a daily basis to supply the needs of St. John's Sanitarium and St. John's Hospital in Springfield.

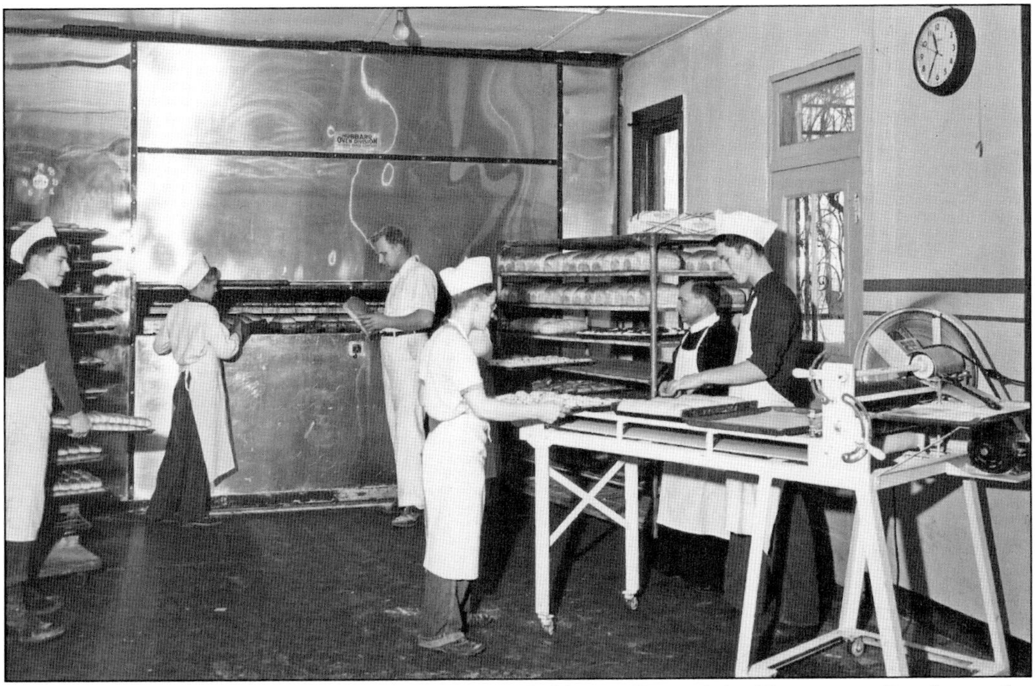

Two views of the bakery at St. James are provided here. One of the Franciscan Brothers who taught dozens of students the fine art of baking was Brother Onuphrius (above, second from right) who was at the school from 1949 to 1959. He was assisted by Stanley Klickna (above, third from left). For many years the school supplied baked goods to several institutions, including St. John's Hospital. Breads, cookies, rolls, and pies, all delicious, were enjoyed by thousands of people. Those pictured in the 1951 photograph below all graduated as apprentice bakers. From left to right are Joseph Ramirez, Donald Evans, John Wilkinson, Brother Onuphrius, unidentified, Arthur Evans, and Charles Jugan.

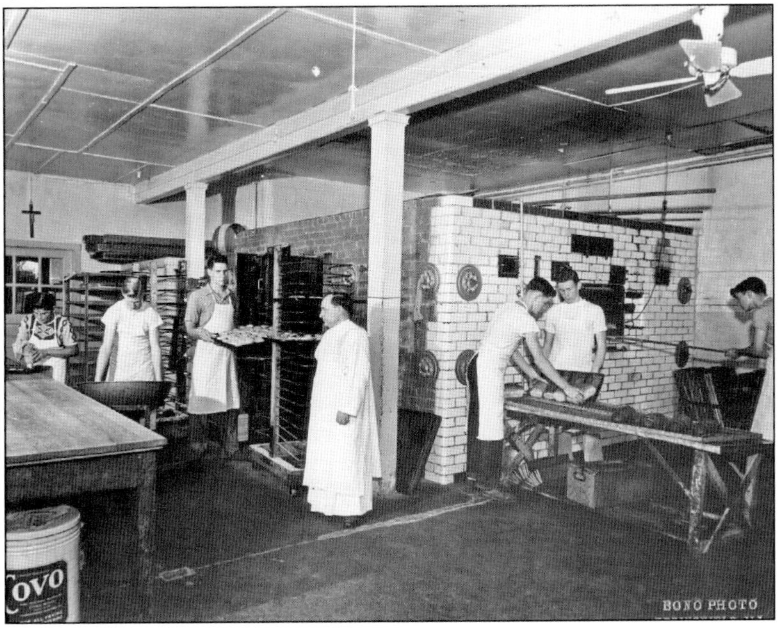

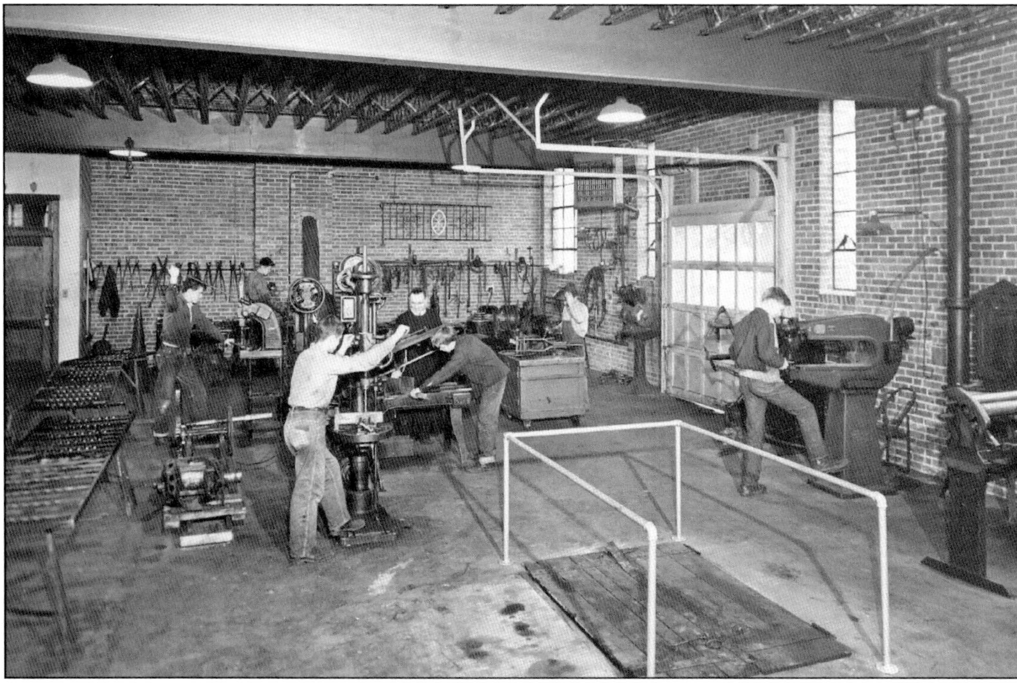

Brother Kolonat (above) spent 18 years teaching in the forge and machine shops. Wrought iron fencing, benches, and flagpoles crafted by the students were in great demand throughout the area. Even 38 years after closing, St. James wrought iron still adorns the grounds of Brother James Court and other places today. This is a testament to the craftsmanship taught by the brothers and the good work of the students.

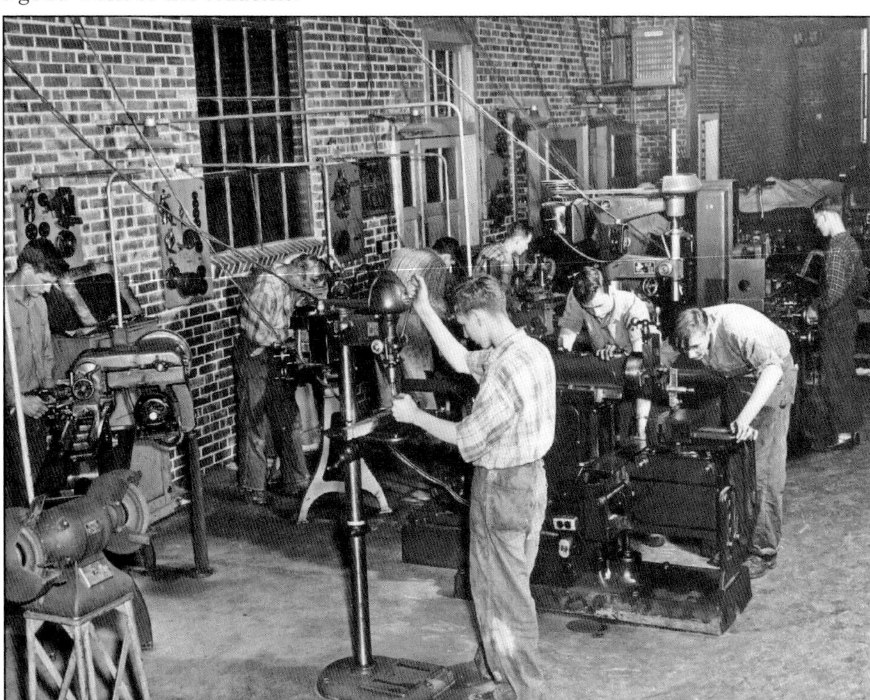

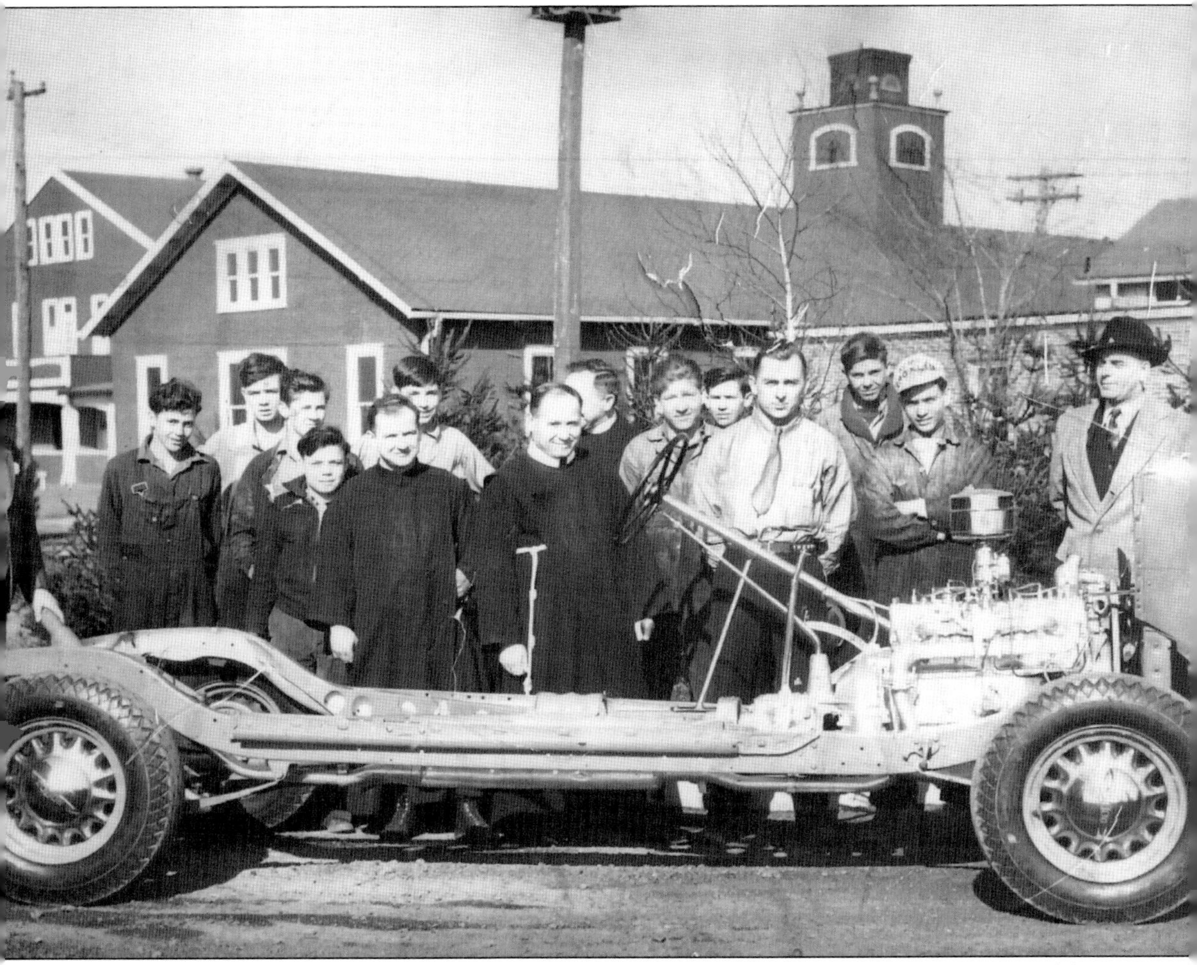

This 1935 Dodge chassis donated by Hatcher-Joseph Dodge dealer was used as a training aid for the mechanics-to-be. Fred Mehlick, auto mechanics instructor, had many contacts among local car dealers and was able to secure the donation. Eventually, the students assembled the chassis into a road-worthy car by the addition of rods, pistons, seats, and other parts, and a complete body from a salvage yard. The Dodge was licensed and turned over to the brothers, who drove it for several years. The adults in the photograph are (from left to right) Oliver C. Joseph, president of Hatcher-Joseph Dodge; Brother Banthus; Brother Egbertus (superior); Fred Mehlick, instructor; and Harry Small, general manager of Hatcher-Joseph Dodge.

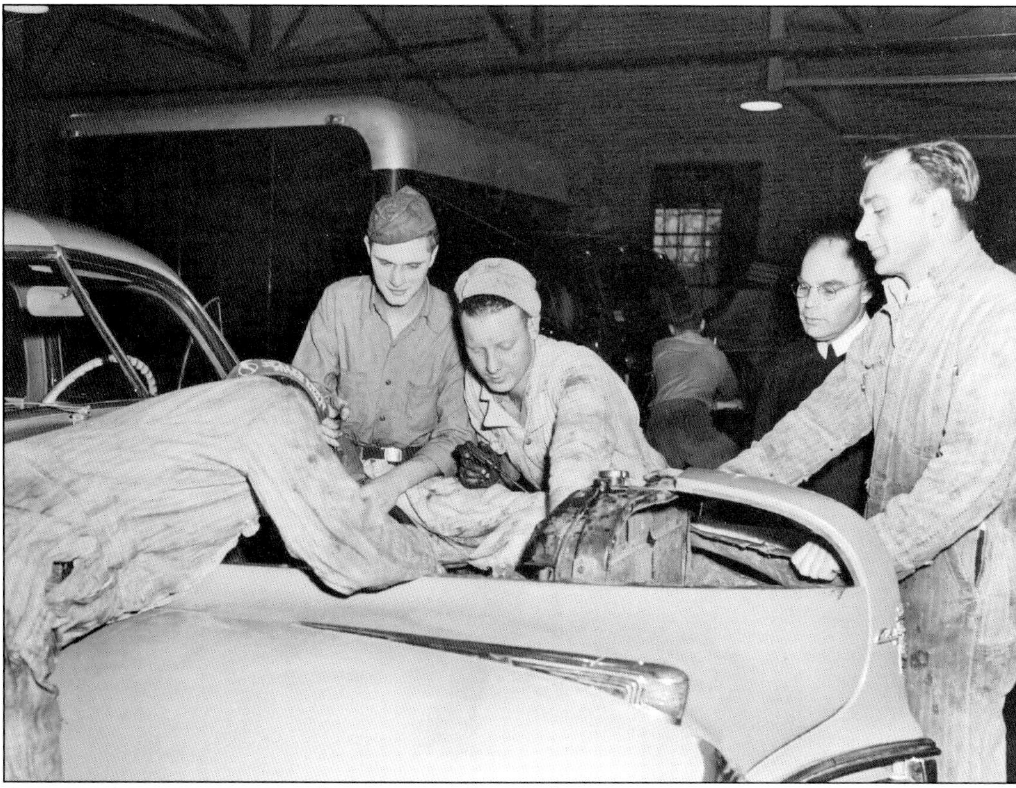

Auto mechanics was a popular program that had its first apprentice graduate in 1938, and certificates continued to be given through the final class in 1972. Fred Mehlick (back to camera) taught at the school from 1936 to 1972, while Brother Fabian was there for its entire existence. Maintaining the school's fleet of vehicles as well as body work and engine overhauls were skills taught to the students. As St. James' reputation for good work became known, many of the public became regular customers.

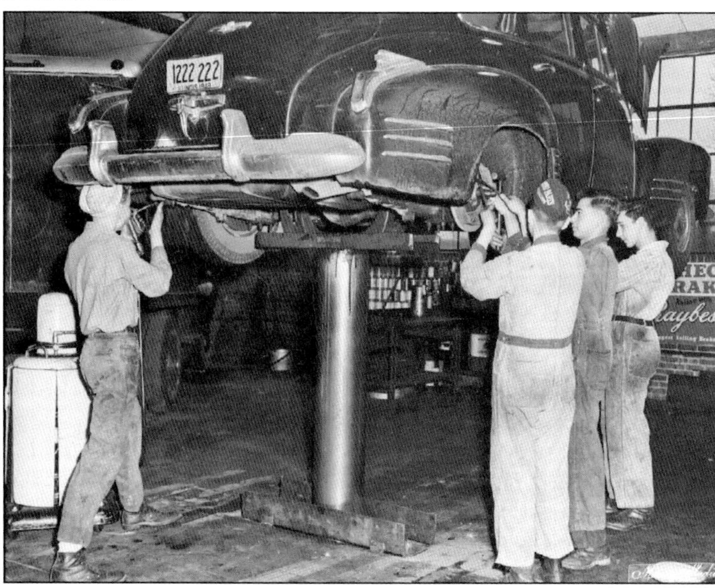

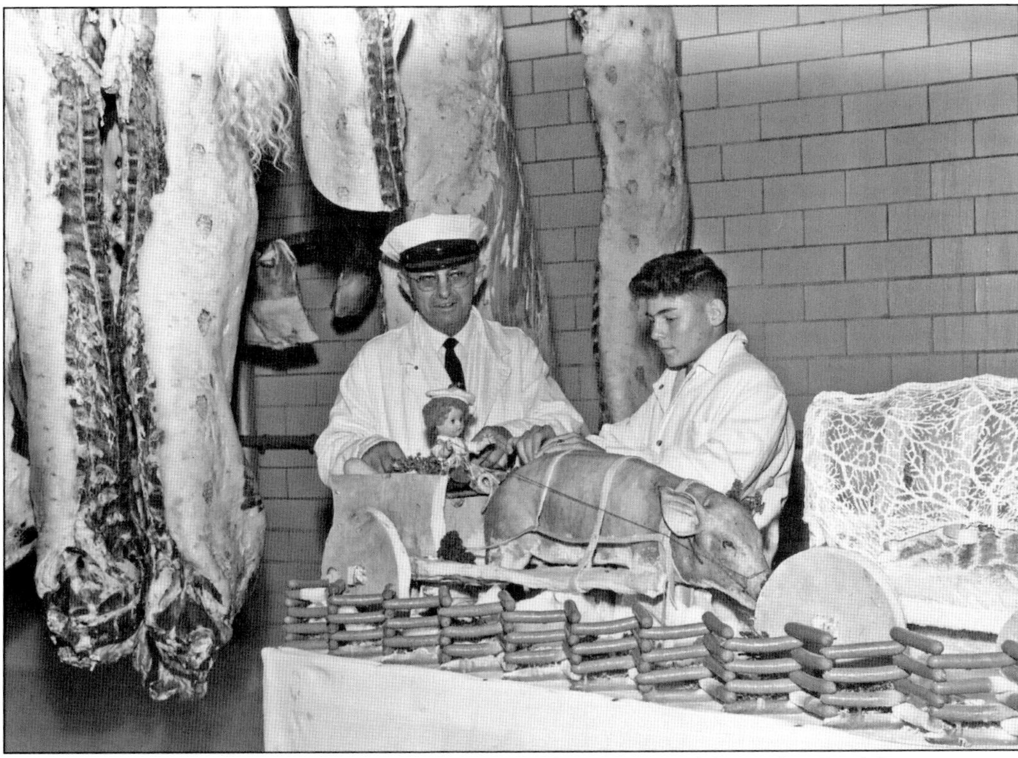

Although individual customers experienced much of the expertise of the trade school departments, at times an open house, such as the one in these 1961 photographs of the meat-processing department, effectively expanded the presentation of the wares. Above, instructor Alvin Altepeter aids the creative work of John Pershing, a student. Below, two ladies enjoy the displays with Altepeter and Frank Romano (1933 graduate), also an instructor in the meat-processing department and butcher shop.

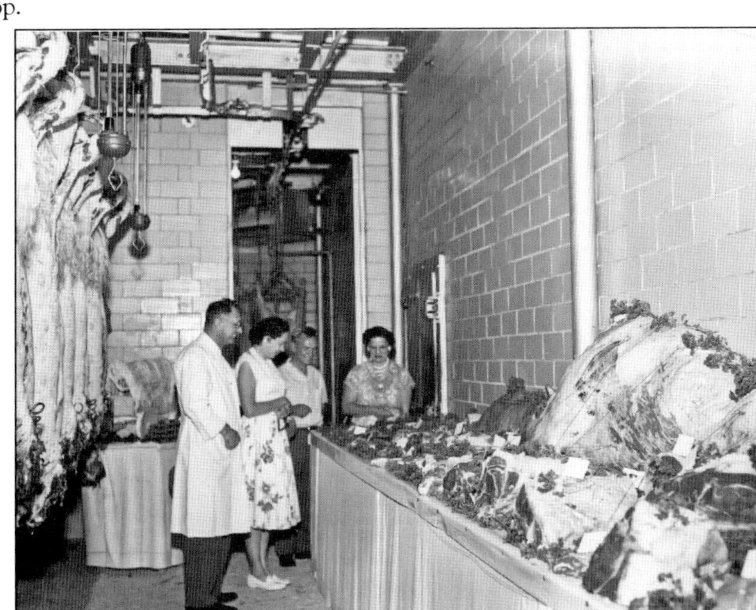

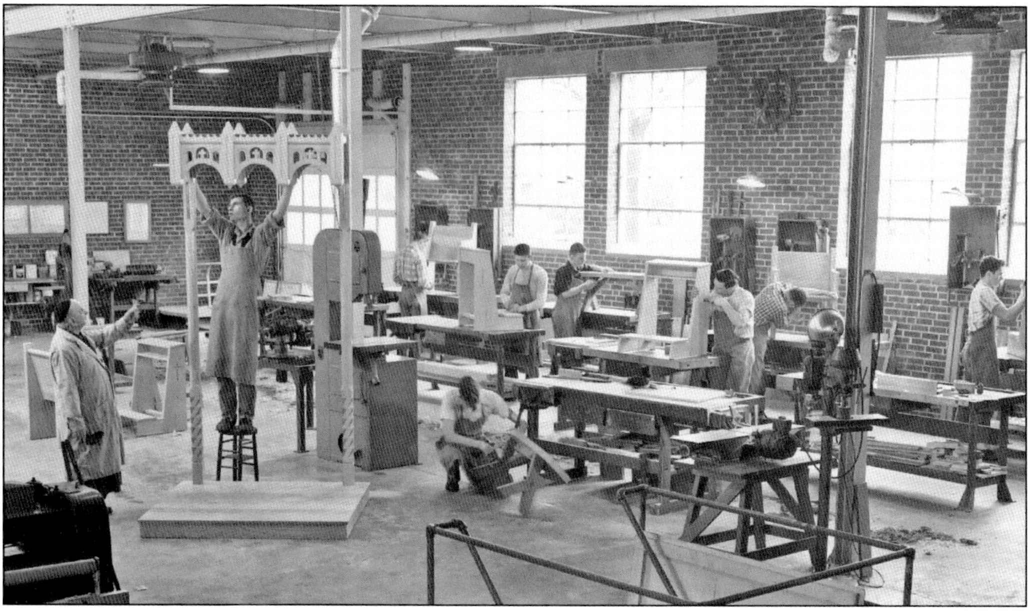

One of the most popular trades was carpentry. Here the students are cabinet makers-in-training, fashioning furniture that would be used throughout the school. Brother Rembert gives directions as the student works on a frame that will be used over the bishop's throne when he comes for graduation in the chapel.

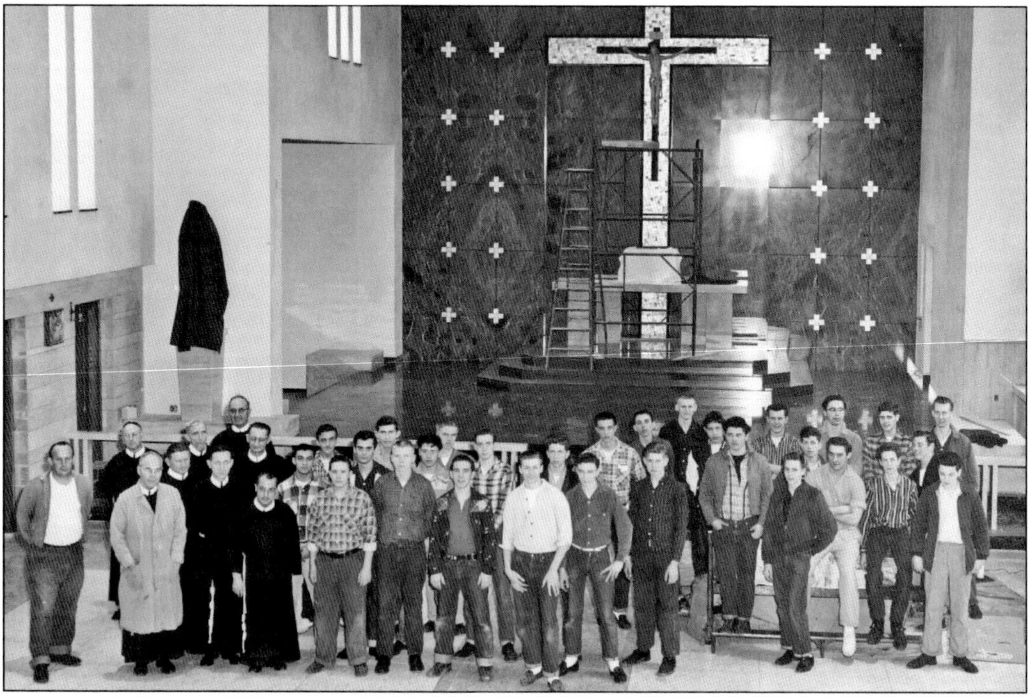

The students received hands-on training in their chosen trade; many times this experience involved actually building the "new" chapel used by the students, brothers, teachers, and staff. This picture is from 1959 on the occasion of the completion of St. Joseph the Worker Chapel on the school grounds.

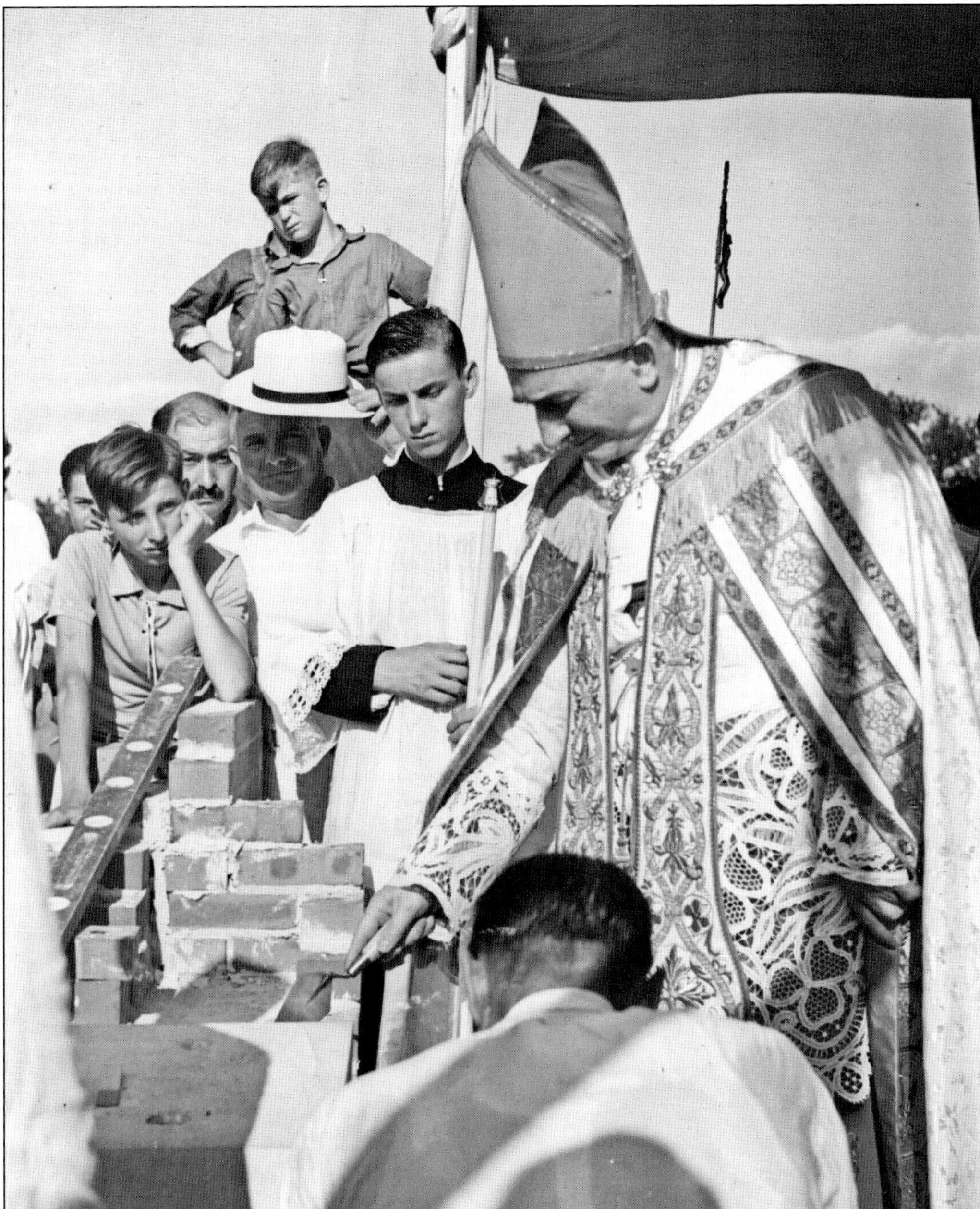

On July 17, 1938, Bishop James A. Griffin of the Diocese of Springfield places cement for the laying of the cornerstone of the gymnasium. The inscription on the stone, now visible in the atrium of Brother James Court, reads "Through Christ The Corner Stone To The Holy Trinity." The gym was completed in time for the first basketball season in 1941 and continued to be used until the 1990s. Bishop Griffin was a great benefactor of St. James and attended numerous functions at the school.

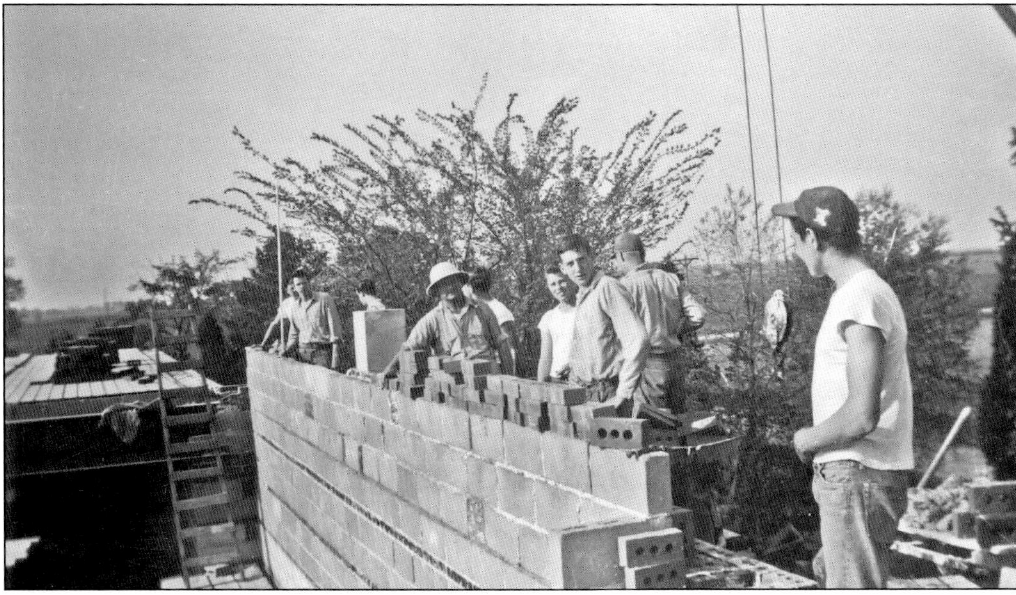

Construction of St. Joseph the Worker Chapel began in 1954 and was completed in late 1958. Student carpenters, electricians, bricklayers, and others all worked on the project. Brother Elpidius, instructor from 1948 to 1958, and Brother Nicodemus, 1948–1972, led the students on this project. Tile walls, terrazzo floors, and stained glass windows are beautiful examples of the work done by the students and brothers. As the walls go up, it is evident that many hands are involved. Some of the student workers in the above photograph are Charles Peters, Bill Eddington, James Guyon, Gerald Bryan, and Ron Runkles. Brother Elpidius is seen sporting his safari hat. The photograph below shows the progress of the chapel construction in August 1955.

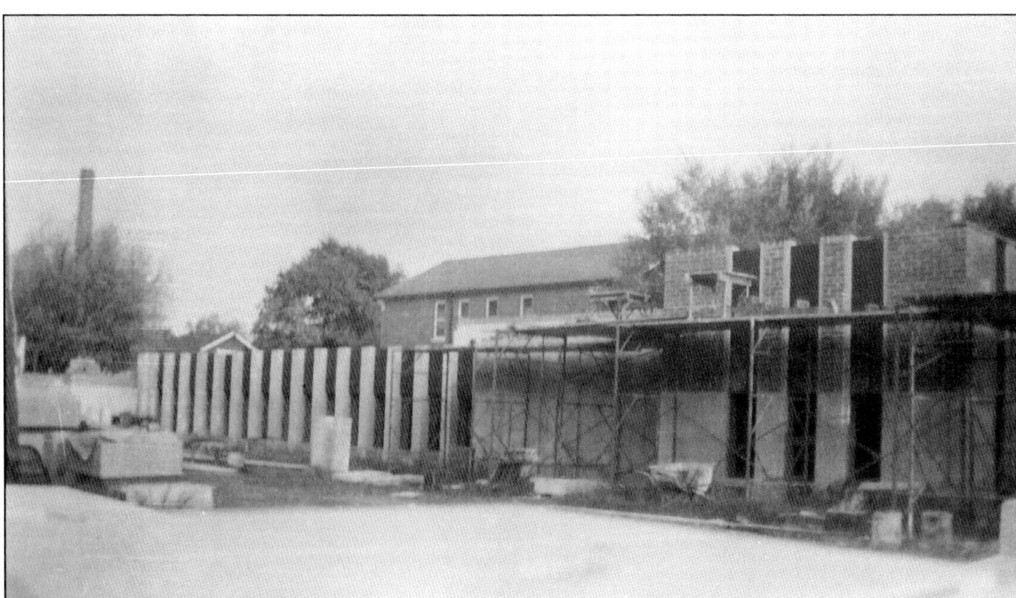

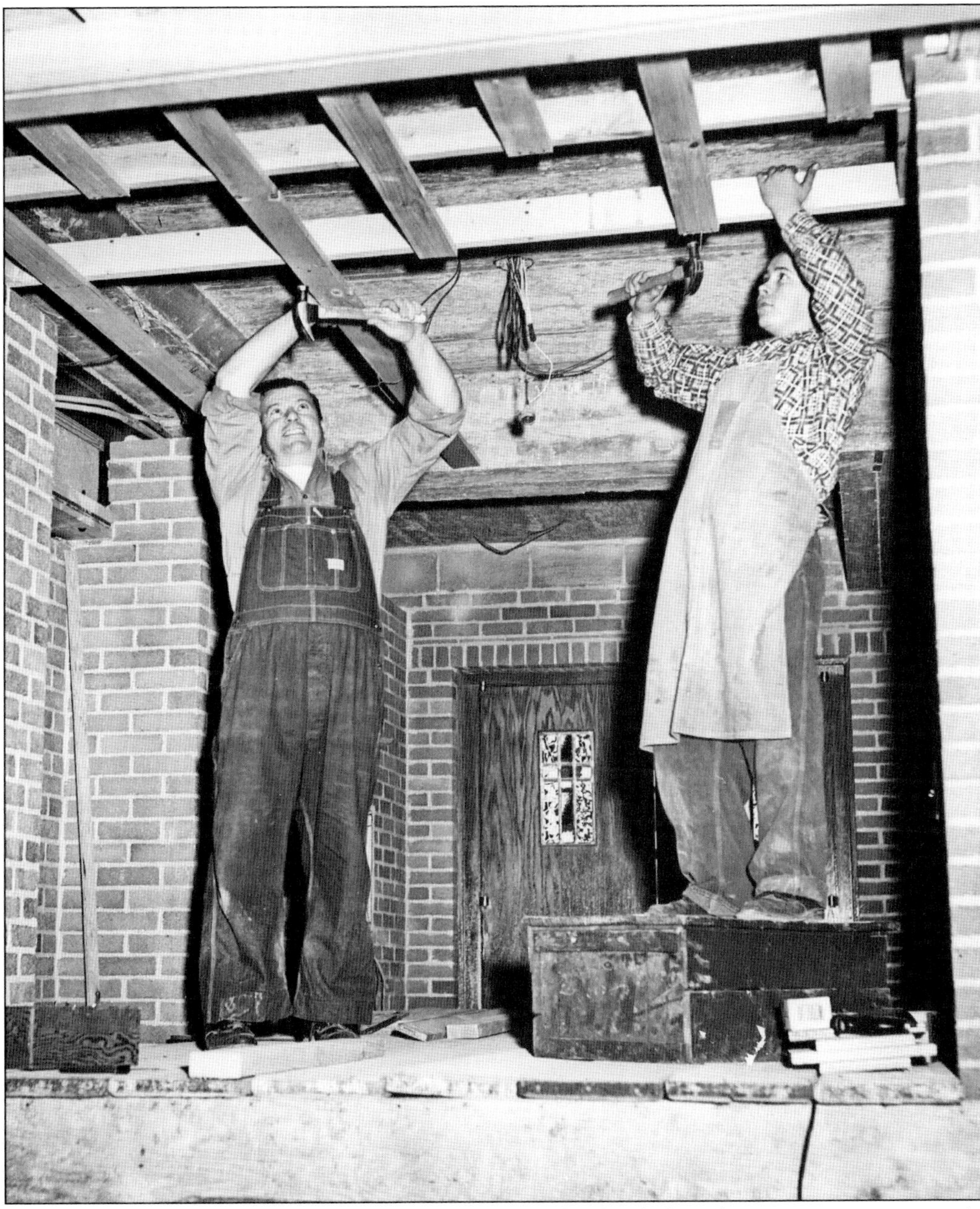

A certified electrician shows student-apprentice Michael Schubert how to string wires in the entrance to the chapel.

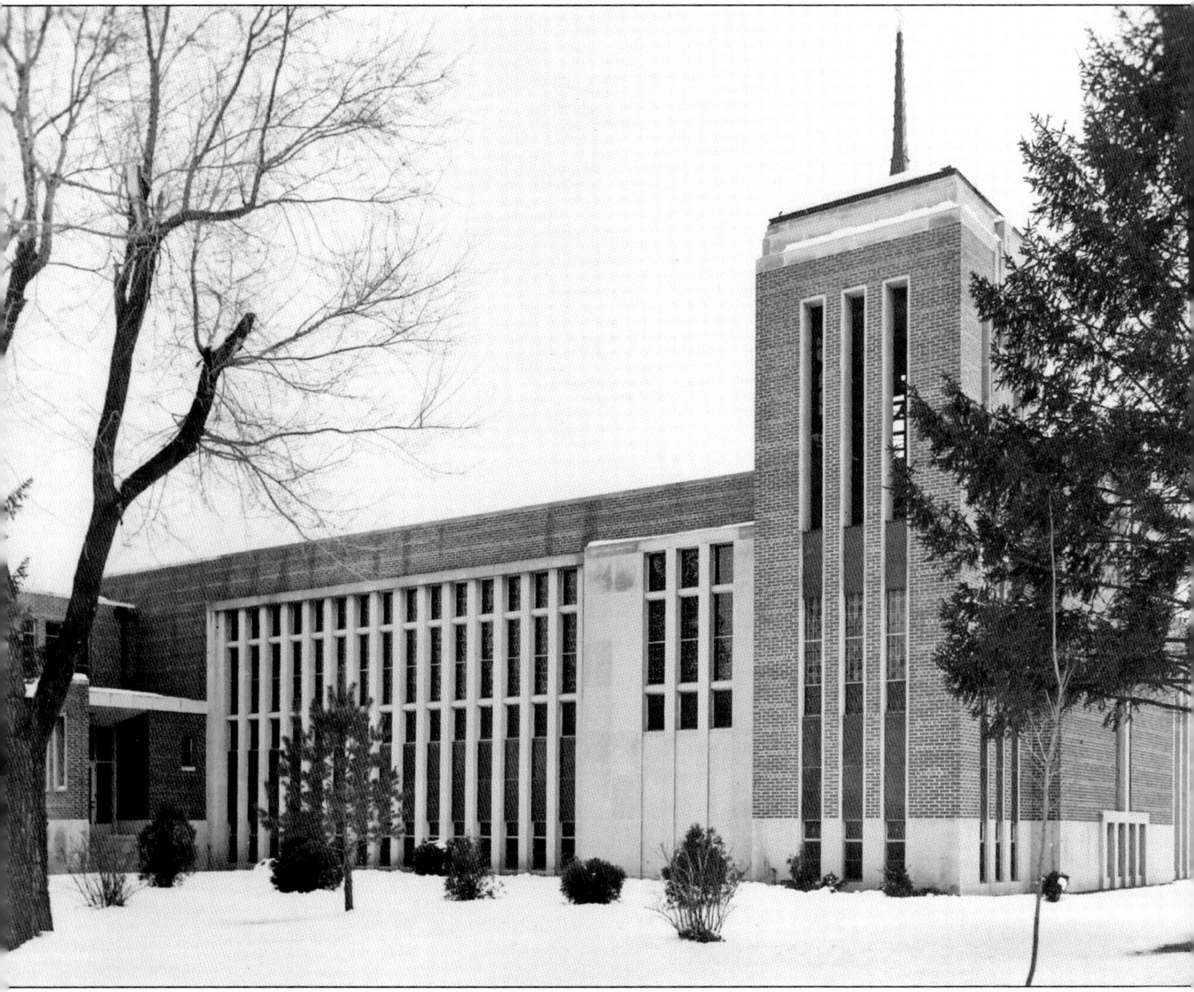

The finished house of worship stands ready for use, and is still in use to this day.

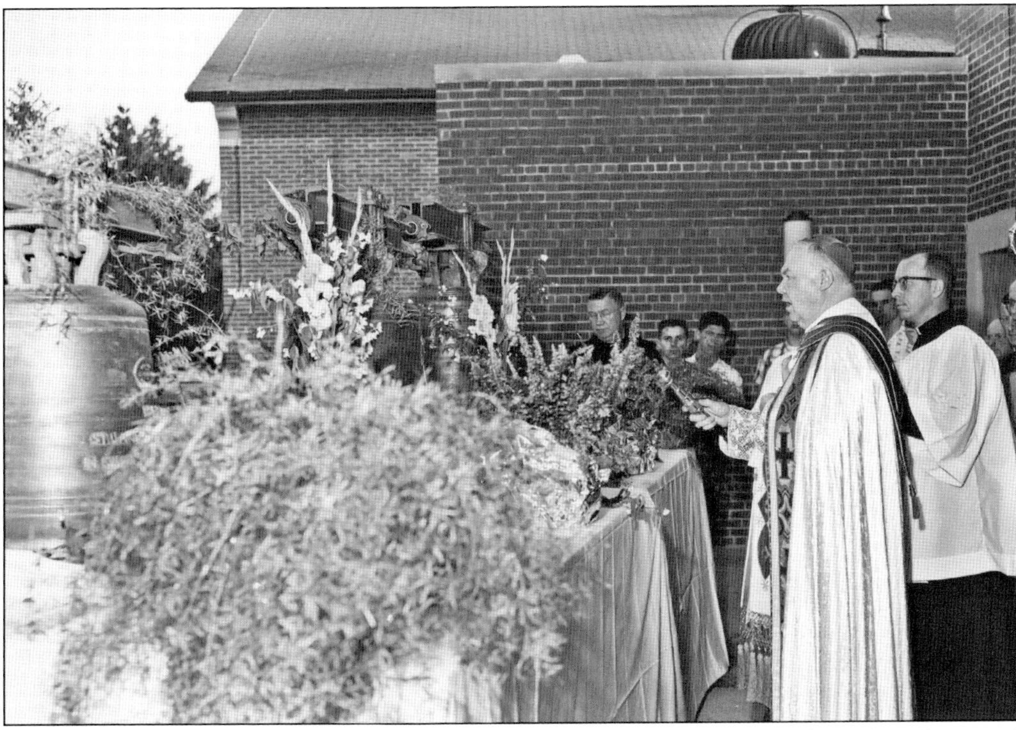

The blessing of the chapel and the baptism of the bells occurred on September 15, 1962, to mark the 100th anniversary of the founding of the religious congregation in Germany. A stained glass window depicting St. Francis of Assisi also commemorates the 100th anniversary for the Franciscan Brothers of the Holy Cross. The photograph above shows Bishop William O'Connor of Springfield blessing the bells. The photograph below shows a flag with the papal colors of white and gold and an early insignia of the congregation.

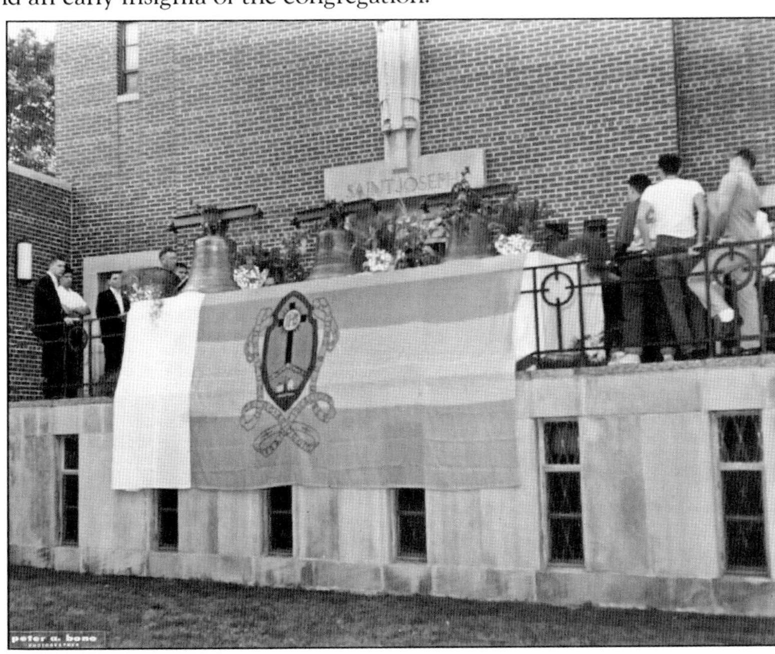

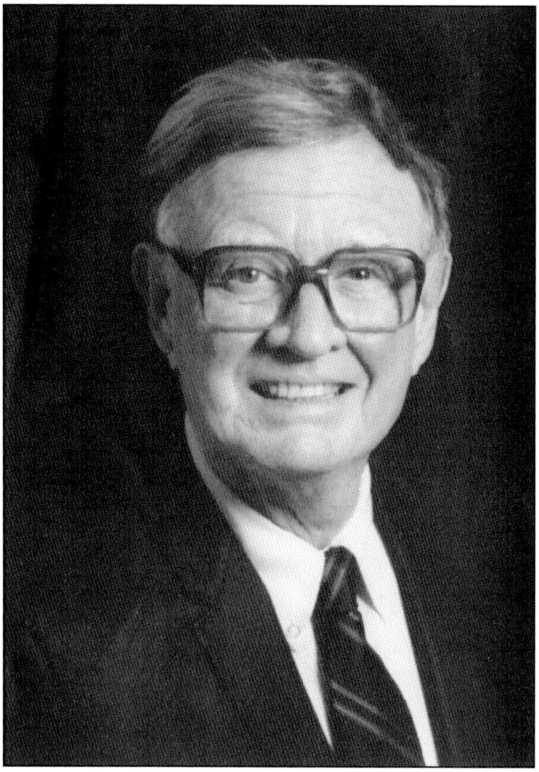

The late McCaffrey brothers, John (left) and Donald, authored a detailed and well-written account of the history of St. James titled *The St. James Story, 1928–1972* published in 1995. Both men grew up in orphanages and graduated from St. James in 1939. Donald apprenticed as a carpenter and John as a baker. They were veterans of World War II—Donald had a 29-year army career, retiring in Virginia as a lieutenant colonel, while John, who had been in the Army Air Corps, became an educator in California. Donald and John both married (Edith and Tina, respectively). Their book was a project of several years, and many alumni and their wives helped in the preparation of the story. Also contributing were Br. Michael Groesch, superior/principal at the school, and Br. David Sarnecki, a later principal at St. James. (Photographs courtesy of Tina McCaffrey.)

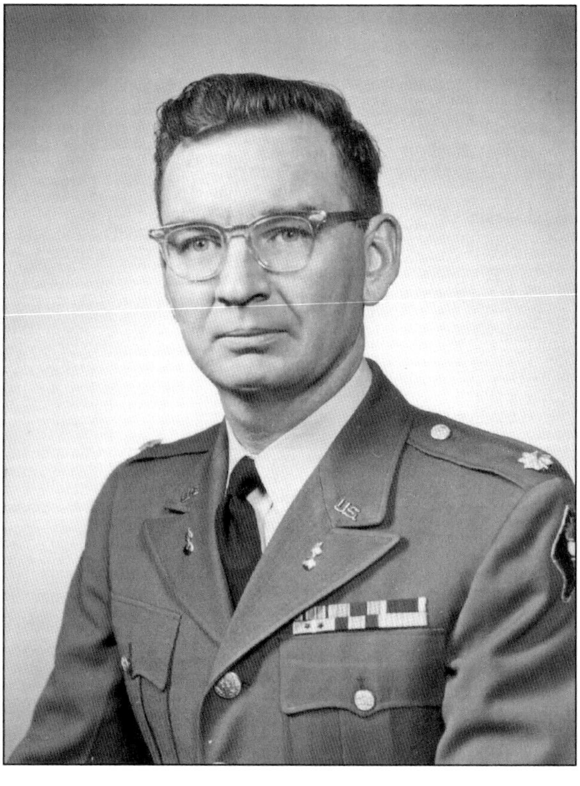

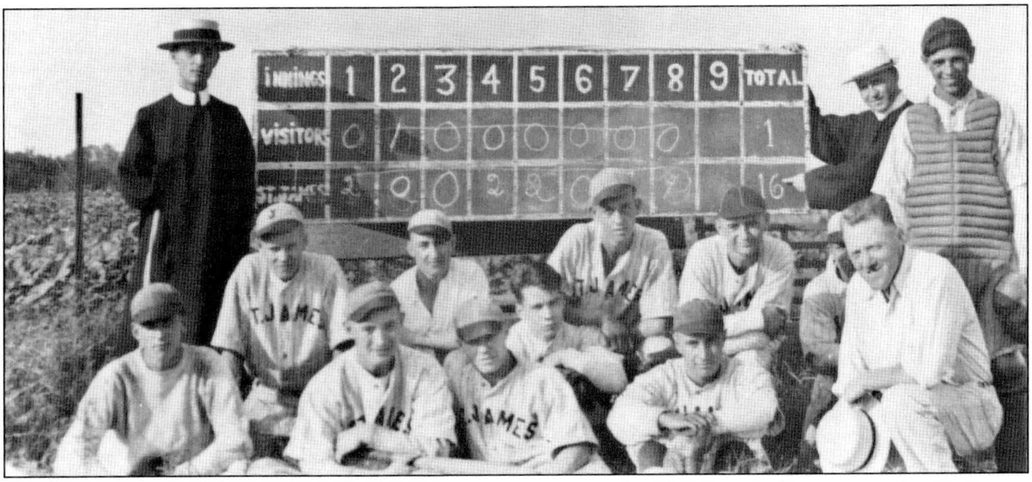

Brother Egbertus (superior) points to the winning score of a 1935 baseball game at the St. James field. The school did not play a full high school schedule until 1942, but it participated in Springfield summer leagues from 1930 to 1941. The team in the early years was a mix of trade school employees and students. Brother Aegidius is at top left, and coach John Taggart is in the first row, right side. Taggart was a 1927 graduate and athlete of Springfield High School. He began the first football program for St. James in 1934, and later worked at the Springfield Post Office for 27 years.

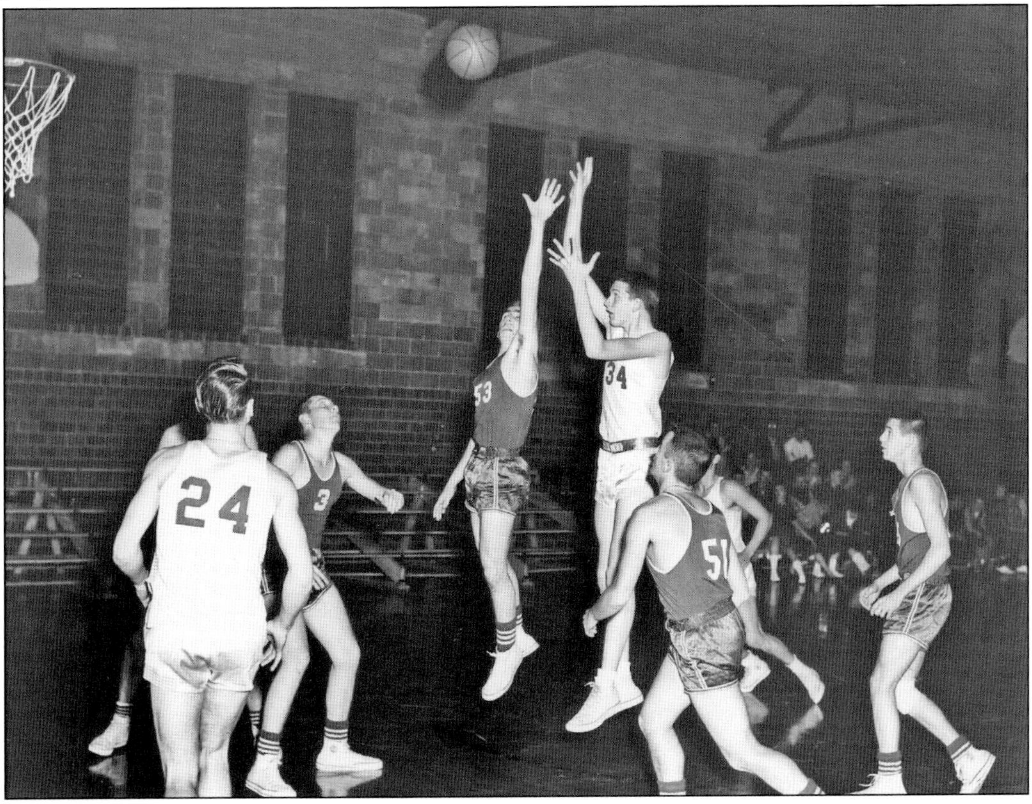

Larry Motley, No. 34, shoots over a defender in this 1958 action photograph taken at the St. James gym. Gerald Even, No. 24, is heading for the basket for a possible rebound, although it is likely Motley made the shot, judging by his 19 points per game average that season.

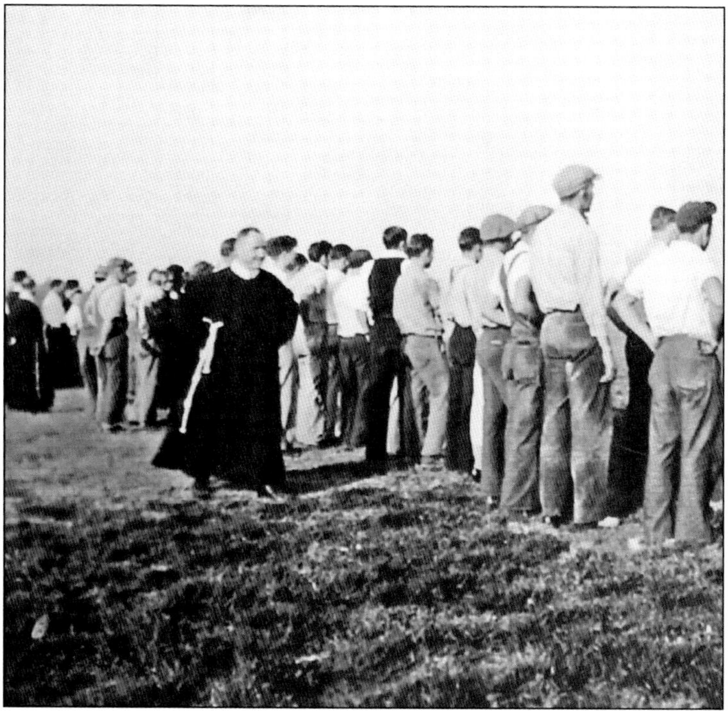

Sporting events were still times of supervision and kindly direction for some of the brother staff members. Here Brother Egbertus quietly walks the line during a football game at St. James around 1936, to ensure that all was going as it should. Bleachers were virtually unknown for games in the early years of the sport. When the public attended the games they were normally charged by the carload, and not individually (25¢ per car). Bleachers were installed in 1941.

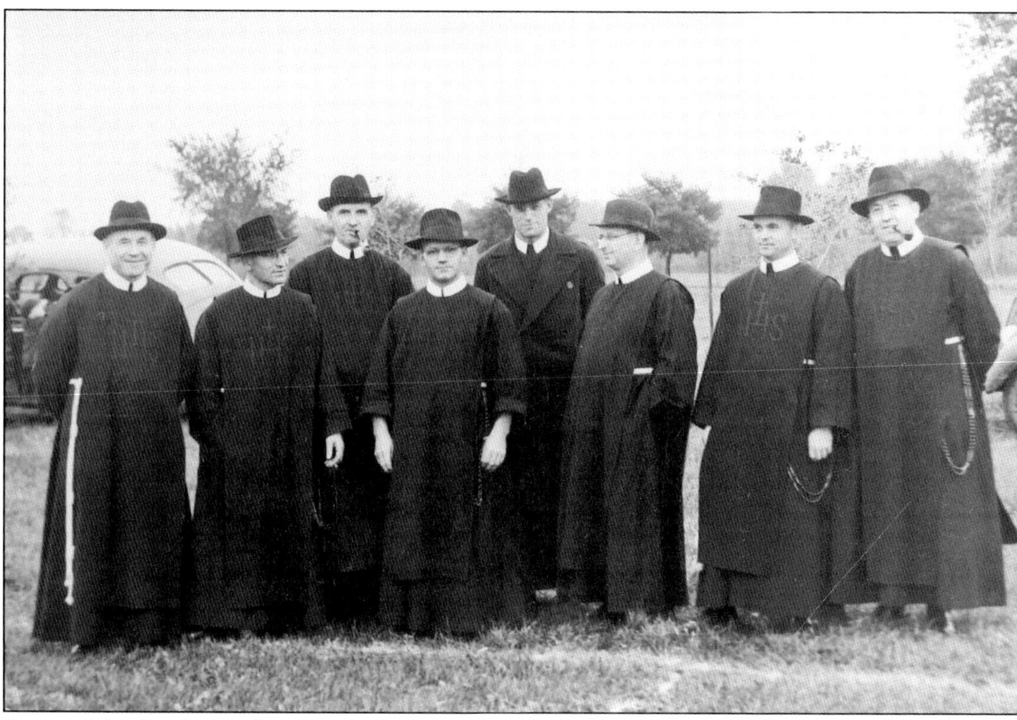

Some of the brothers take an opportunity to be a little less attentive to detail while highlighting their own "good looks." An earlier chronicler said there was no reason why this group did not include all the brothers. From left to right are Brothers Egbertus, Kolonat, Justus, Sergius, Serapion, Rembert, Nicetius, and Juniper. Photograph possibly taken around 1938 on the sports field.

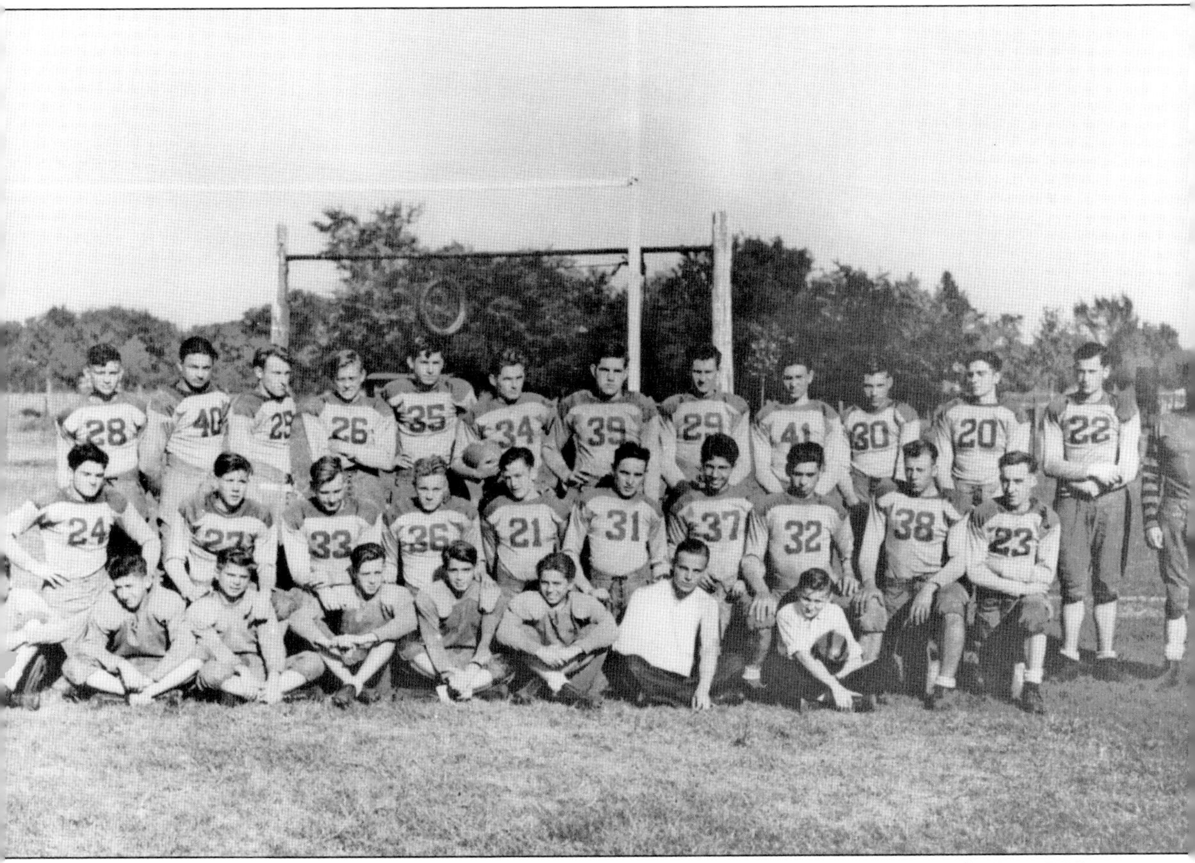

The 1937 football team was the best in the 23-year history of the sport at St. James (1934–1956). Coach Frank "Red" Hartman (third row, far right) rarely had more than 18 players dressed for a game, and nearly all the starting lineup played offense and defense with few substitutions. With a six win, one loss, one tie record, they shared the championship of the downstate Catholic High School Conference. Their only loss was to the Chicago Catholic League's Mount Carmel (with an enrollment 20 times larger than St. James) in a Thanksgiving Day battle at Lanphier Baseball Park in Springfield. More than 1,500 fans were in attendance, paying admission of 50¢ for adults and 25¢ for children. Hartman was the football, baseball, and boxing coach from 1937 to 1941. He also taught history and English. He was a World War II veteran born and raised in Chicago, a graduate of DeLaSalle High School and DePaul University (1930), and he played professional football for a time with the Chicago Cardinals. In the first row of the picture is Paul Britz (arm in sling), whose cousin Andy is a current resident of Brother James Court.

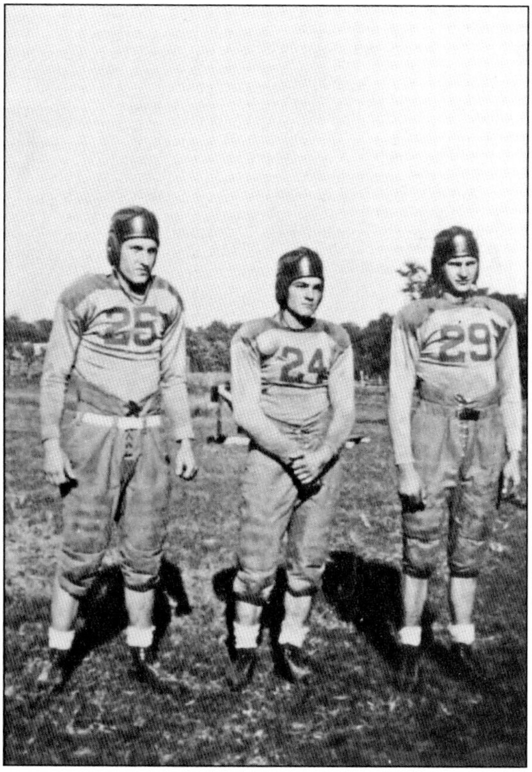

The 1937 football team was led by captain Joseph Wilson (left), Salvatore "Silver" DiGiacomo (center), and Anthony "Mickey" Wysocki. DiGiacomo led the team in scoring in 1937 with 11 touchdowns and Wysocki had four. DiGiacomo scored more points (113) in his four-year career than any player in St. James' history. Wilson did not graduate but the other two received their certificates in 1939: DiGiacomo as a butcher and Wysocki as a welder. After failing as a butcher because he could not stand to look in the eyes of cattle being led to slaughter, and as a baker because he dropped trays of bread dough and forgot to use yeast, Wysocki took up welding, and had a successful career at Caterpillar in Decatur lasting 35 years. (Courtesy The State Journal-Register.)

In 1938 this group of trade school friends got together to celebrate St. James' football co-championship of the 1937 Catholic High School Conference. Brother Fabian (superior) is at first row center, and coach Hartman is at second row, right. (Courtesy The State Journal-Register.)

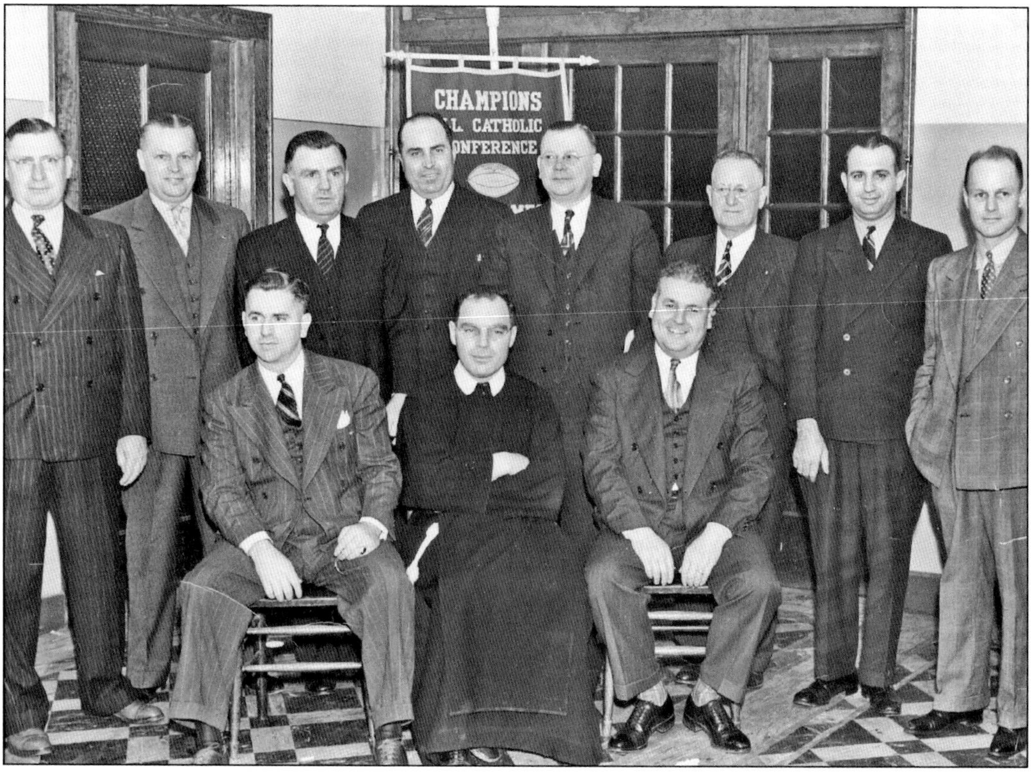

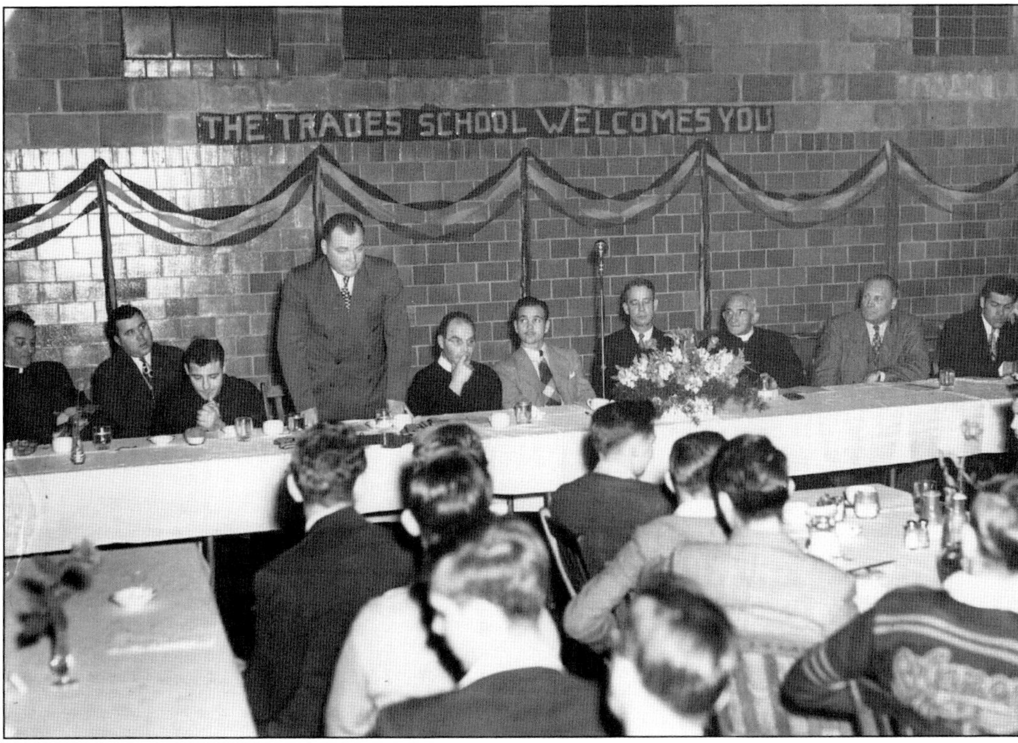

James O'Hara (coach, 1943–1949) addresses the crowd at the 1948 sports banquet in the above photograph. O'Hara had been a star athlete at Quincy College and had a 31-year career at the Springfield Post Office. Present at the speakers table, from left to right, are Rev. F. J. Harbauer (principal, Springfield Cathedral), Luke Gleason (coach, Cathedral), Rev. Evarist Farnand (principal, St. James), James O'Hara, Brother Fabian (superior), William Guinan (1939 St. James graduate), Donald Anderson (coach, Springfield Lanphier), Bishop James A. Griffin, Harry Eielson (mayor of Springfield), and Mac Wenskunas (main speaker; star college football player and team captain for the University of Illinois in its victory in the 1947 Rose Bowl). Below, Charles Gutmann receives his letter from Coach O'Hara.

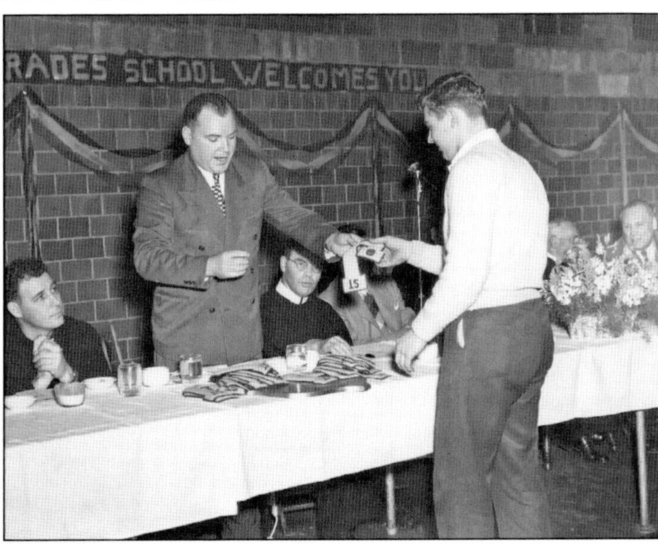

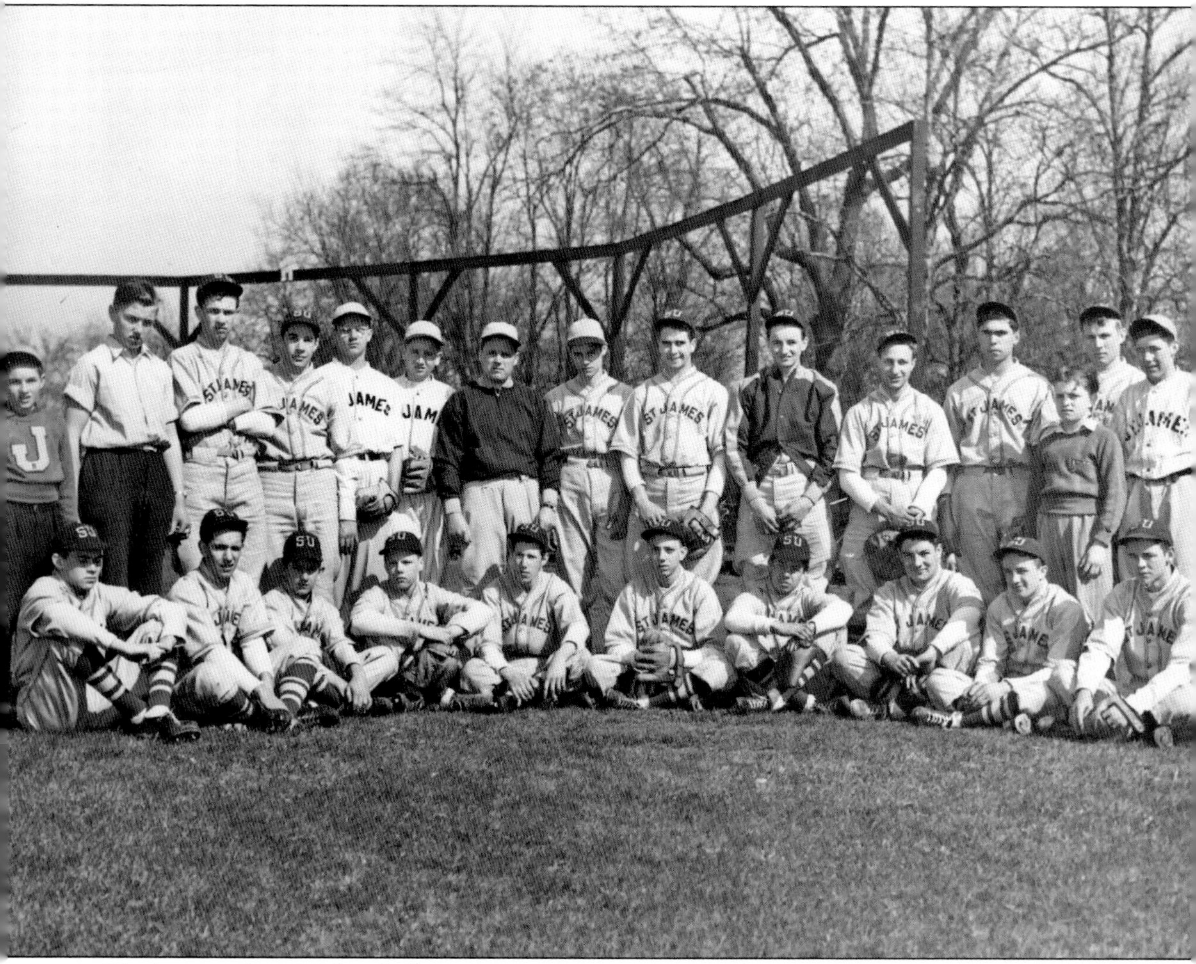

The boys in this 1942 baseball team picture represent more than half of the student body. Coach Albert Lewis (in dark jacket, second row, seventh from left) had a squad that finished first in team batting average among all Springfield high schools. Lewis also coached St. James' first basketball team (1941–1942) and its football squads in 1941 and 1942 before joining the navy during World War II. He was a sports star and graduate of Springfield High School, and was a graduate of Loyola University of Los Angeles, California.

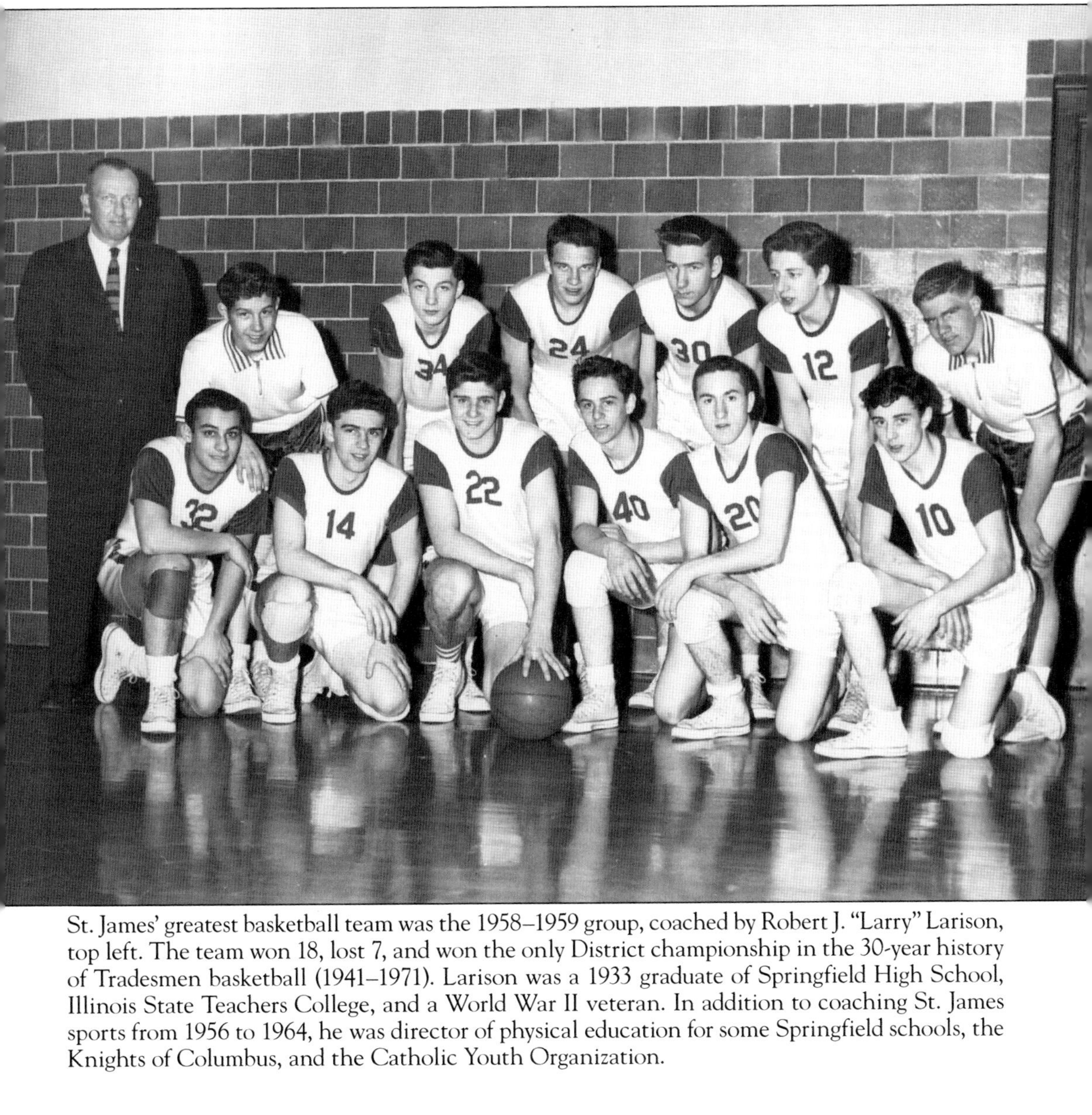

St. James' greatest basketball team was the 1958–1959 group, coached by Robert J. "Larry" Larison, top left. The team won 18, lost 7, and won the only District championship in the 30-year history of Tradesmen basketball (1941–1971). Larison was a 1933 graduate of Springfield High School, Illinois State Teachers College, and a World War II veteran. In addition to coaching St. James sports from 1956 to 1964, he was director of physical education for some Springfield schools, the Knights of Columbus, and the Catholic Youth Organization.

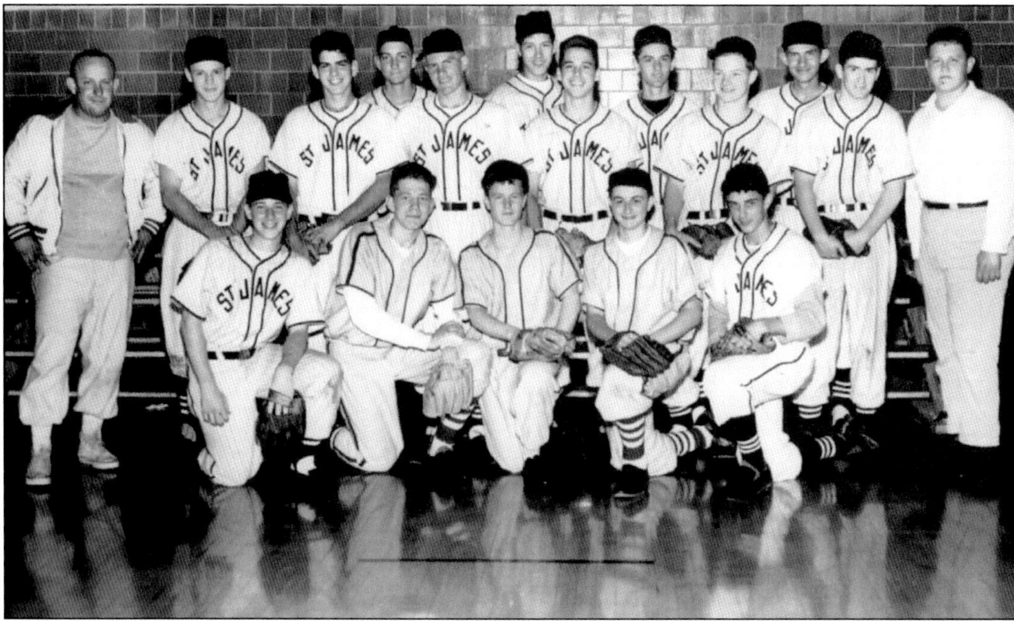

Albert Purgatorio (left) was head coach from 1964 to 1971. He was a 1946 graduate of St. James, earning a certificate as a machinist, and became a teacher in the machine shop. (Courtesy of Dr. Robert "Larry" Larison.)

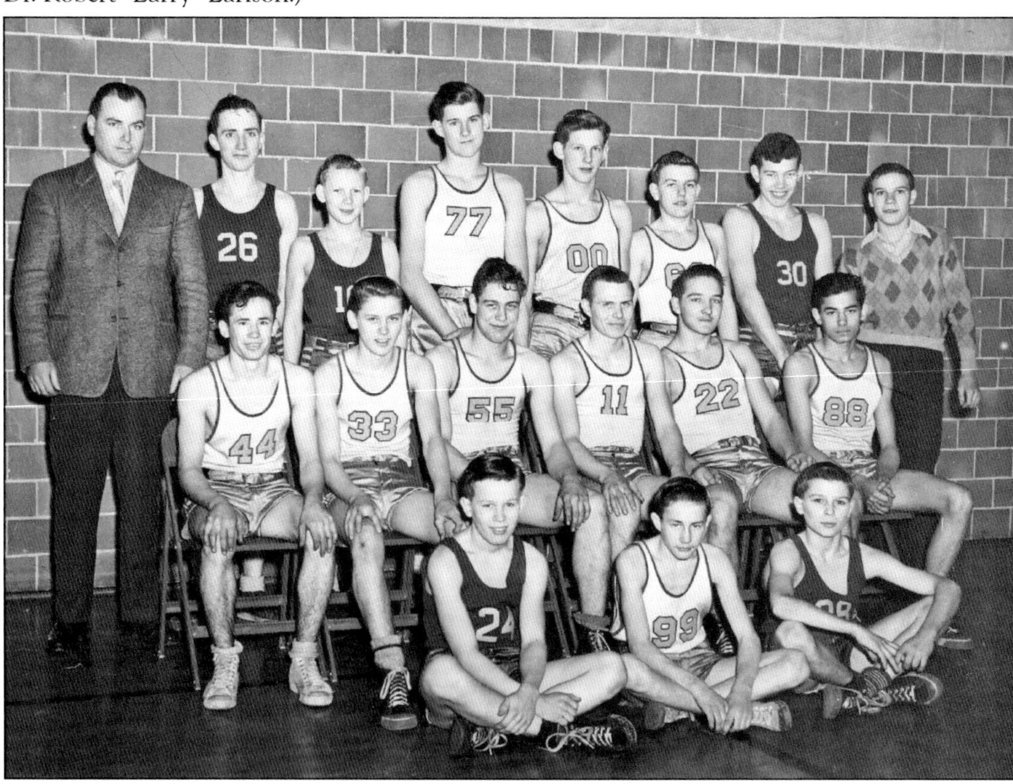

Coach O'Hara (top left) and his 1947–1948 basketball team consisted of freshmen as well as other classes. The Tradesmen had a difficult season, winning 4 while losing 17.

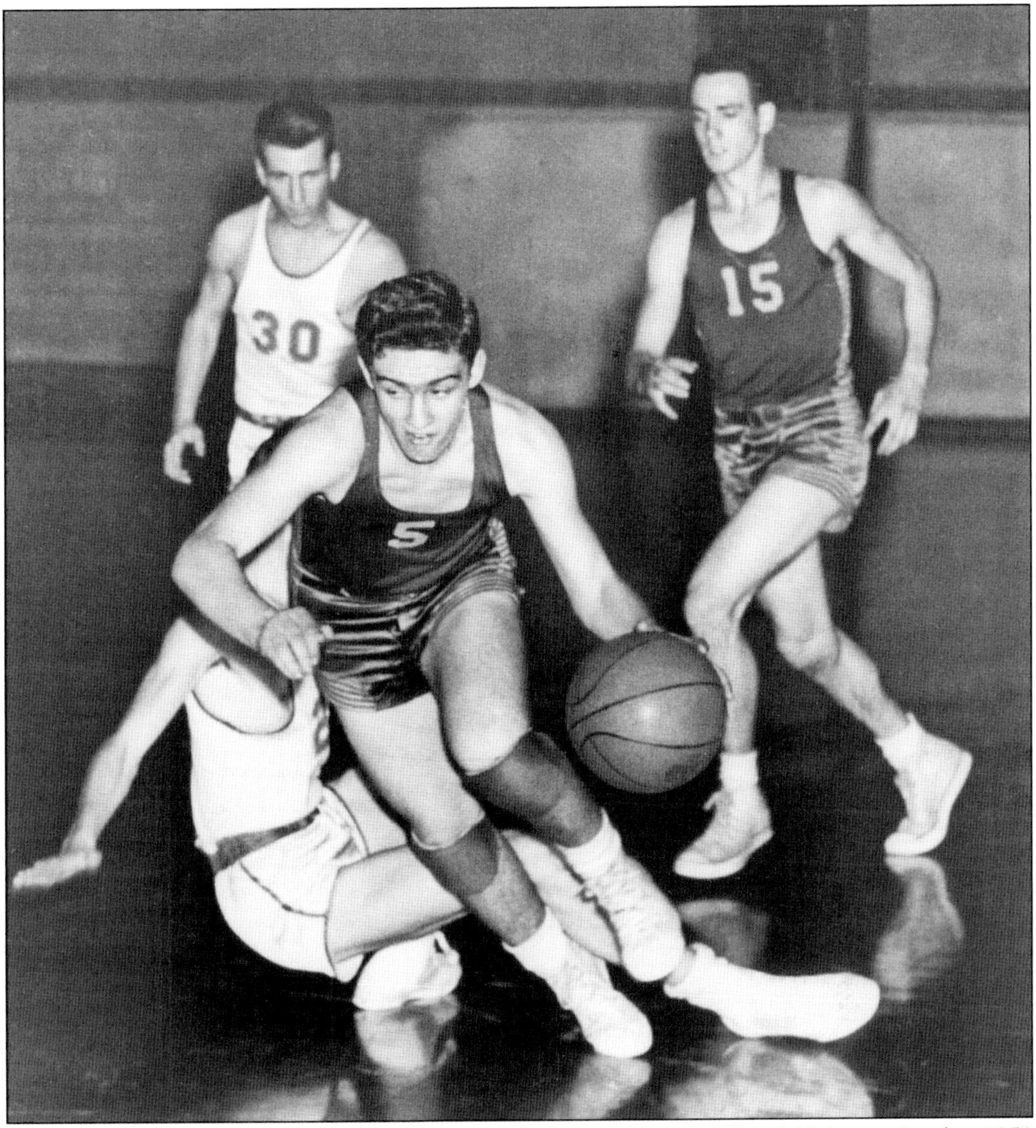

Coach Larison's 1957–1958 team fared a little better with 10 wins and 13 losses. In this 1958 photograph in the opposition's gym, Thomas Benedict, No. 5, drives around an opponent while Gerald Even, No. 15, follows.

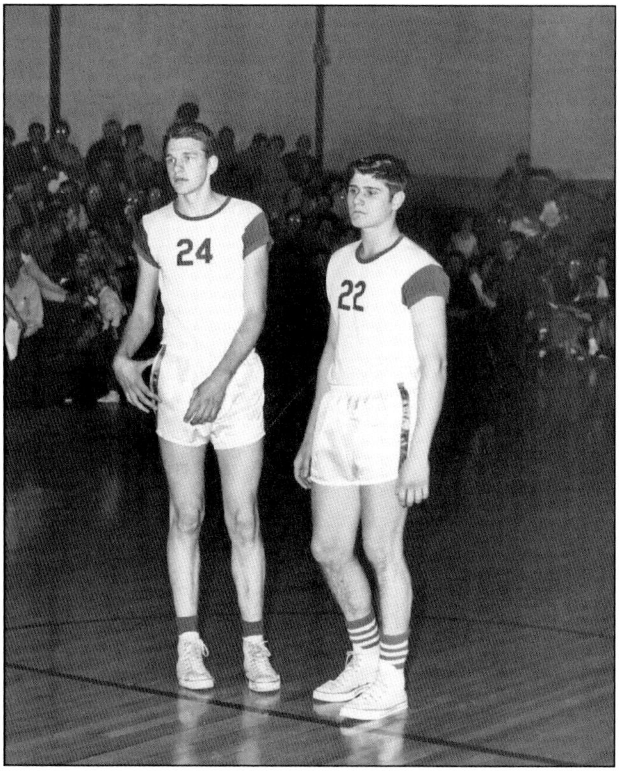

The highest-scoring basketball players in St. James history were Larry Motley (left) and Barry DeNardo. They were teammates for two seasons (1957–1958 and 1958–1959), with Motley totaling 974 points and DeNardo 953. Motley was the school's all-time leading scorer, garnering 1,158 points in his three-year career. Robert Fredrick has the single season scoring record of 624 points, accomplished in the 1961–1962 season.

In this 1959 gym class scene, some of the varsity basketball players demonstrate the skills needed to compete in the sport. From left to right are (first row) Tom Benedict, Warren Range, Barry DeNardo, Bob Heeley, Paul Hughes, Larry Motley, Gary Benedict, and John Termine.

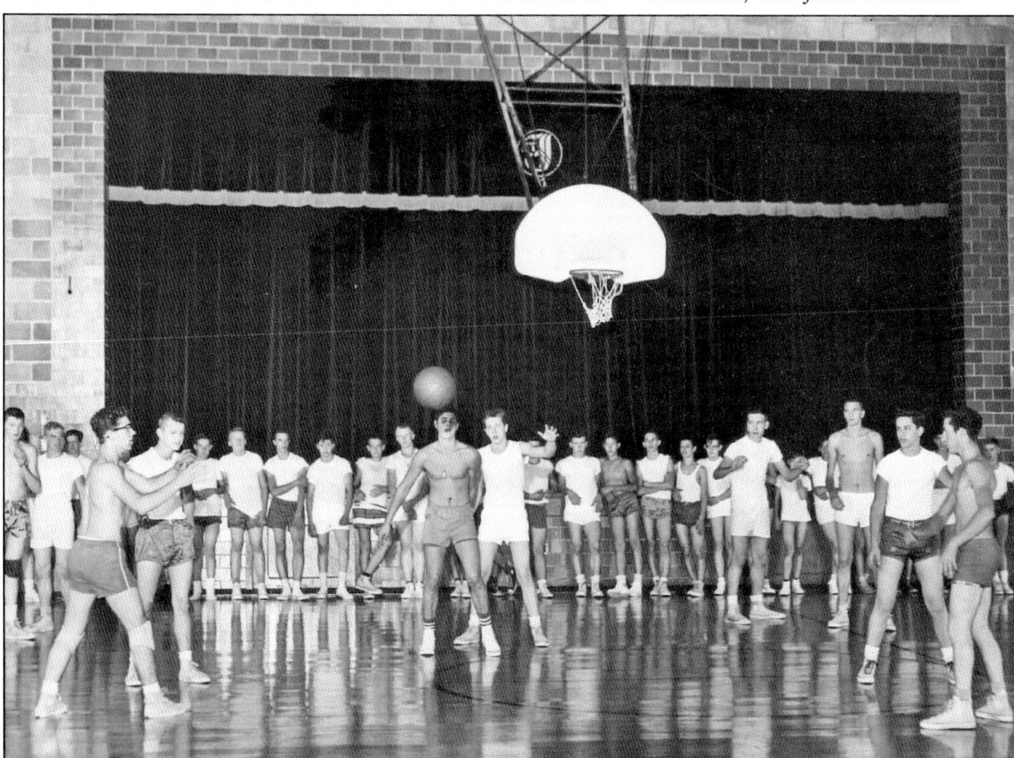

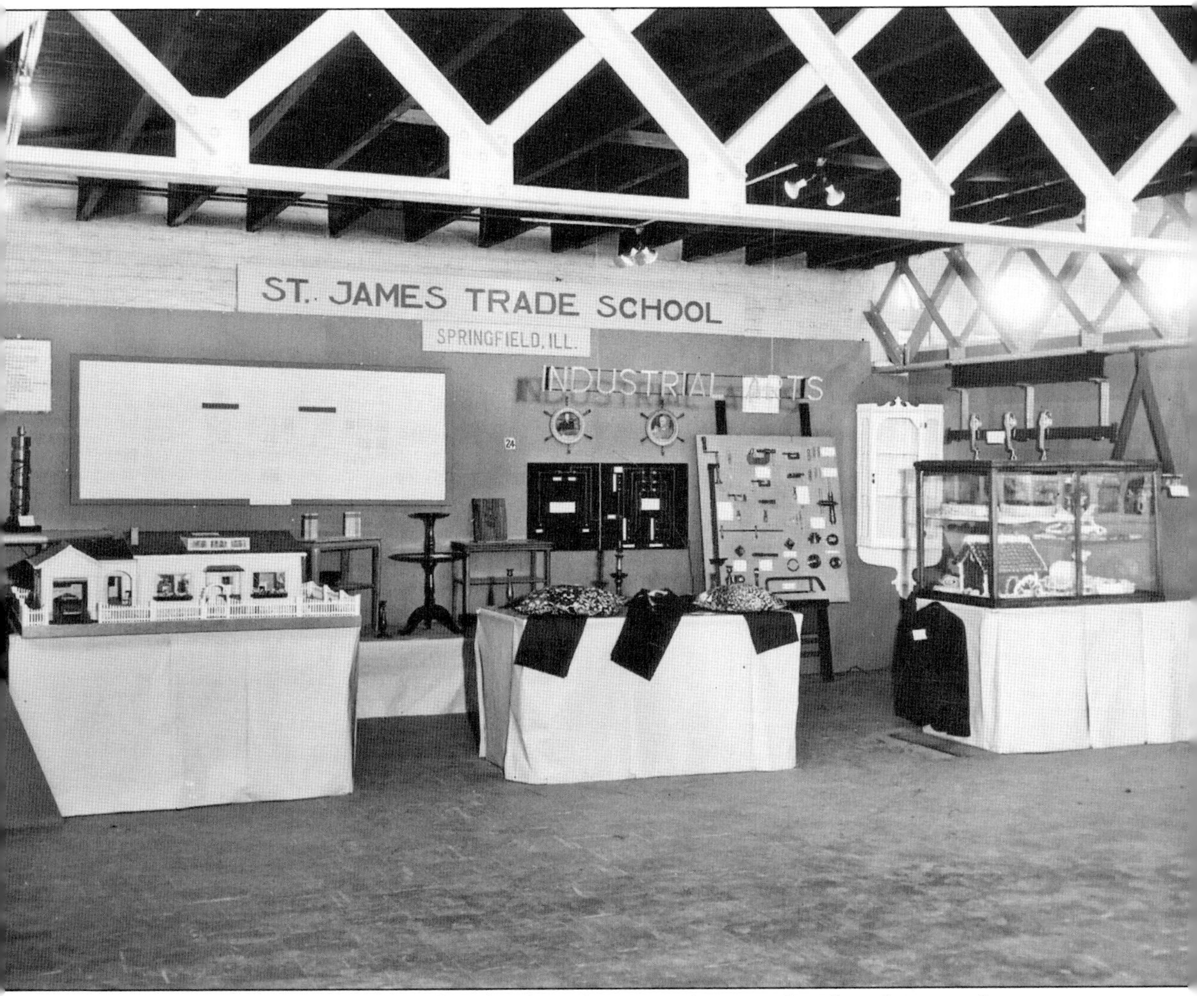

The above display of St. James Trade School products was showcased at the education department at the 1954 Illinois State Fair. Trades represented were bakery, tailoring, electronics, carpentry, painting, and machinery. Student submissions from the mechanics shop were so good that they always took first place and the officials had to ask the boys not to compete each year.

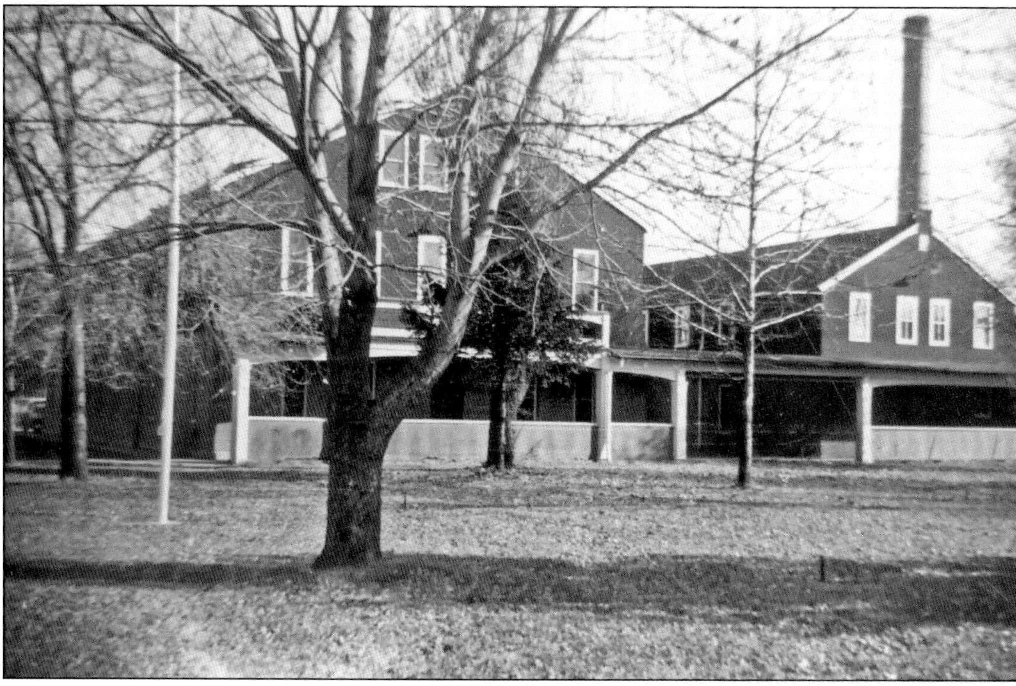

The Boys' House is seen on the left side of this photograph.

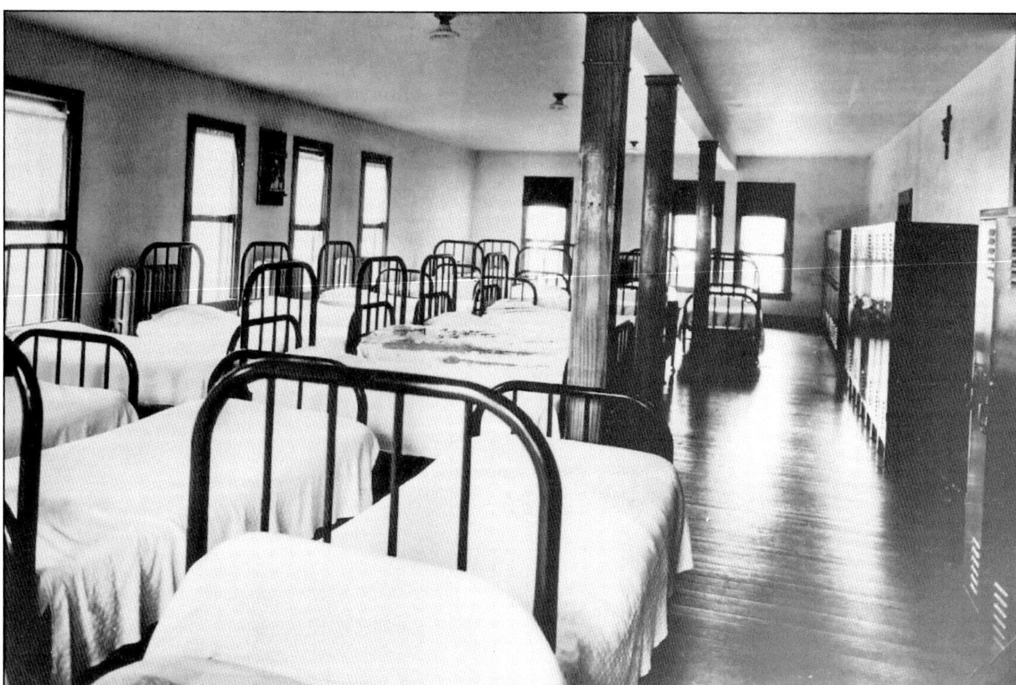

This 1934 photograph shows one of the dormitories, where 50 boys usually resided.

Three

BIRTH OF BROTHER JAMES COURT

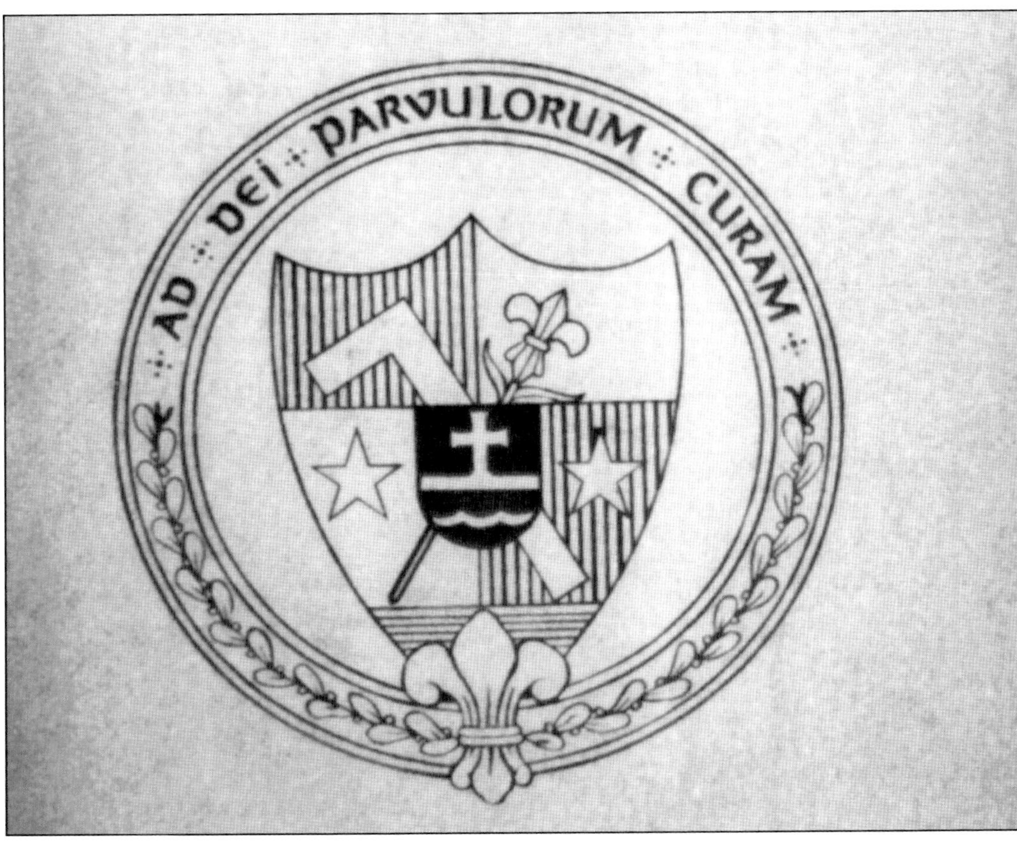

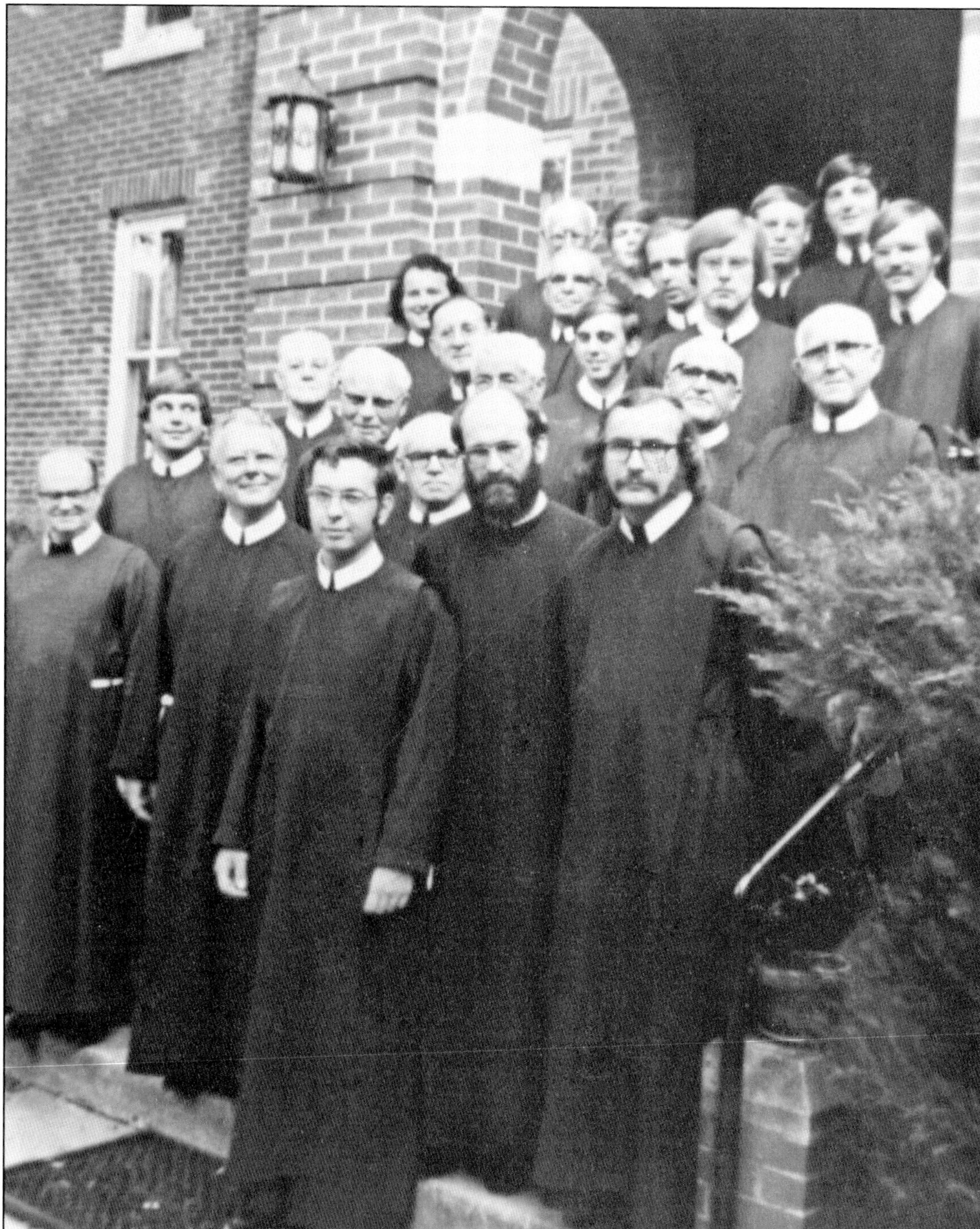

In 1973, the community gathered after a meeting in front of St. James Monastery with their superior general, Brother Hieronymus, and his companion, Brother Gunther. It was at this meeting, called a chapter, that the decision was made to proceed with plans to build Brother James Court. At this time there were 14 American brothers and 9 German brothers in the American region.

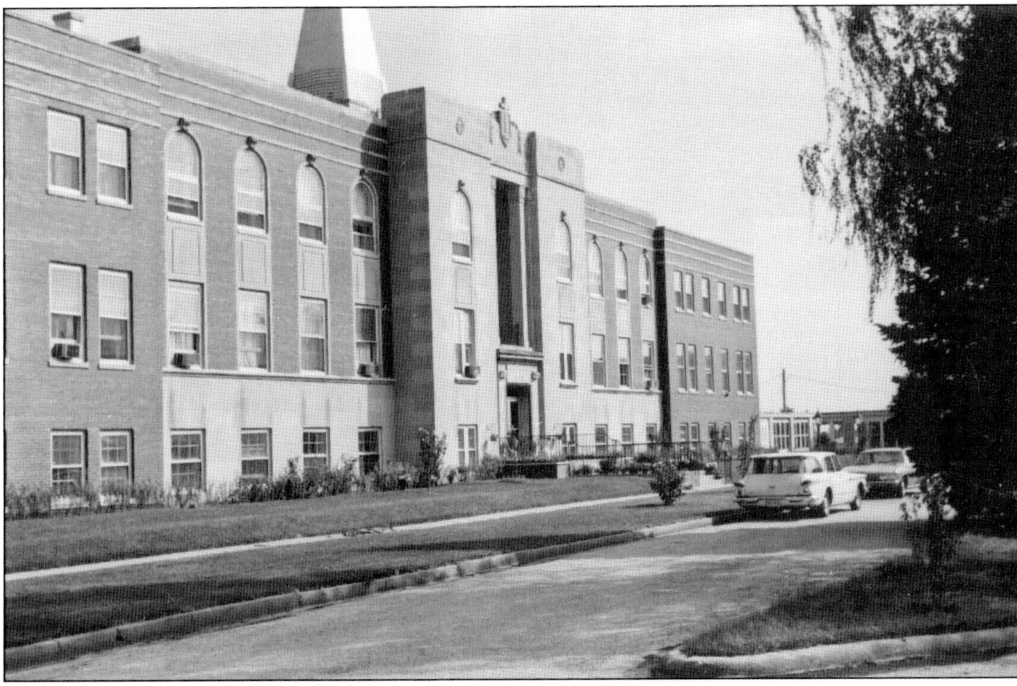

Brothers who would be future workers at Brother James Court also received excellent training in direct care of the developmentally disabled at Good Shepherd Manor in Momence, Illinois. They were trained under the watchful eyes and caring guidance of the Brothers of the Good Shepherd, a male religious community also dedicated to the this type of work. A few even received college training with the sisters who ran St. Coletta School at their Milwaukee Cardinal Stritch College, and the University of Wisconsin-Whitewater. Both schools specialized in special education.

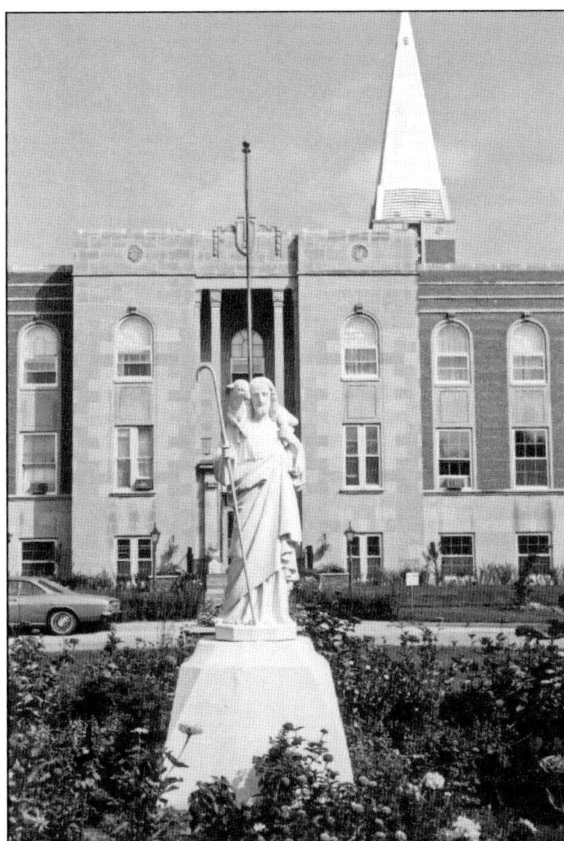

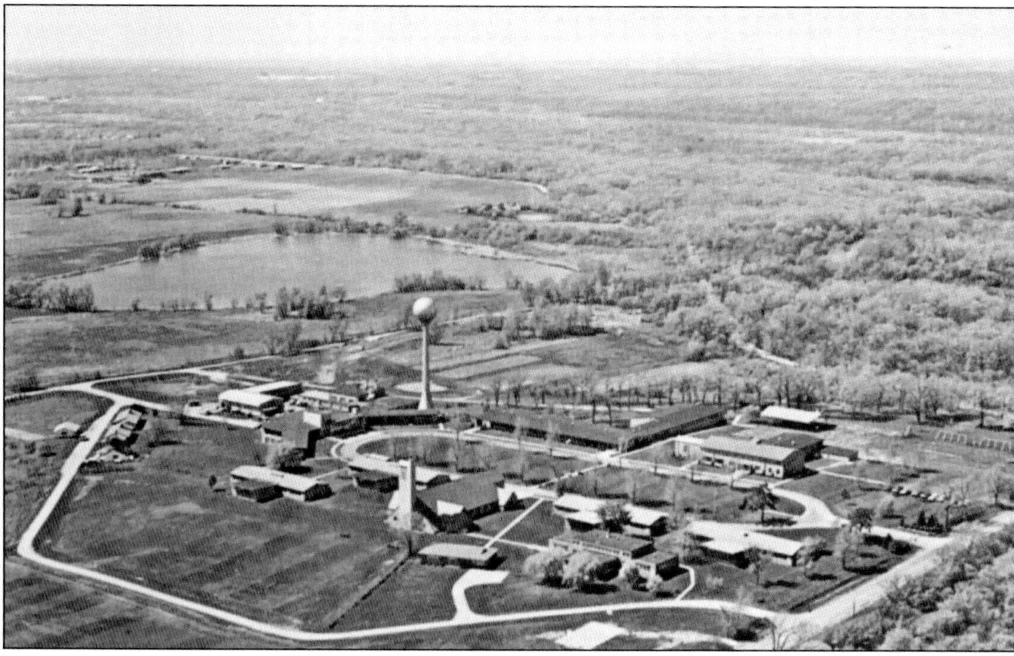

With the closing of St. James Trade School, other works had to be embraced by the brothers. As early as 1969, the brothers had begun on-the-job training as direct care staff at Lt. Joseph P. Kennedy Jr. School in Palos Park, Illinois (above). This was a residential school for developmentally disadvantaged youngsters (and a few "lifers"). In 1970, the community expanded its on-the-job training, with the same Franciscan Sisters from Milwaukee at St. Coletta School in Jefferson, Wisconsin (below). Some of the brothers sent there worked with the school-age residents, and some worked with adult residents. This was another great preparation time for those who would later work at Brother James Court.

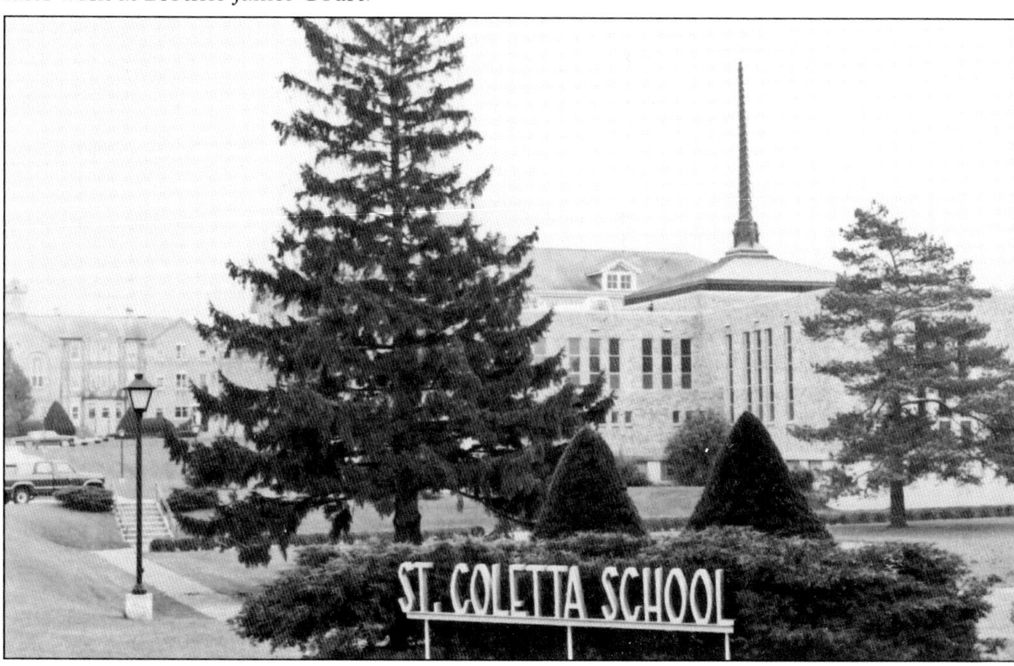

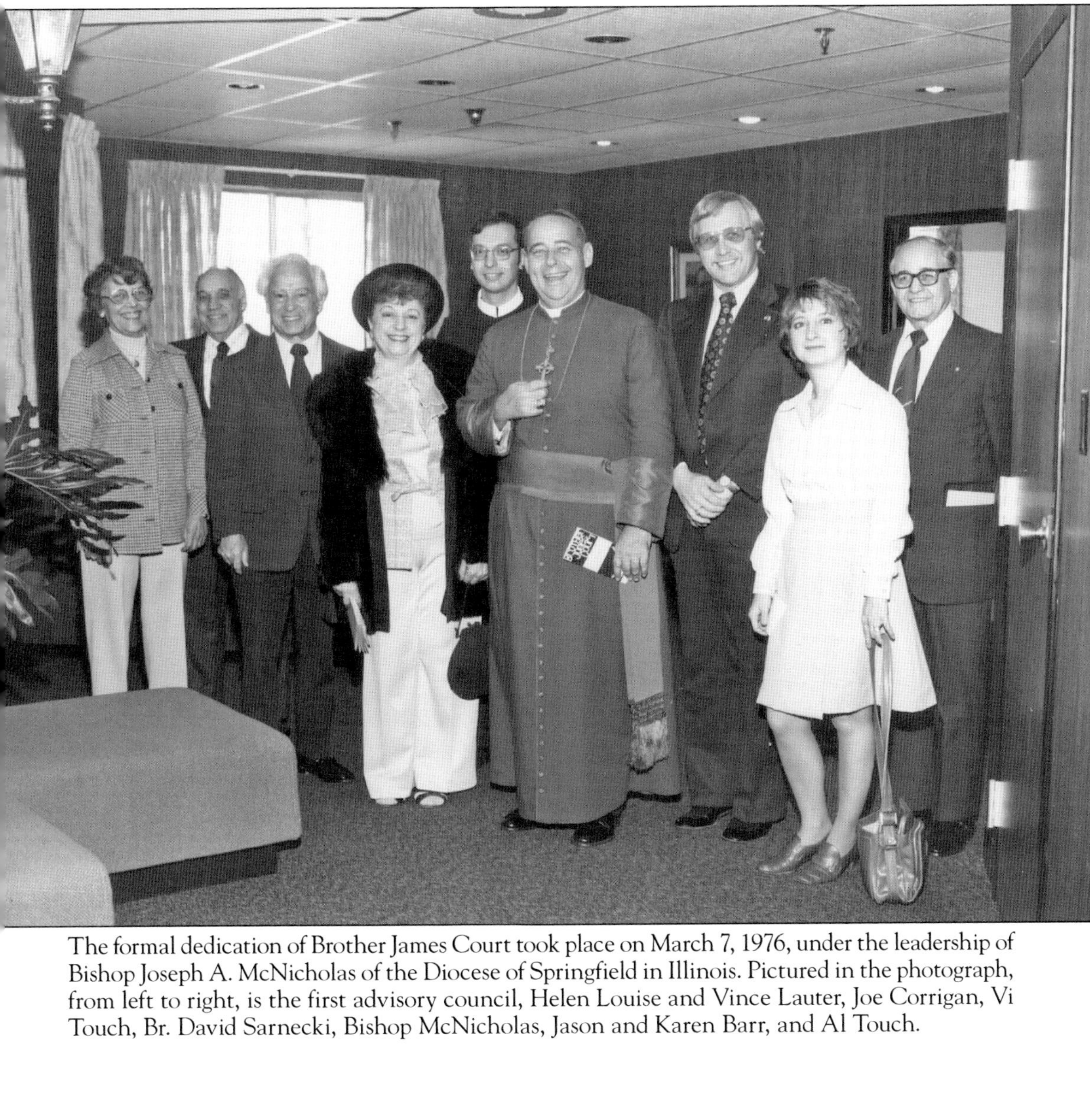

The formal dedication of Brother James Court took place on March 7, 1976, under the leadership of Bishop Joseph A. McNicholas of the Diocese of Springfield in Illinois. Pictured in the photograph, from left to right, is the first advisory council, Helen Louise and Vince Lauter, Joe Corrigan, Vi Touch, Br. David Sarnecki, Bishop McNicholas, Jason and Karen Barr, and Al Touch.

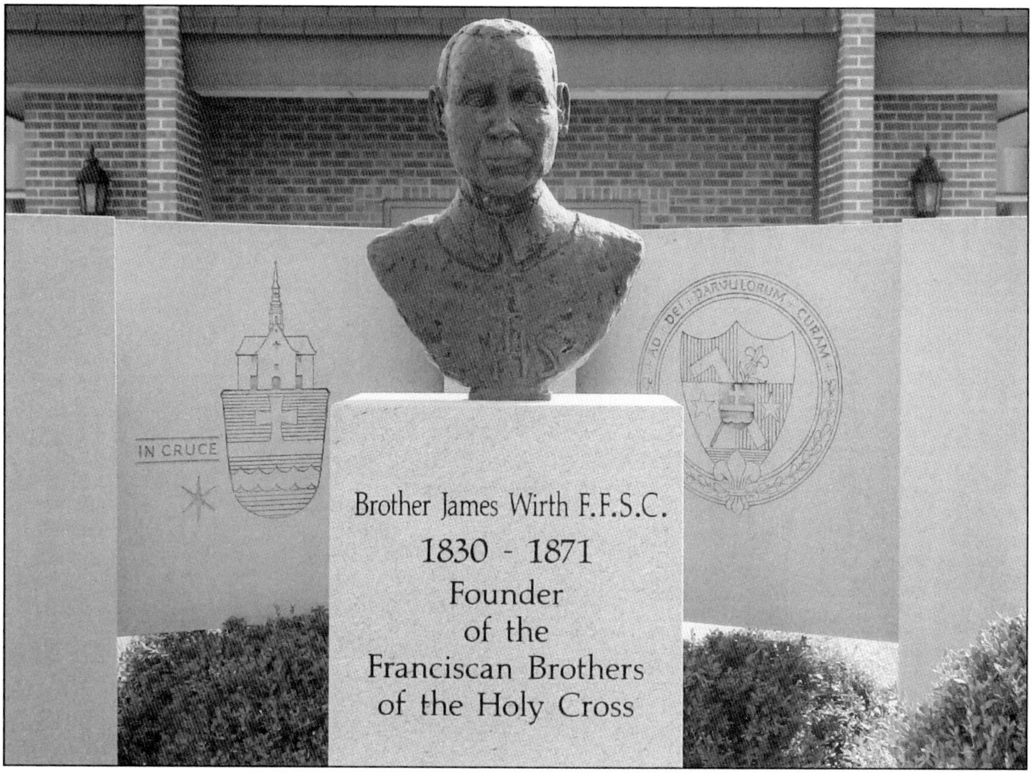

While the quality care of the developmentally disabled adults continues at Brother James Court, there is a continual awareness of the inspiration the founder, Br. James Wirth, has been for the religious community since the early years (the devotion and care for these special men began in Germany in 1887). There is a wonderful reminder of this connection to the founding brothers whenever anyone enters the front door of the Court. The monument shown in these photographs has a beautiful bronze bust of Brother James and crest of the congregation and the crest of the Court.

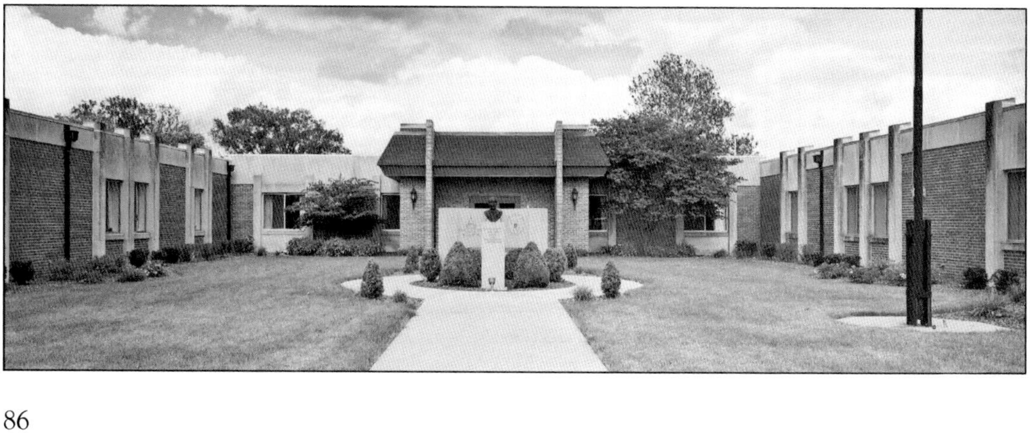

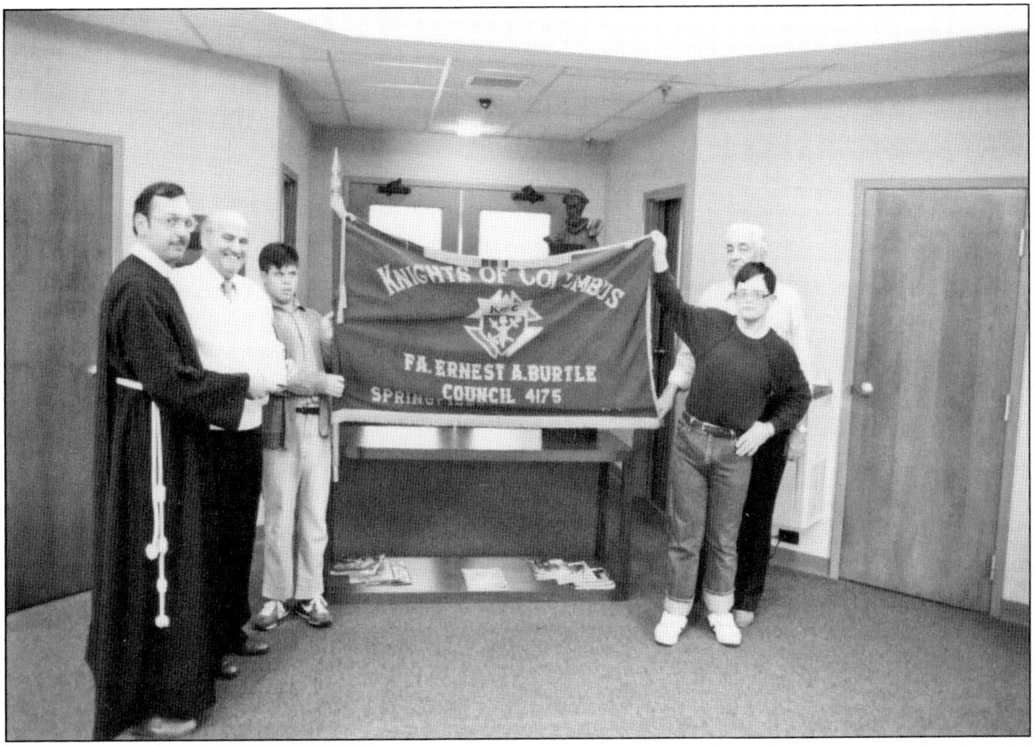

Brother James Court has always been blessed by the friendship of the Knights of Columbus (K of C) and their financial support, especially from their Tootsie Roll Drive, which raises funds to aid in the care of the developmentally disabled. Also important is the ongoing support of the Association of Brother James Court that helps with many special projects to improve the quality of life for the residents. The 1986 photograph above shows K of C Council No. 4187. The 1979 picture below shows, from left to right, Ann Gawlik, Brother David, Rudy Gawlik (president), and Virginia Schneider (publications chairperson).

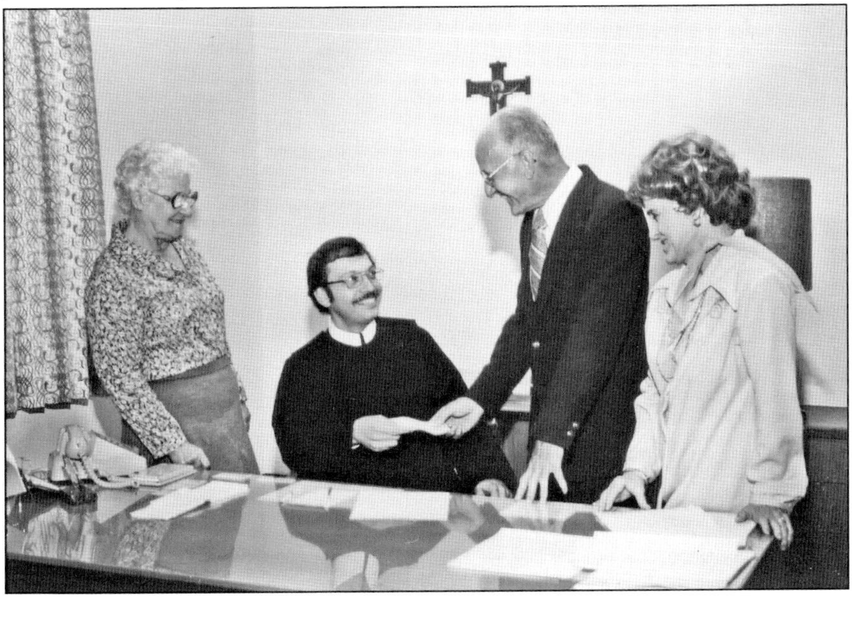

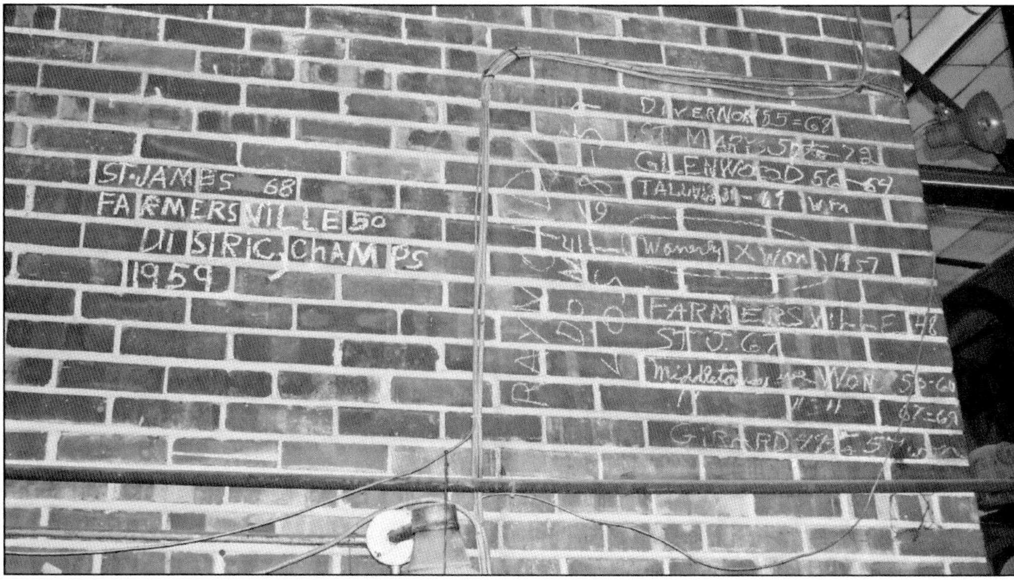

In the garage where auto mechanics were once taught, and which now houses the many vehicles used by Brother James Court, one can still see the intense activity of some of the sports fans at the trade school. Basketball scores from the 1950s remain printed on the wall high above the vehicles. They went unnoticed until a group of alumni toured the building in 2009 and pointed out the work of unknown Tradesmen. One never knows what the alumni gatherings are going to add to the "living history" of Brother James Court! (Courtesy of Bill Prose.)

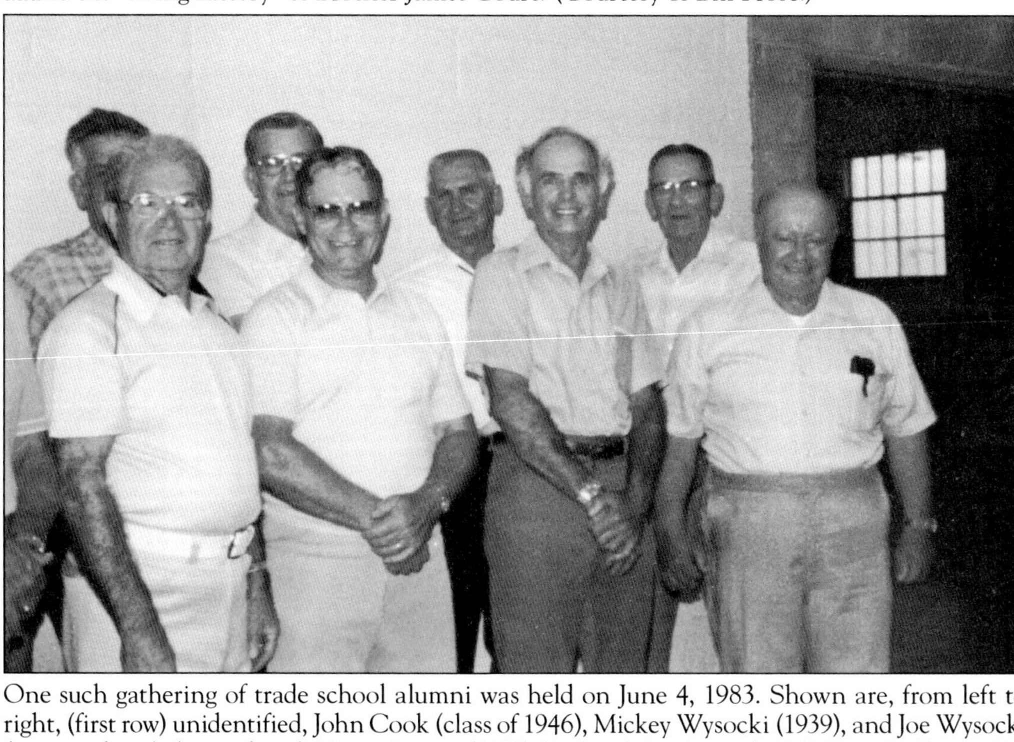

One such gathering of trade school alumni was held on June 4, 1983. Shown are, from left to right, (first row) unidentified, John Cook (class of 1946), Mickey Wysocki (1939), and Joe Wysocki (non-graduate); (second row) Mario Caruso (1932), Richard Atteberry (1936), Tony Keller (1939), and Hank Buhnerkemper (non-graduate).

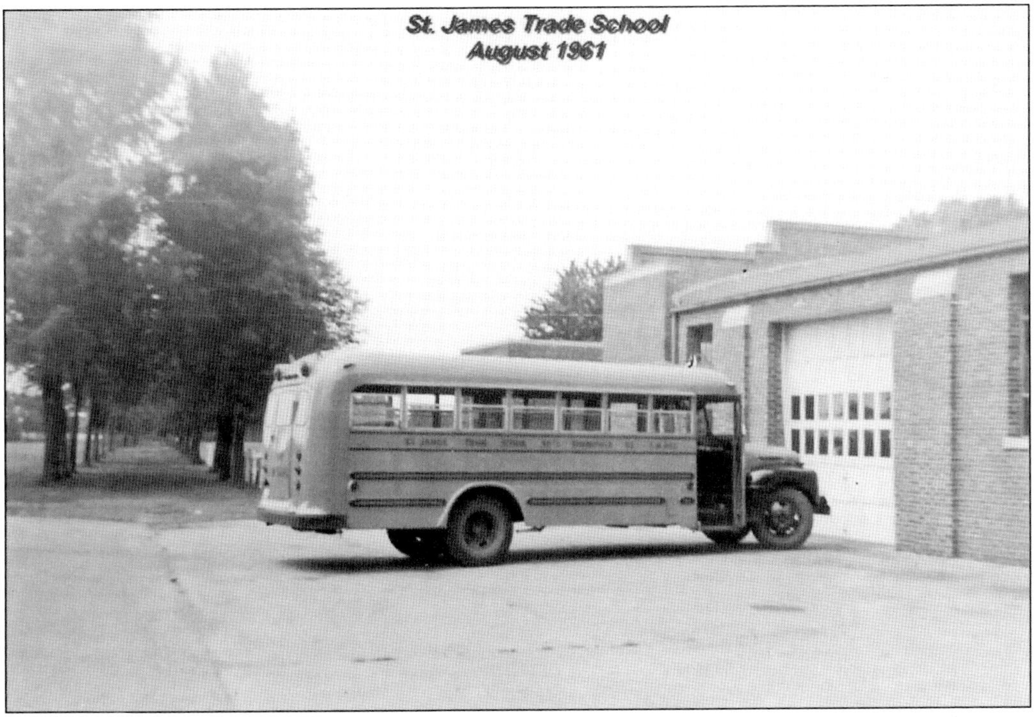

In the above photograph from 1961, the St. James Trade School bus is parked in front of the auto mechanics garage. The double line of trees creates an access road to the Brothers' Cemetery. This garage is still in use at Brother James Court and a newly refurbished bicycle and walking track has replaced the double row of trees. Below, a sunny day makes walking the new track at Brother James Court very enjoyable. (Photograph below courtesy of Bill Prose.)

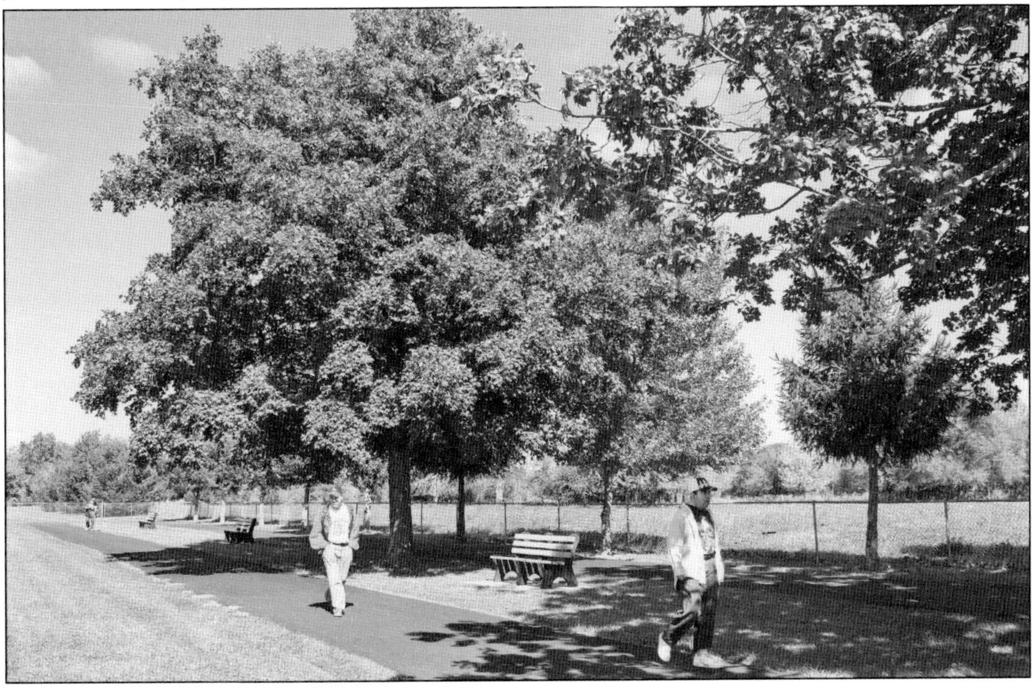

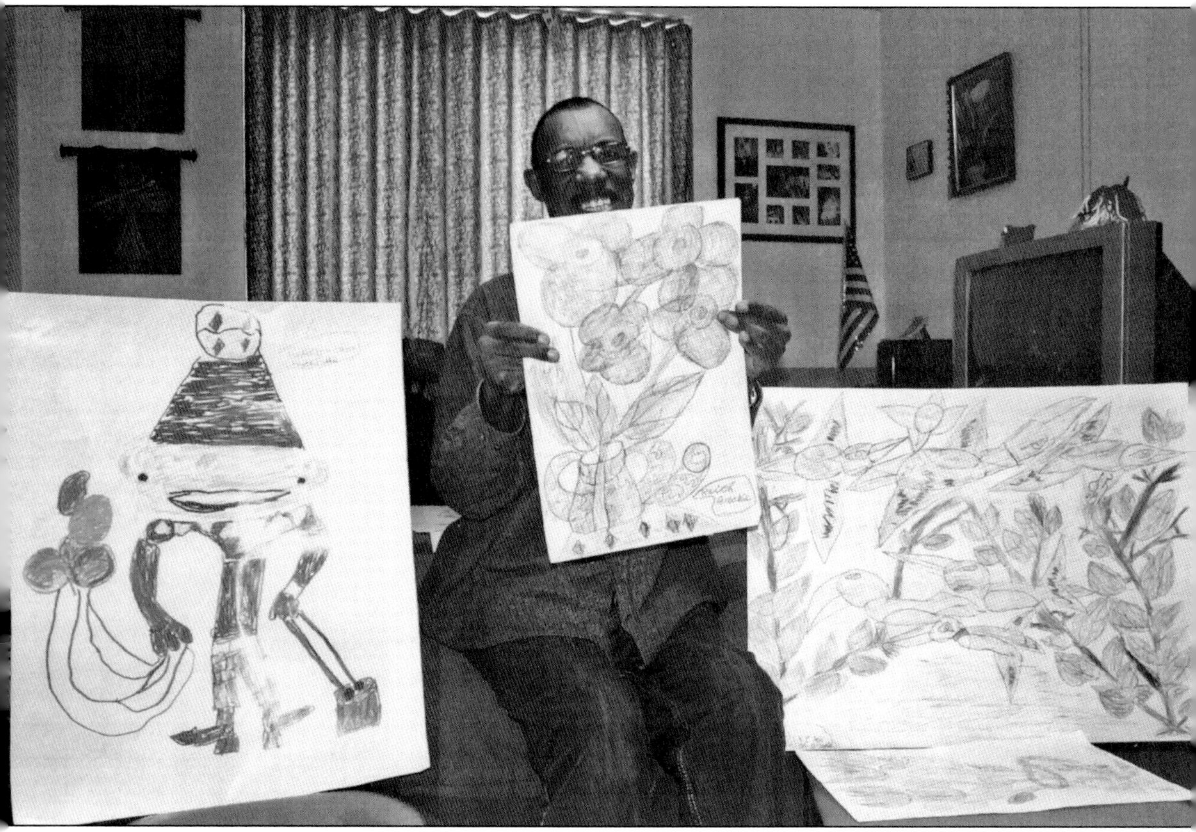

In the work at Brother James Court, the whole person is considered and programs and living situations are adjusted accordingly. Just as with Special Olympics, there is an awareness of other life skills that individual residents have. In keeping with the vision statement, which reads "empowering individuals with special needs to achieve their highest potential through life skill training," Brother James Court is delighted when it can spotlight the artistic achievements of the residents. Pictured here is Keith, whose artwork has given many pleasure over the years. (Courtesy of Bill Prose.)

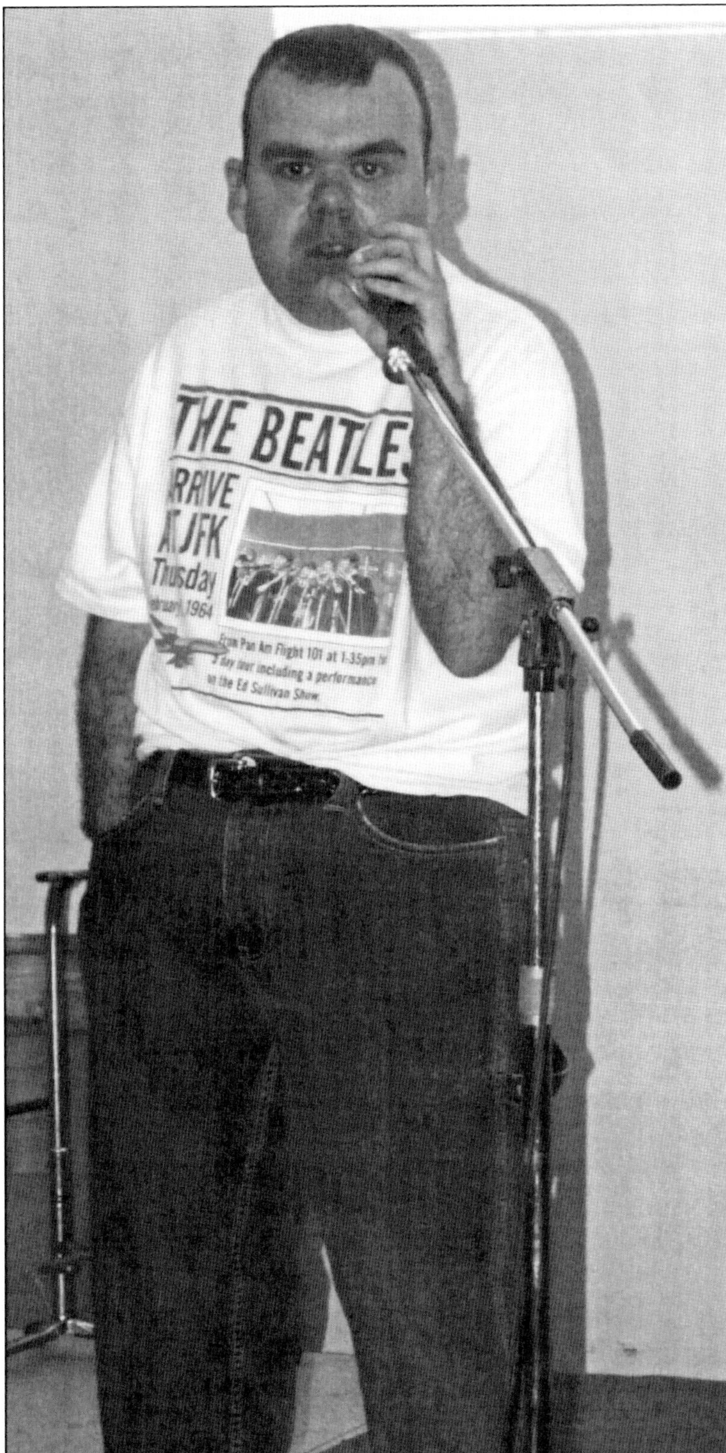

Tim is a gifted singer who loves the Beatles and shares his music with residents and friends alike. (Courtesy of Jim Kiesow.)

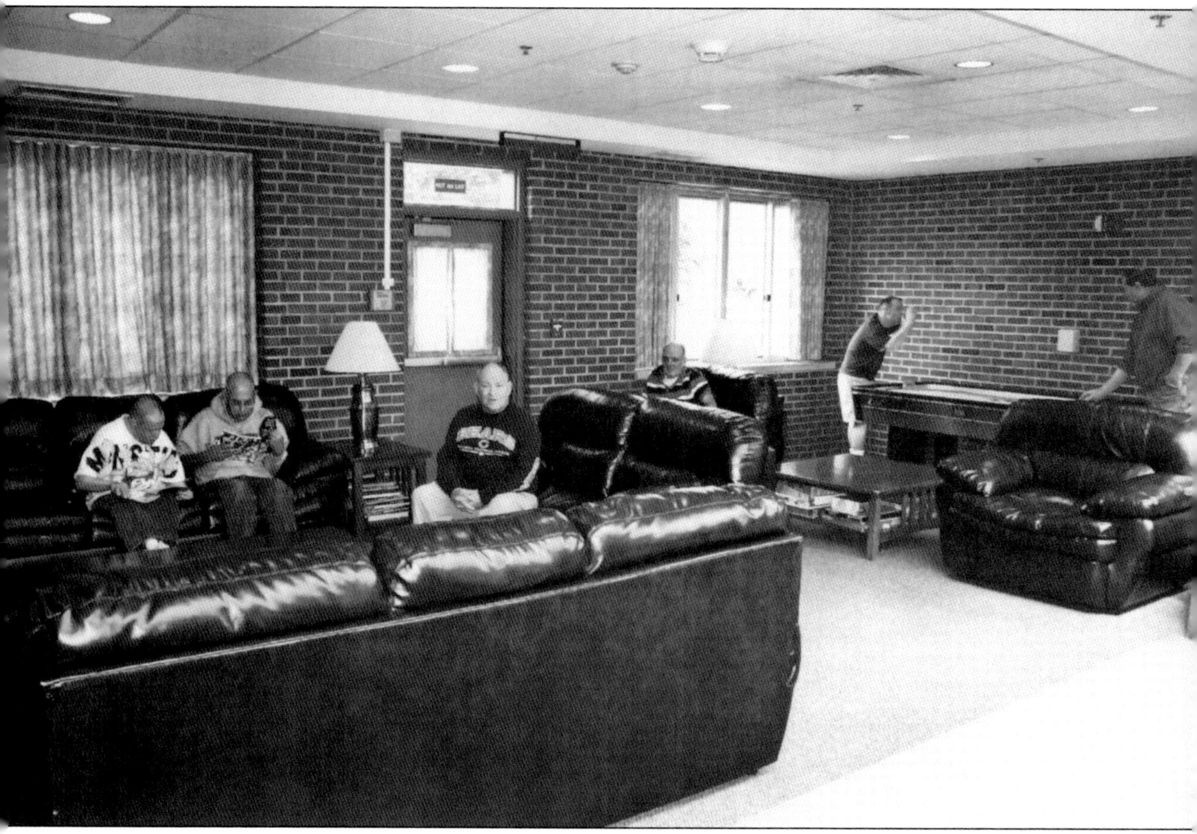

Relaxation is a necessary part of anyone's day and the men of Brother James Court are no exception. The men in this photograph are obviously enjoying the new furniture in their day room, along with a friendly game of air hockey. (Courtesy of Bill Prose.)

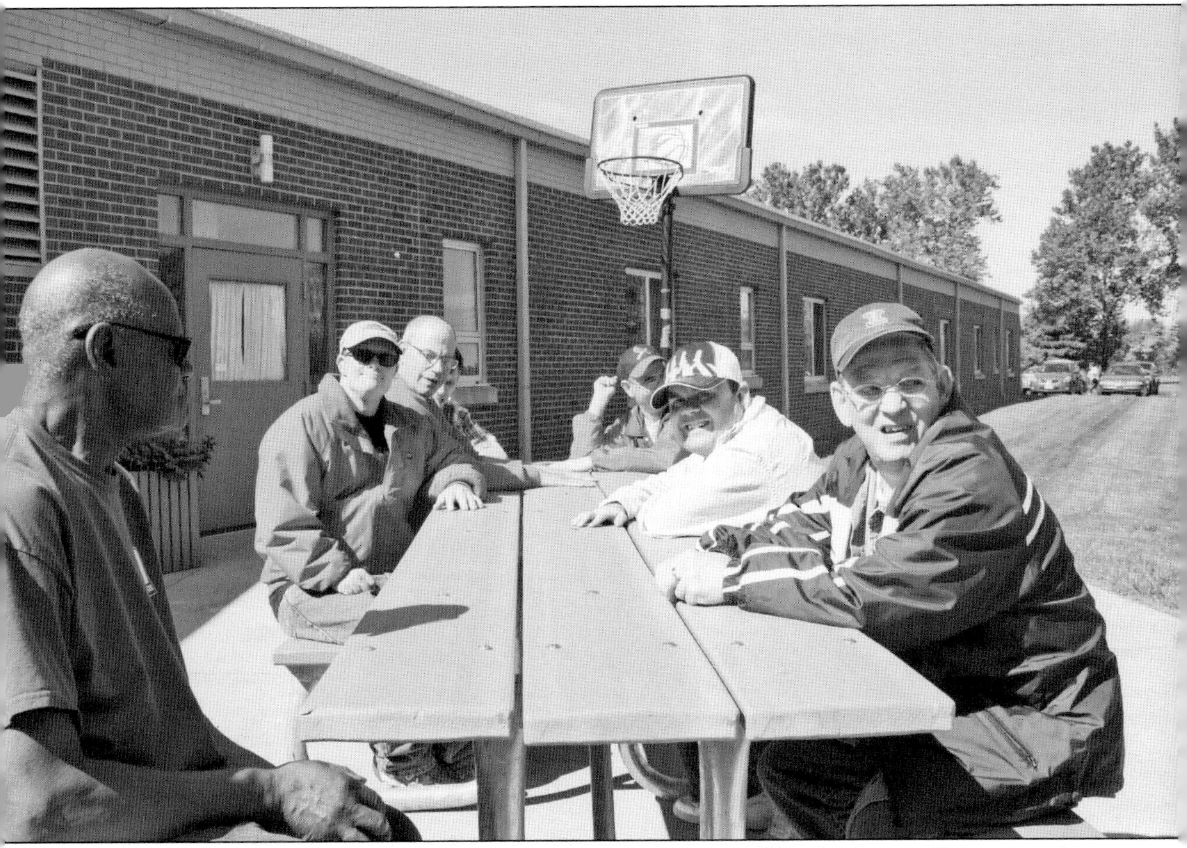

The Outdoor Project, taken on by the very active Association of Brother James Court, was the challenge that materialized in the outfitting of the four patios (one per wing), and the upgrading and resurfacing of the walking track and its infield to the tune of $40,000. The facility is grateful to its supporters who enhance the daily living of the men so enthusiastically. (Courtesy of Bill Prose.)

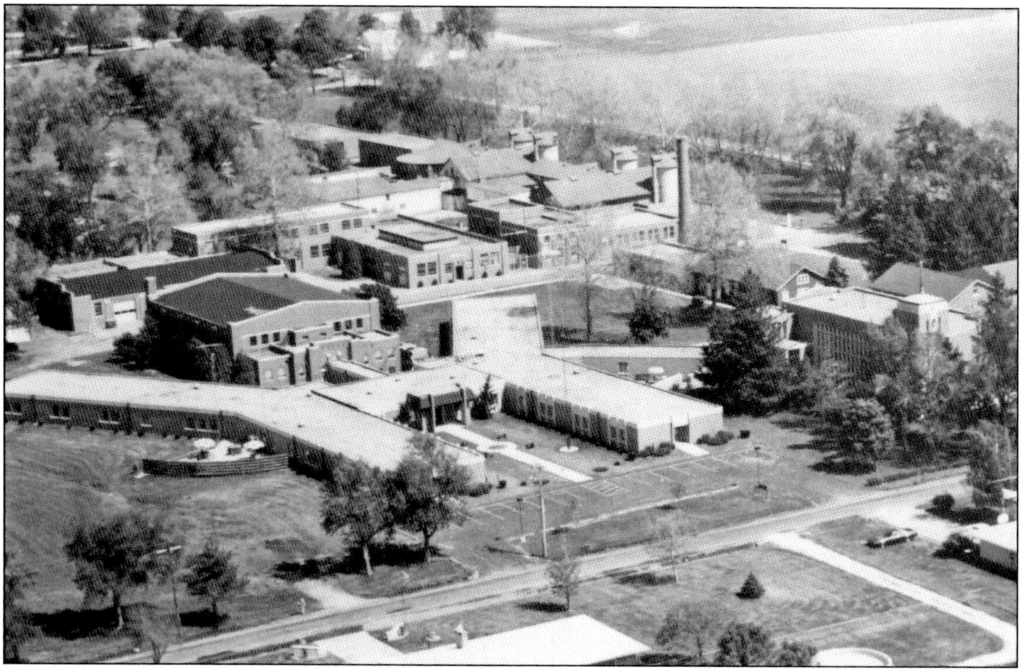

The cornerstone, which once was part of the trade school gymnasium, is still visible in the building that replaced the gym, and the inscription is a constant reminder of the focus for the work with the Tradesmen and the men of Brother James Court. The picture above shows the gym behind the Court building, with wings that fan out to surround it. The gym in the early days of the Court was the place for physical activities, entertainment, and some classes. It was used from 1940 until 1997, when the new dining room, kitchen, and atrium replaced it. (Photograph below courtesy of Bill Prose.)

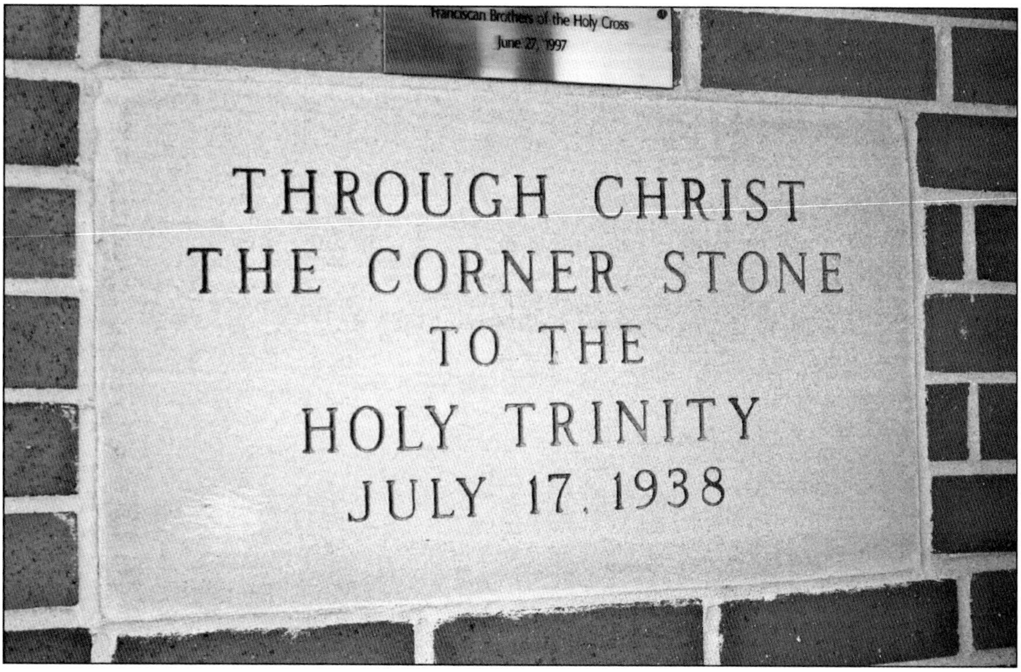

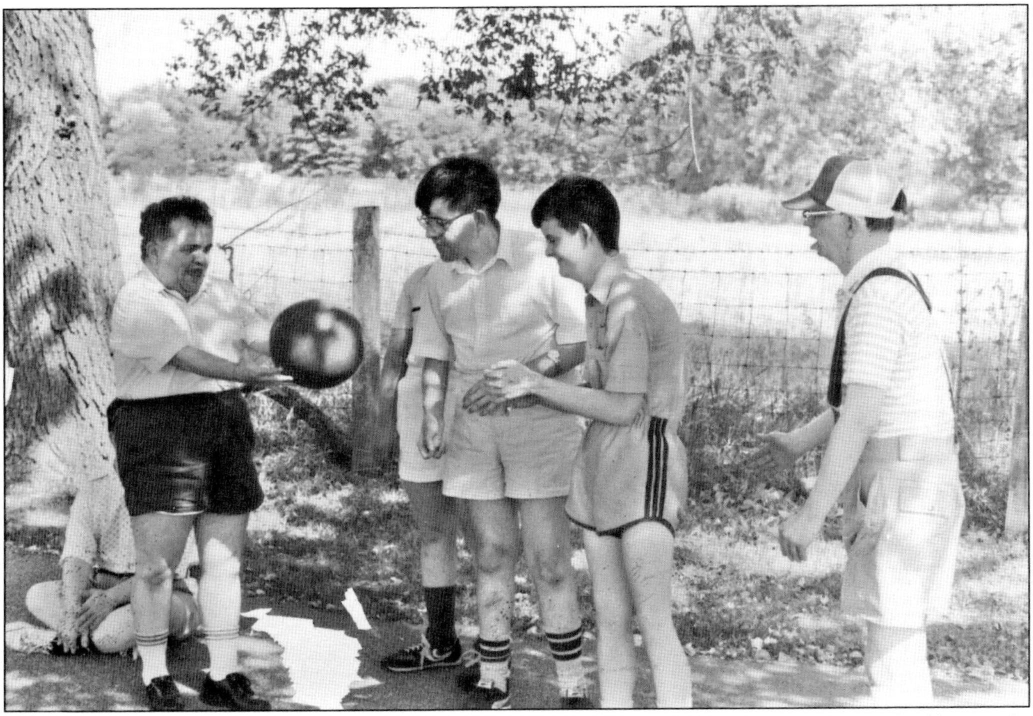

Here residents at Brother James Court are seen outdoors on the track. (Courtesy of Bill Prose.)

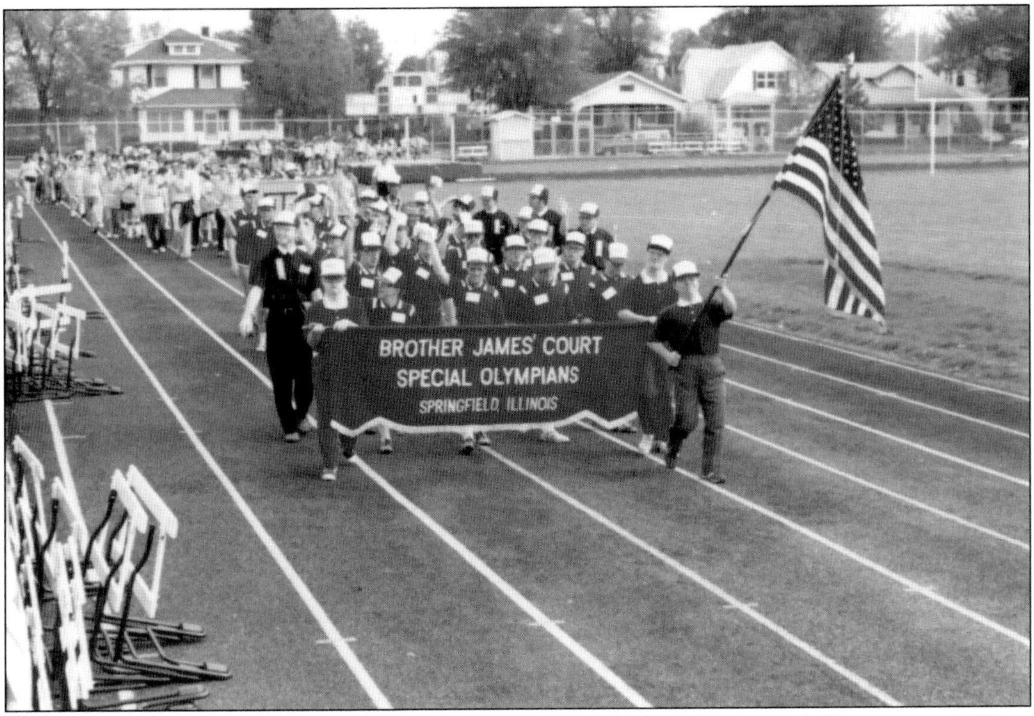

This contingent of men from Brother James Court marched in the Special Olympics in 1982 in Bloomington, Illinois. (Courtesy of Charlotte Dormal.)

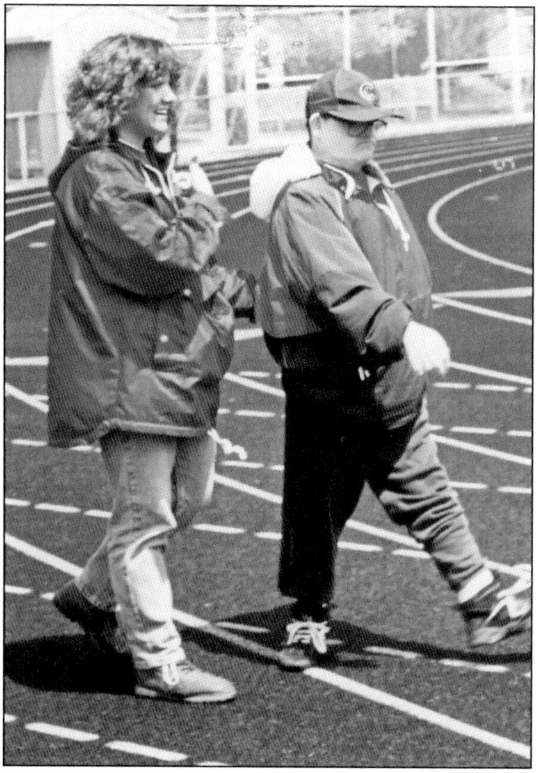

Sports are important to the men who are fans of and who enjoy participating in them. One of the favorite activities of the clients of the Springfield Developmental Center, located at Brother James Court, is their participation in Special Olympics each year. As the men age, some racing is done at a walking pace and the sport of bowling becomes more popular.

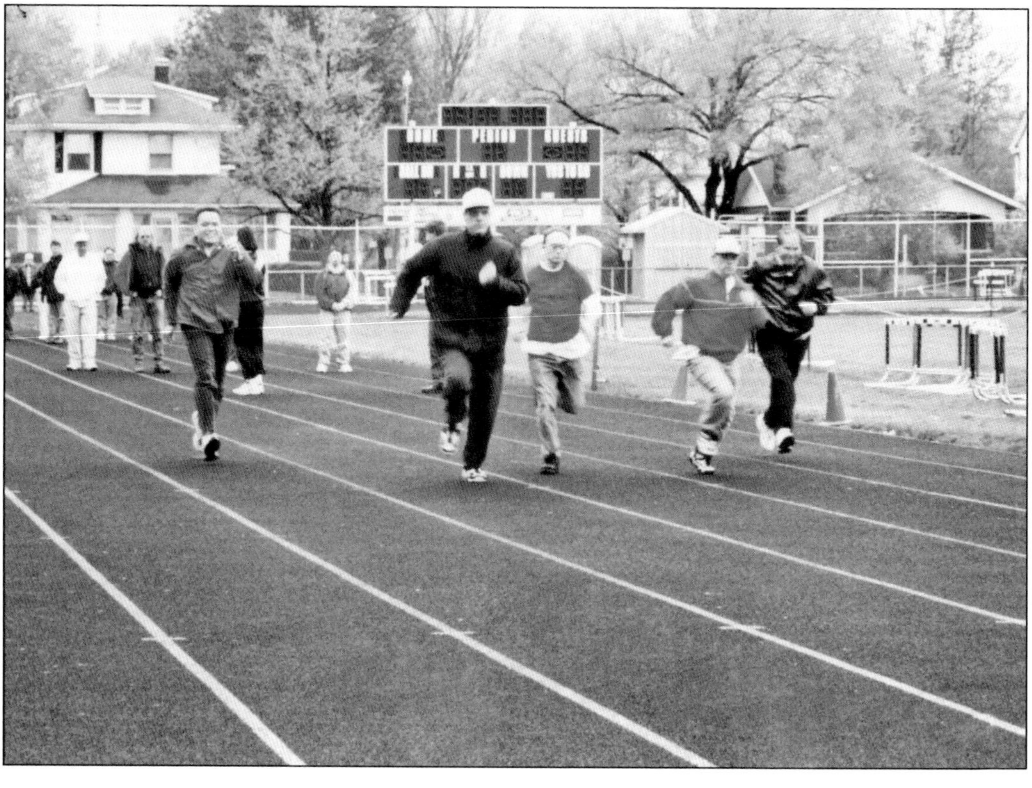

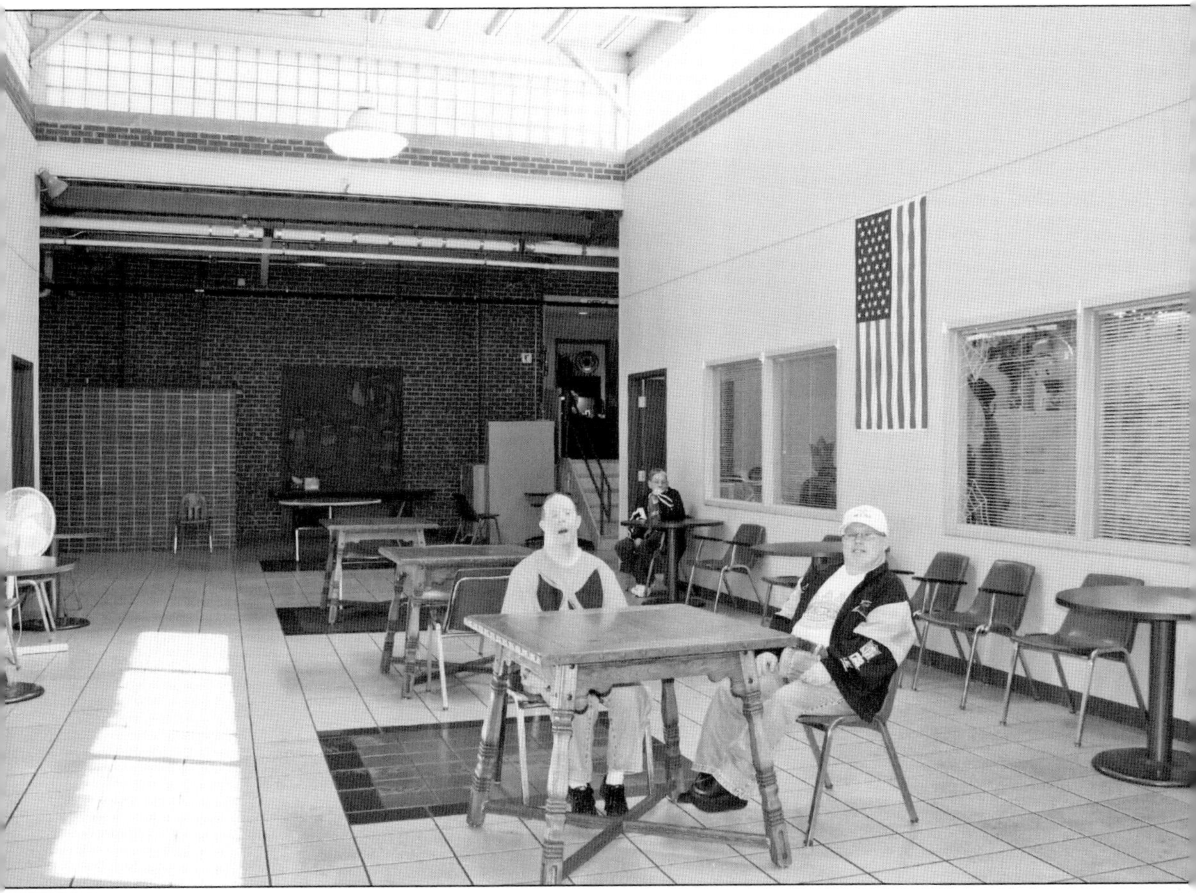

The interior of the old carpentry shop never looked so good as when the men from Brother James Court are relaxing in the newly renovated classroom space. Small groups according to ability level are the order of the day. This classroom/atrium also serves Springfield Developmental Center as a gathering space for tours and the clients who come from other facilities or their homes (a few of these clients are female). Court residents are part of the over 100-person client base at SDC. (Courtesy of Bill Prose.)

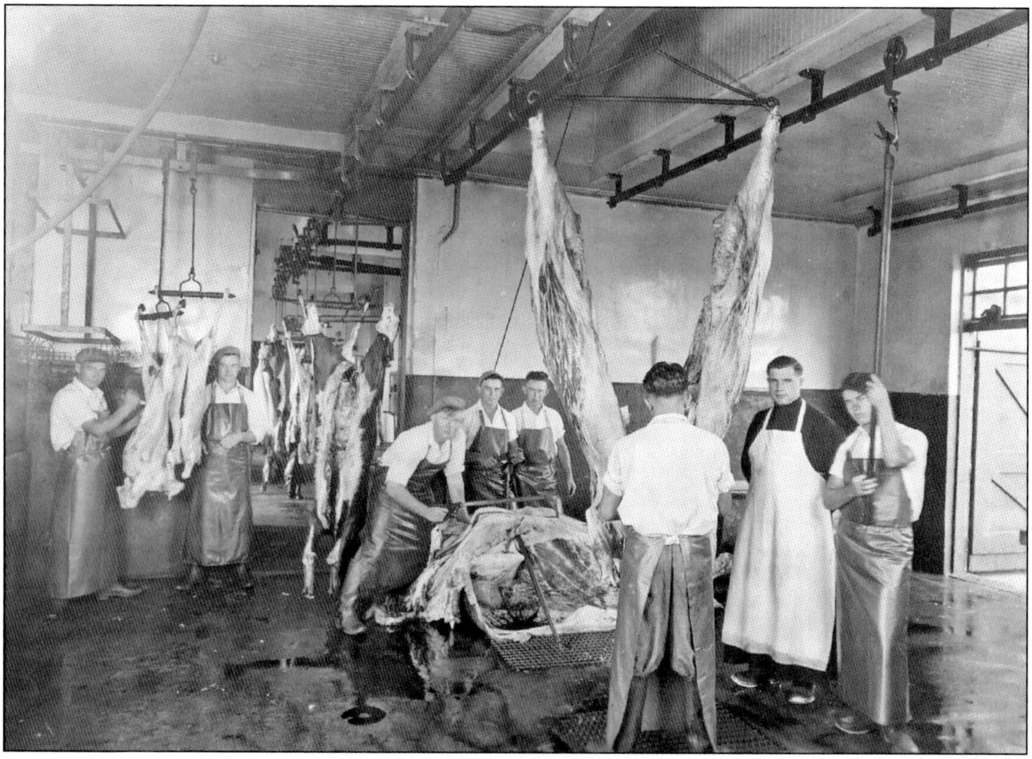

Brother James Court residents have a wonderful space in which to handle their sorting and other contract work and even have their annual talent show. The above photograph is the meat processing/butcher shop, which was built in 1950. The look of this building has improved a hundredfold, as shown by the photograph below, where even the metal tracks once used for hanging carcasses are gone, and everything is bright and airy. (Photograph below courtesy of Bill Prose.)

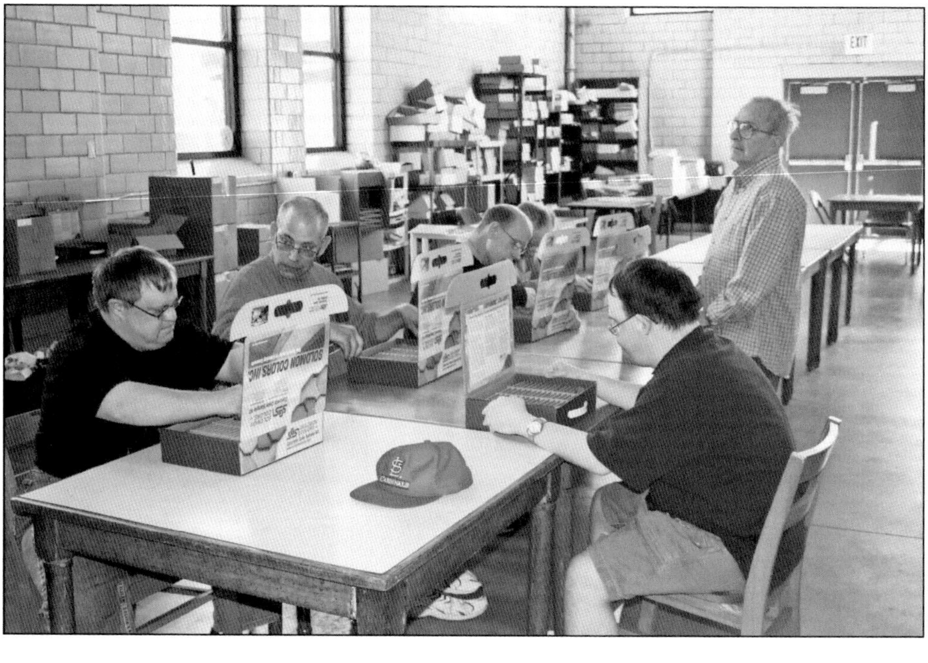

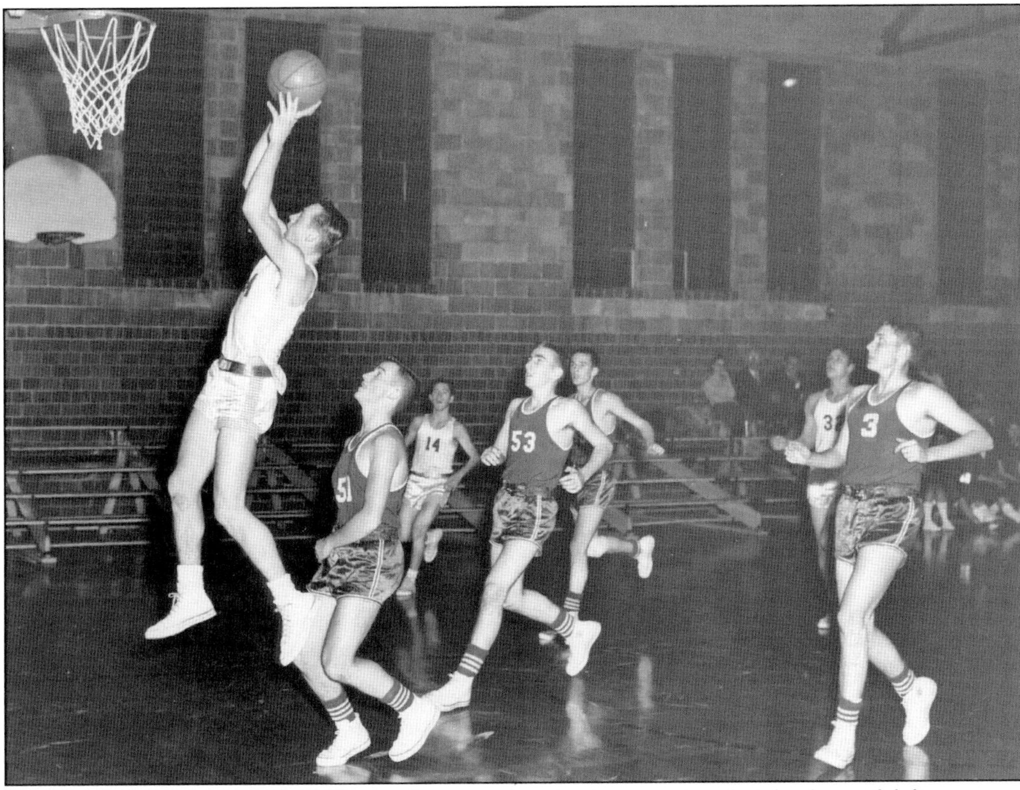

A space once filled with the activities of teenage boys has been replaced with a beautiful dining room and kitchen that bustles three times a day with the eager activities of 98 hungry residents.

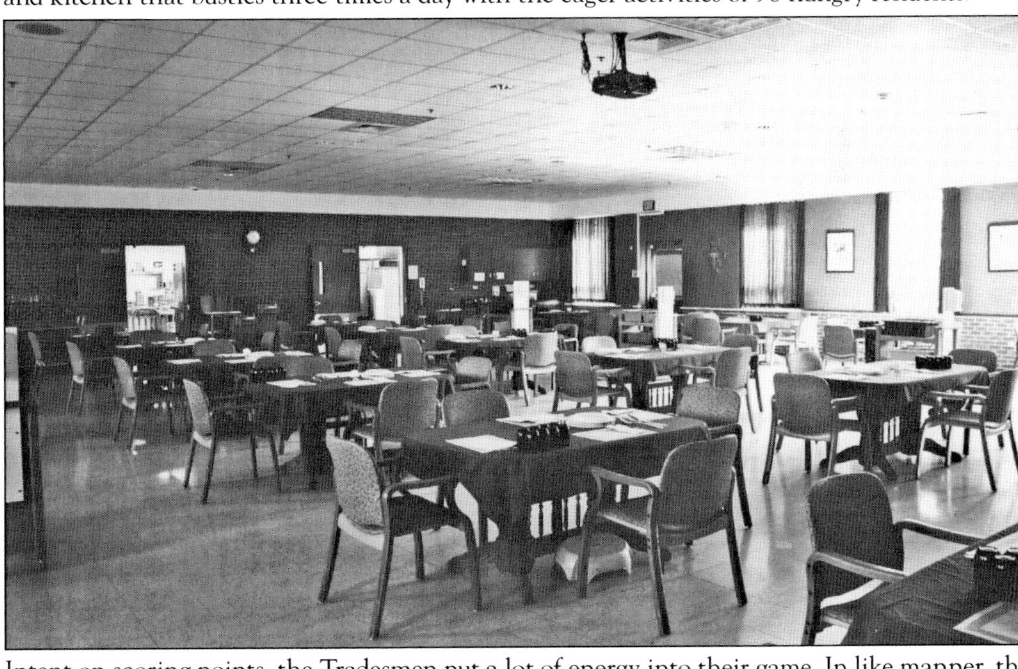

Intent on scoring points, the Tradesmen put a lot of energy into their game. In like manner, the men of the Court put a lot of energy into the wonderful meals they have in the dining room.

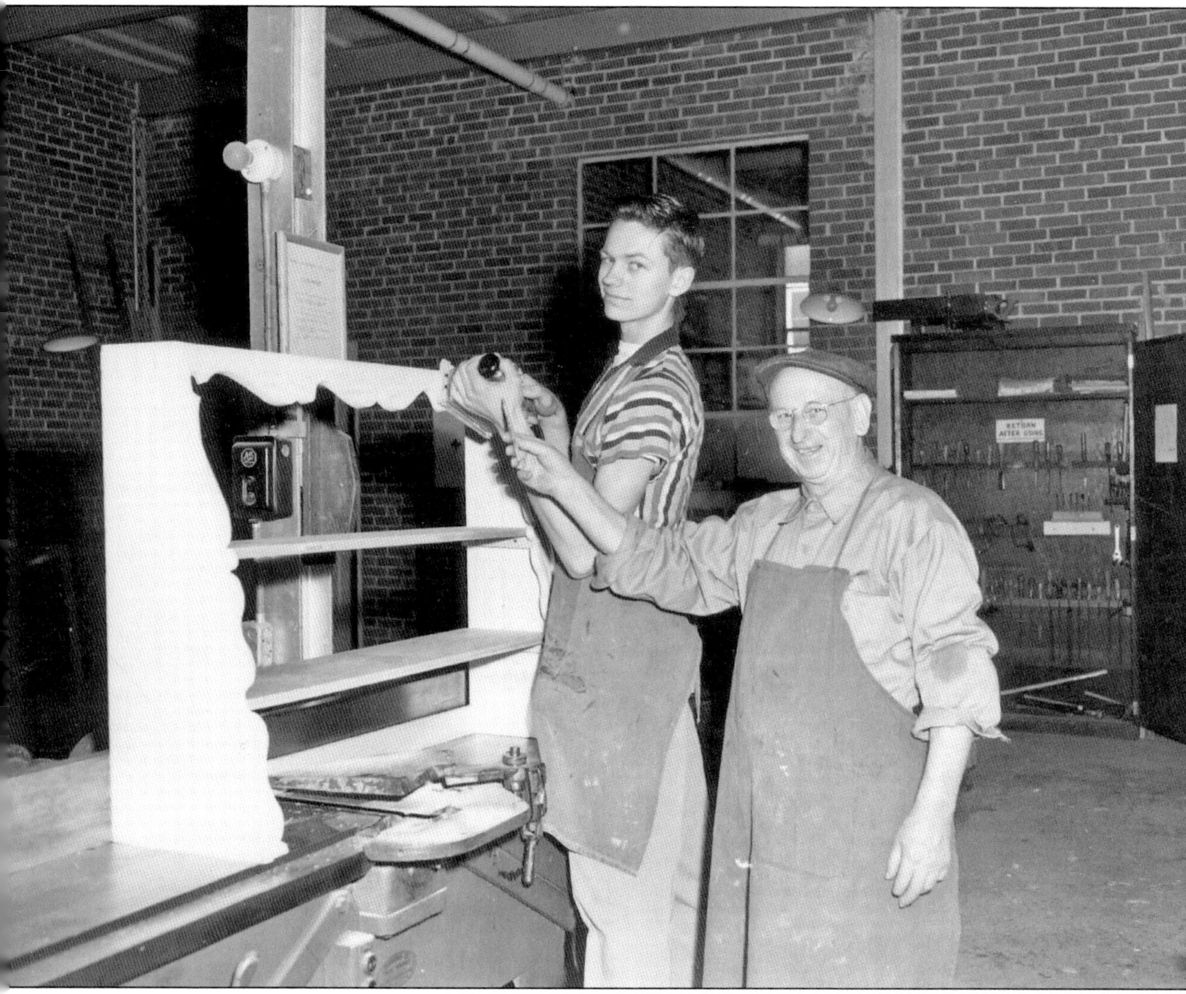

In the carpentry shop, teenagers learned the trade that would give them a leg up in life. Brother Rembert is shown here instructing an unidentified student.

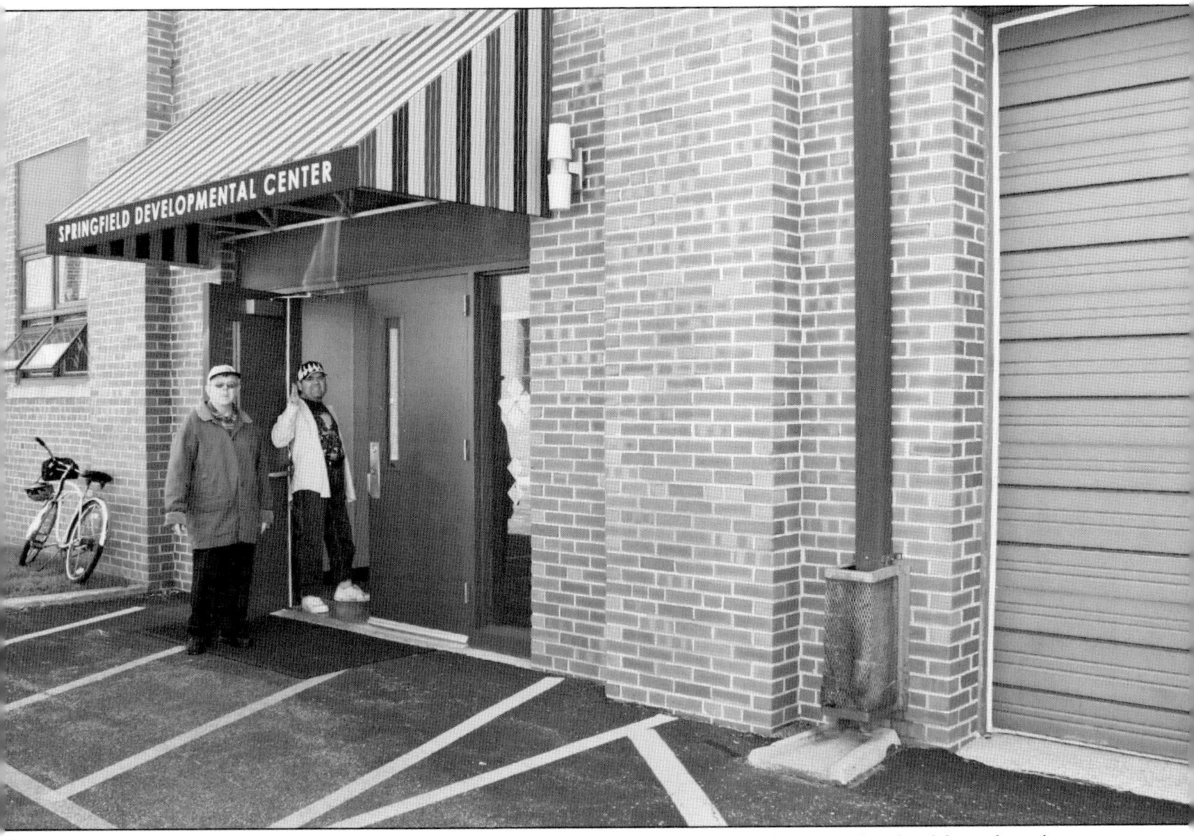

An activity program for the developmentally disabled has taken place in this building five days a week since 1975. This program, now called Springfield Developmental Center, is a fully accredited sheltered workshop that Brother James Court residents enjoy. The building, constructed in 1953, is the boast of the center's director, who has approximately 7,000 square feet across multiple buildings for her program, which also assists a few clients from other agencies.

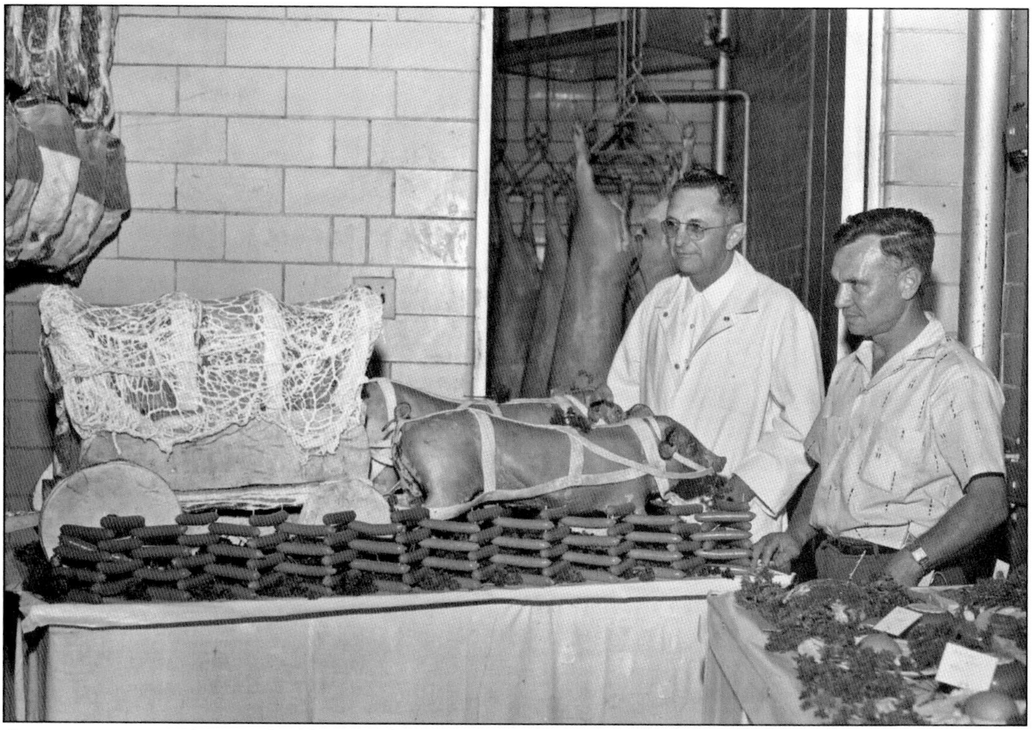

A room once used to cool off meats for the butcher shop now heats up with the fevered exercises enjoyed by the men during their day at the Springfield Developmental Center. About two-thirds of the residents are enrolled in the exercise programs accessible to them across the driveway separating the Court from the Center. (Photograph below courtesy of Bill Prose.)

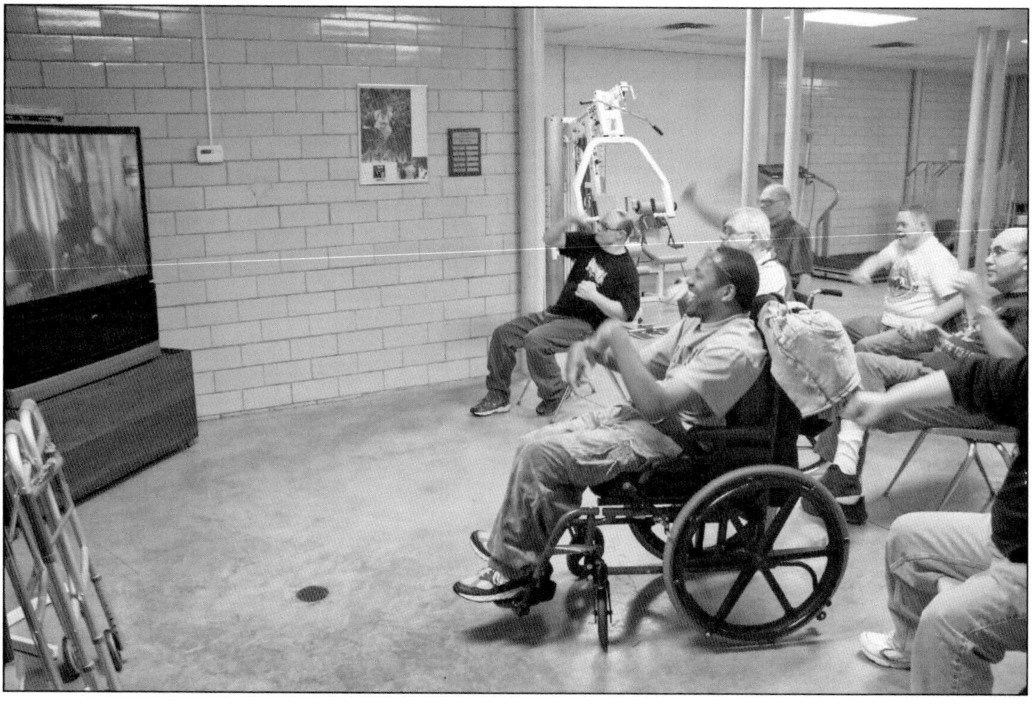

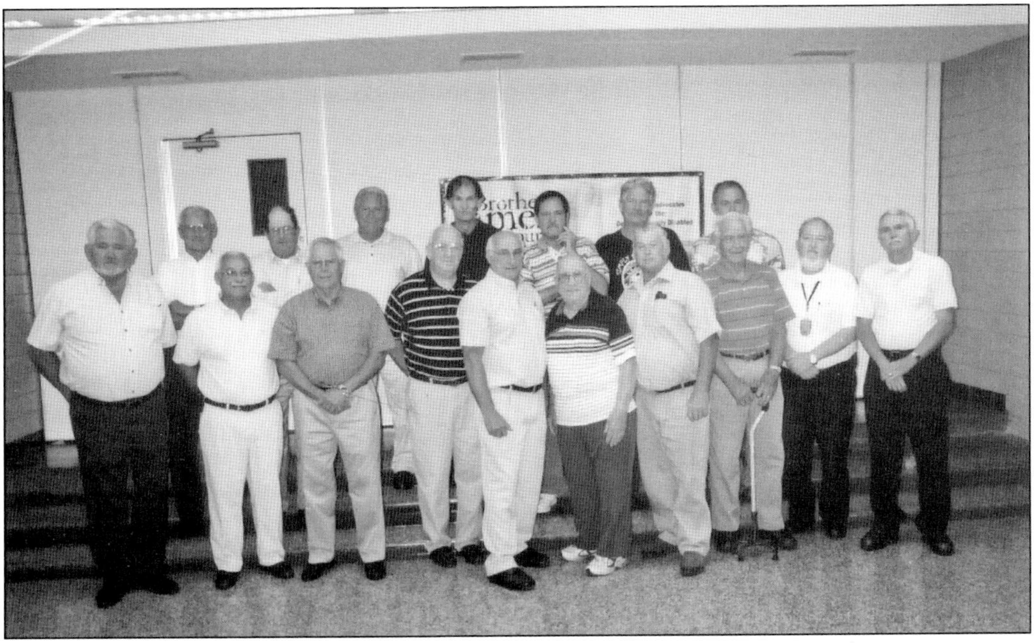

The photograph above is from a trade school reunion on July 19, 2009. As alumni, the men pictured know first hand the work of the Franciscan Brothers. As local men, they and their families are great contacts who support Brother James Court. The reunion was a gathering of those who graduated as far back as 1936 and as recently as 1972, the last year the school was open. In the first row, sixth from left, is Pete Bono, class of 1936, who took many of the pictures used in this book. The class of 1959, celebrating its 50th graduation from high school, had the most attendees at the reunion. Some of the buildings the students helped to construct are still in use today. Below is a photograph of some of these men when they were at St. James.

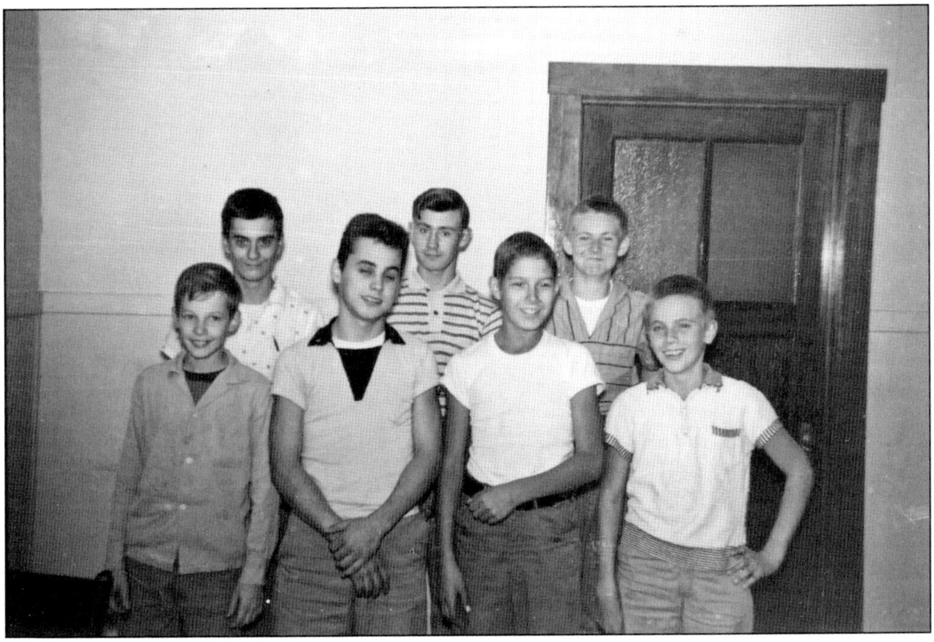

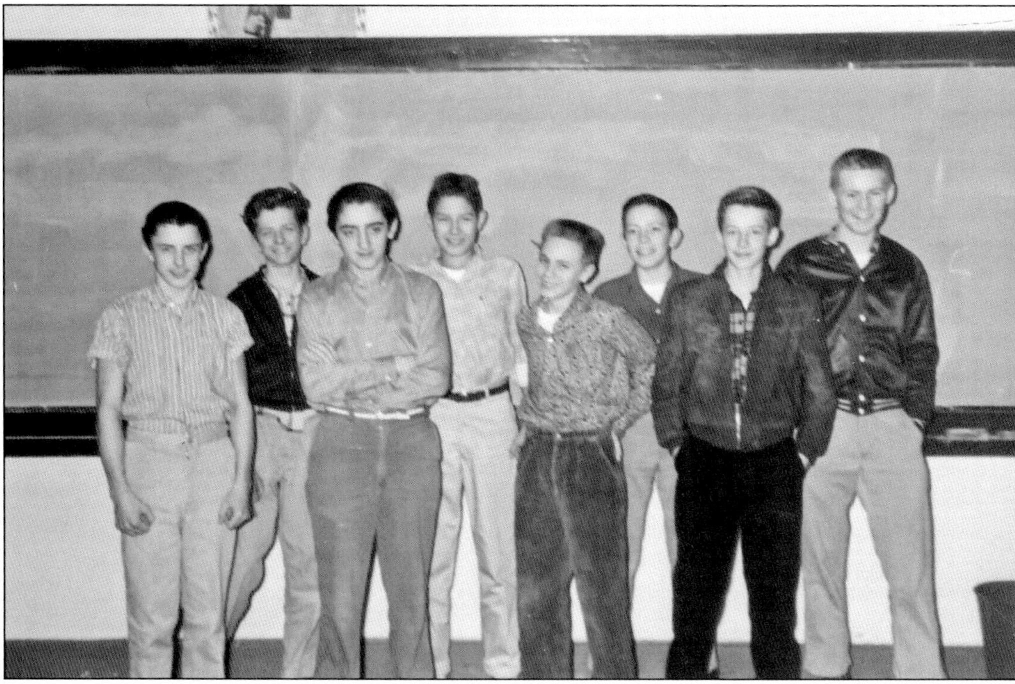

The next two pages show boys in their freshman or sophomore years at St. James Trade School, 1955–1956.

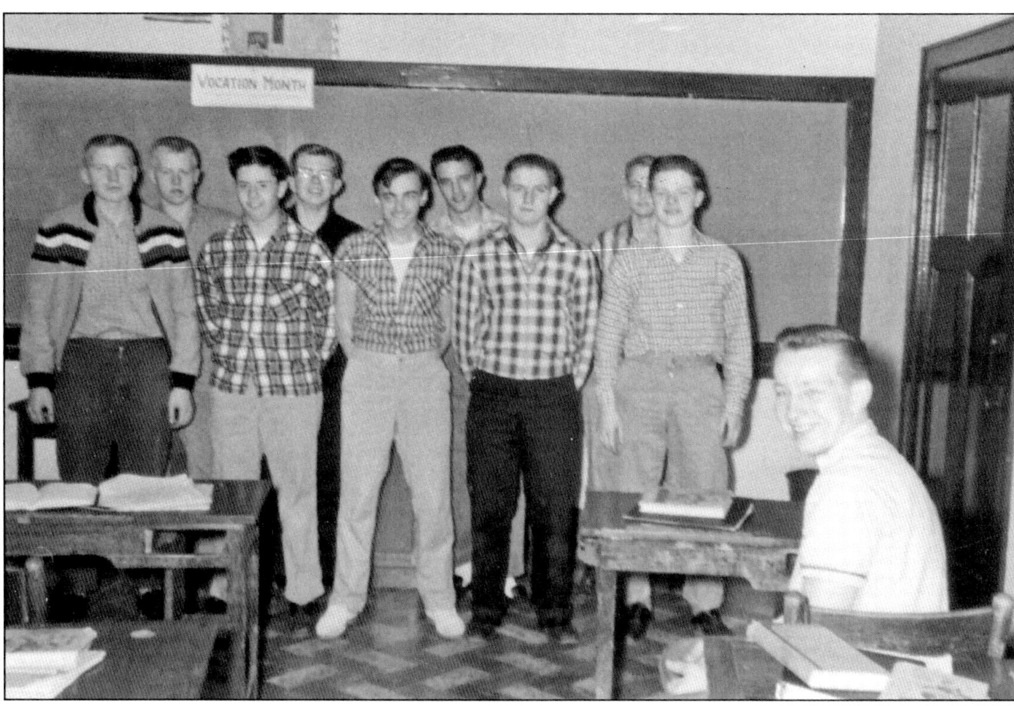

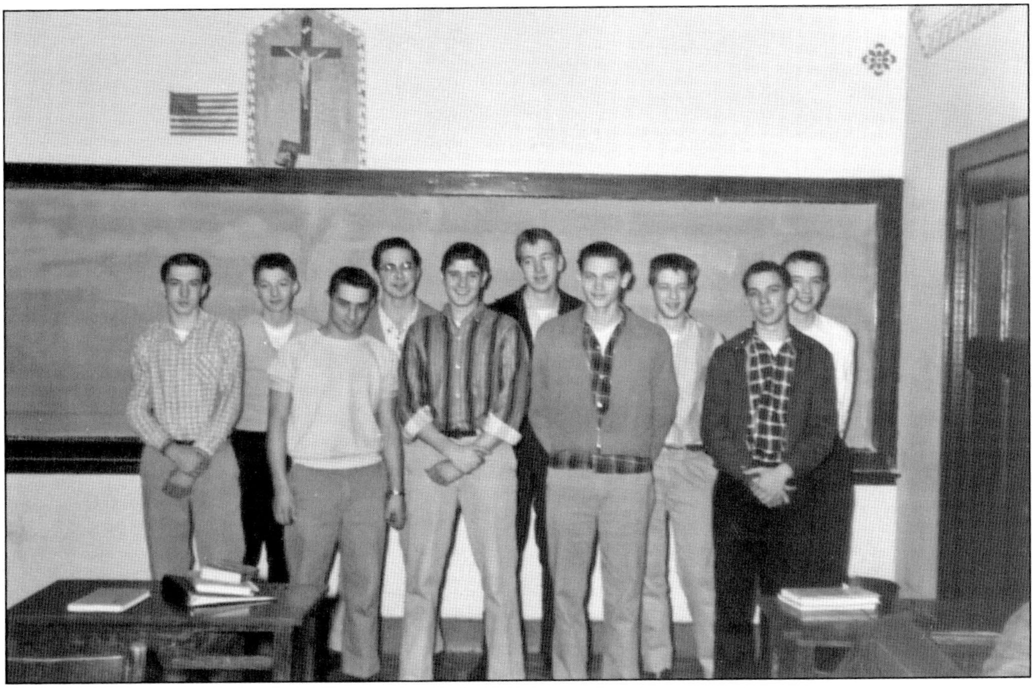

Perhaps the reader can identify one or more of these boys of the Trade School from around 1956.

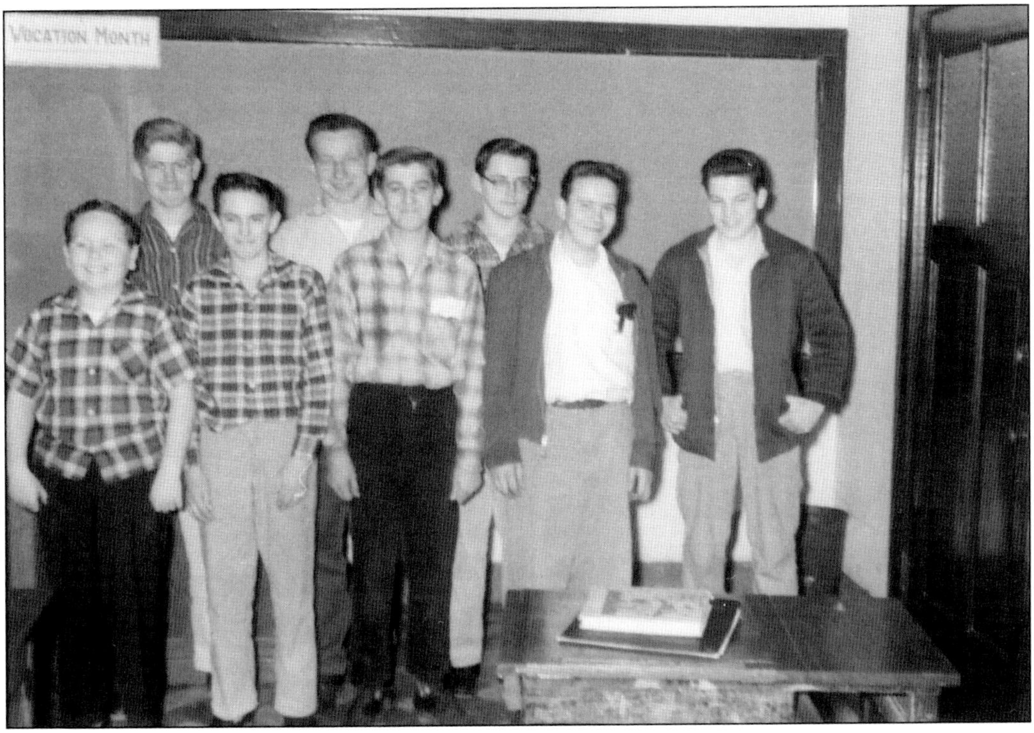

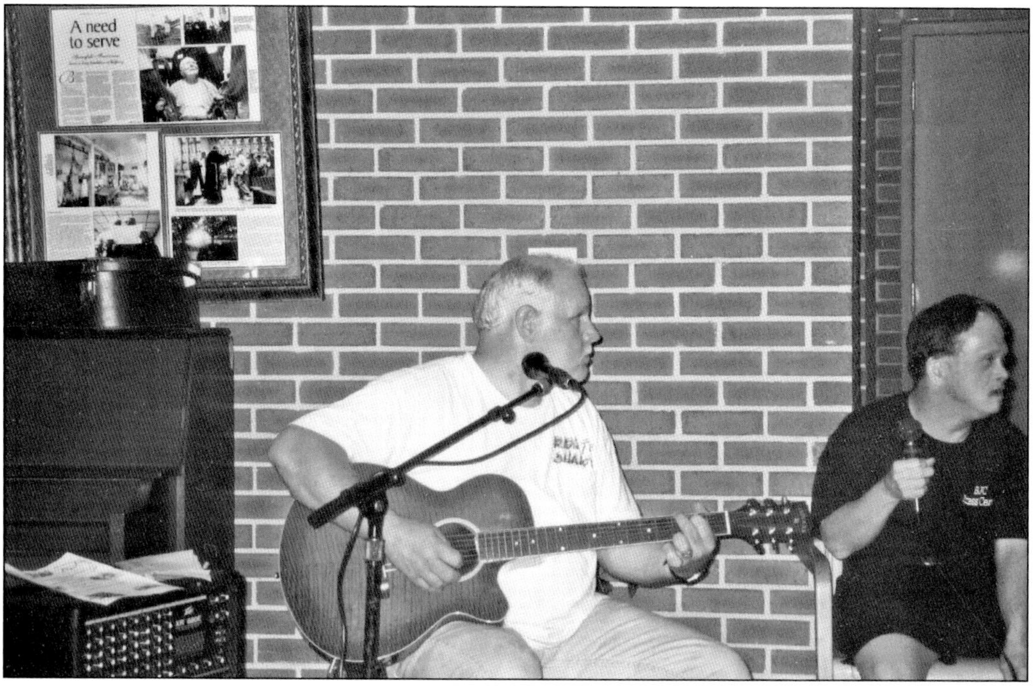

Sing-a-longs are very popular at Brother James Court. Musician Dan Wilson leads the men in some of their favorite songs in these 2007 photos.

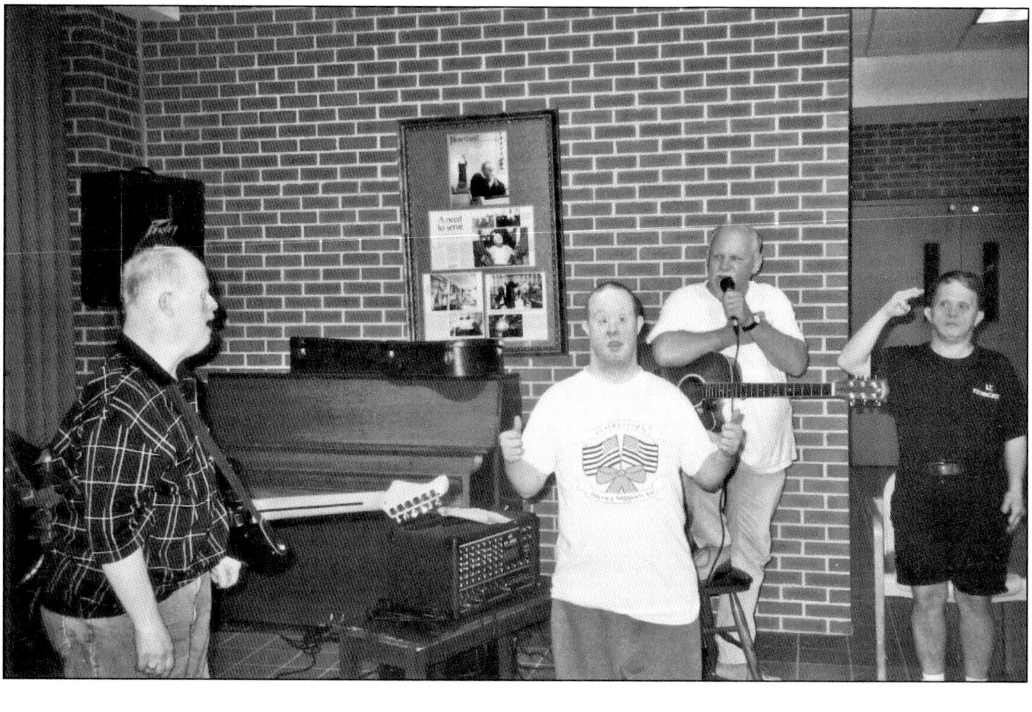

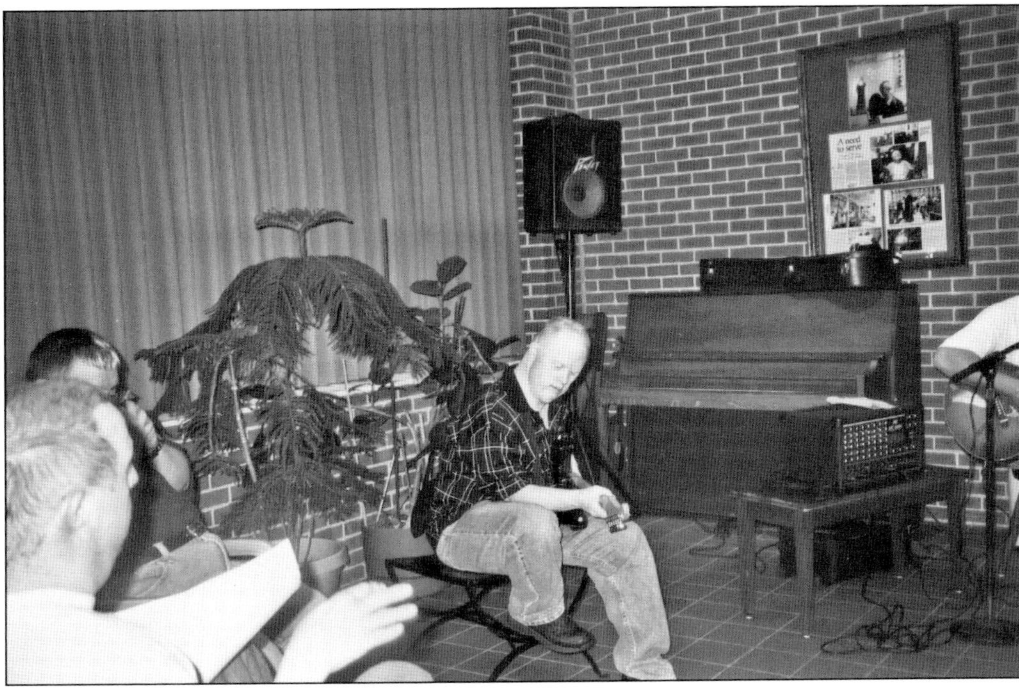

With Dan Wilson as accompanist, one of the men tries his hand at the guitar, while another takes the spotlight as the singer.

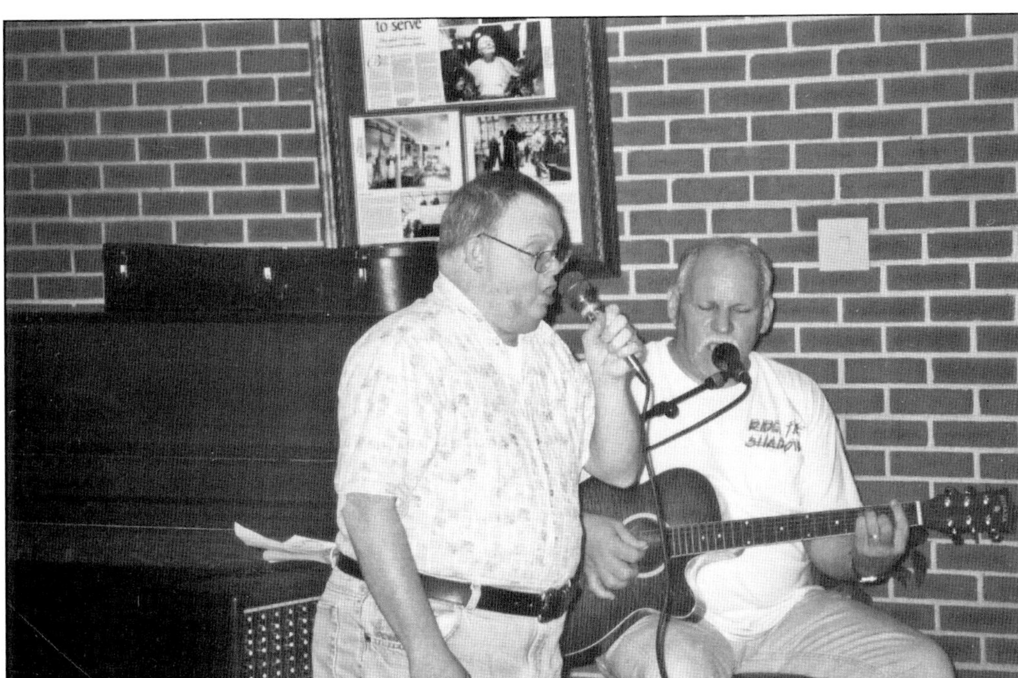

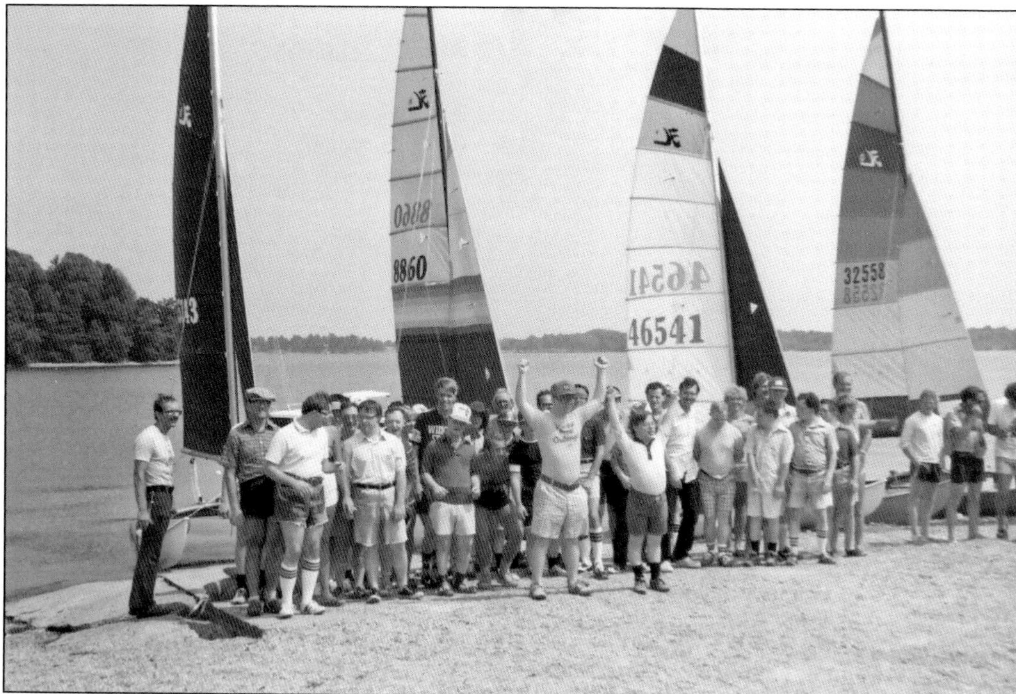

Highlighting a picnic at Lake Springfield in the early 1980s, the Brother James Court men pose in front of beautiful sailboats with Br. David Sarnecki. Below, they are having a good time at the picnic.

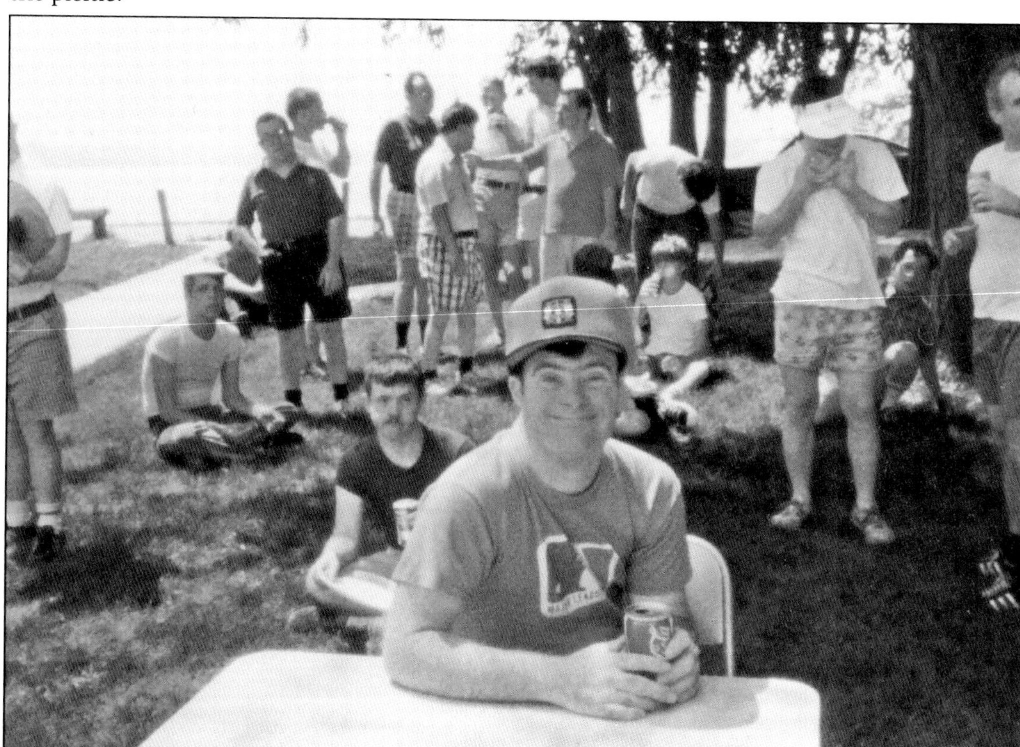

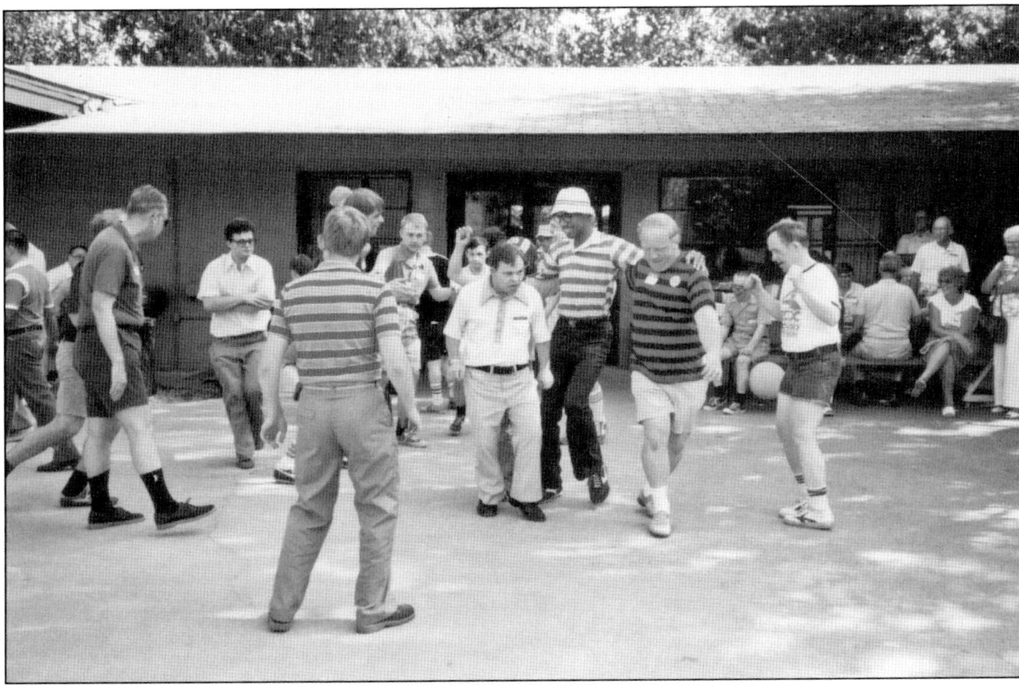

The Brother James Court men and their families get together at the annual family picnic, around 1985.

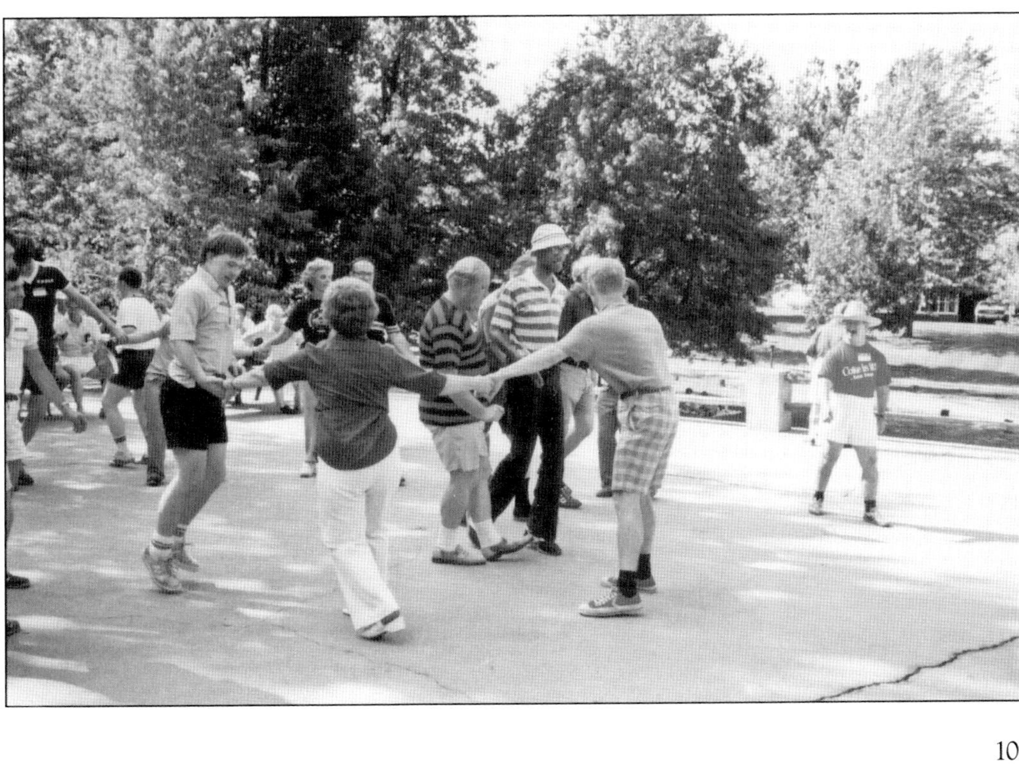

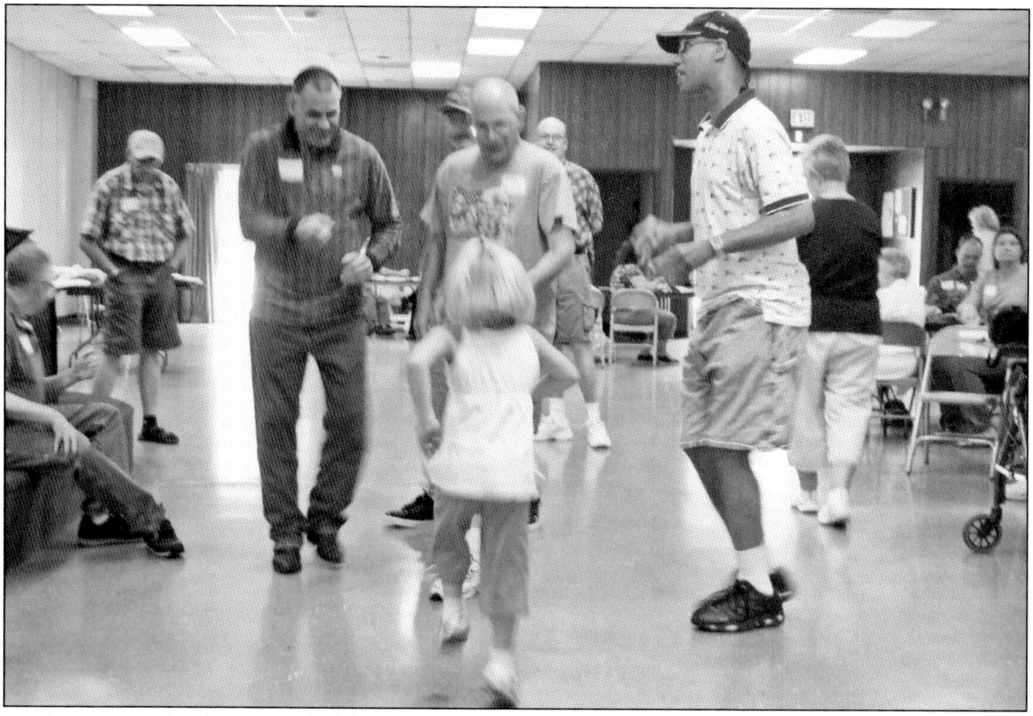

At the annual family picnic, held in 2009 at a Knights of Columbus hall, the men enjoy dancing. (Courtesy of Jim Kiesow.)

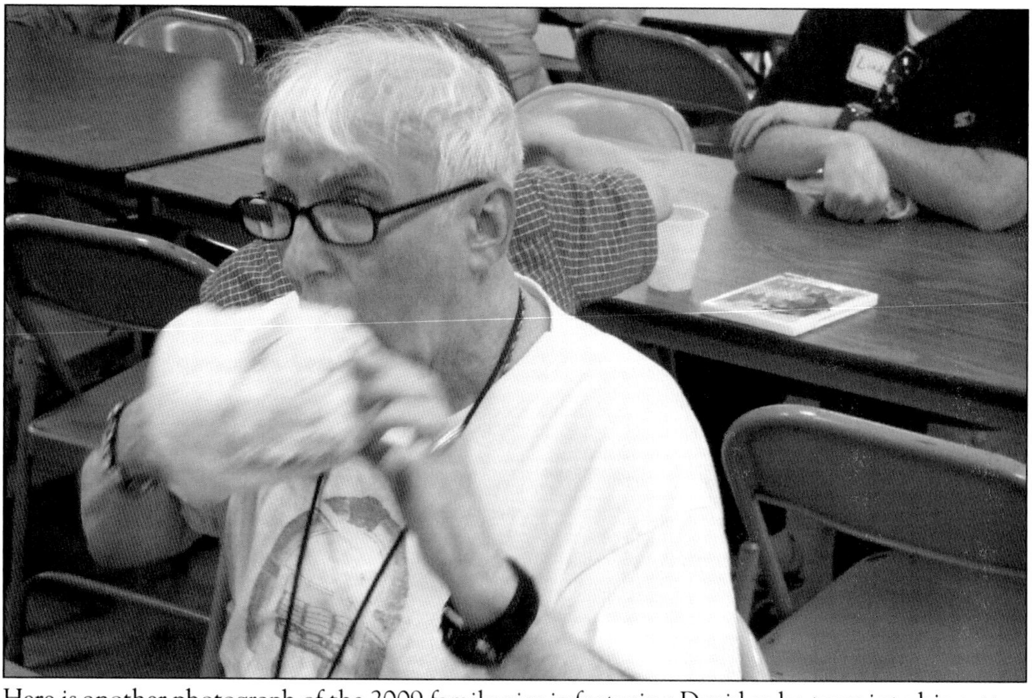

Here is another photograph of the 2009 family picnic featuring David as he tears into his cotton candy. The picnics usually will attract about 250–300 family members and the men of Brother James Court. (Courtesy of Jim Kiesow.)

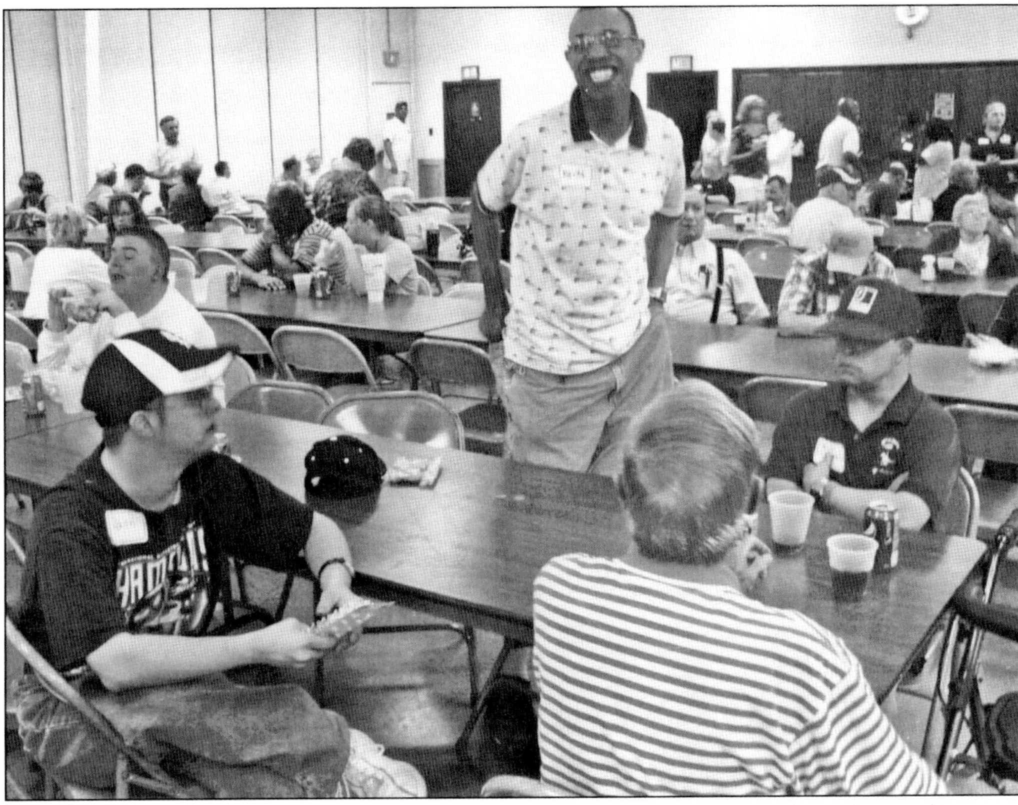

The men have a good time visiting with each other and their families in the cafeteria. (Courtesy of Jim Kiesow.)

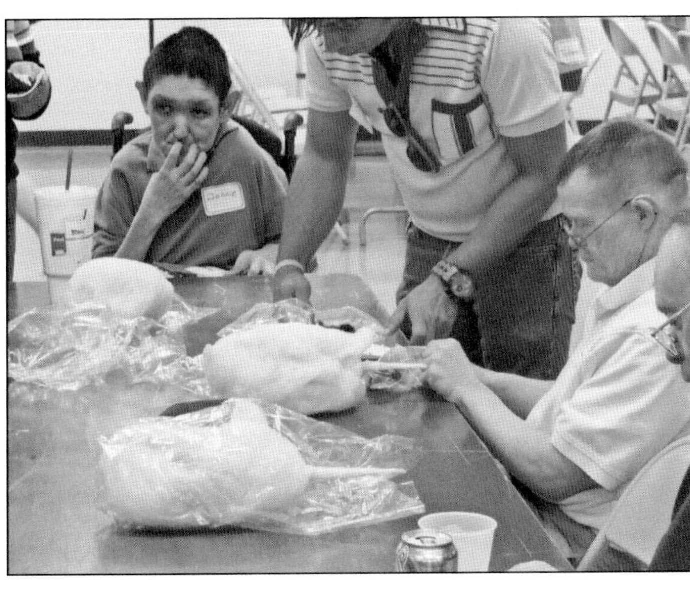

Cotton candy is on the snack menu at the picnic, along with plenty of other good food and drinks. (Courtesy of Jim Kiesow.)

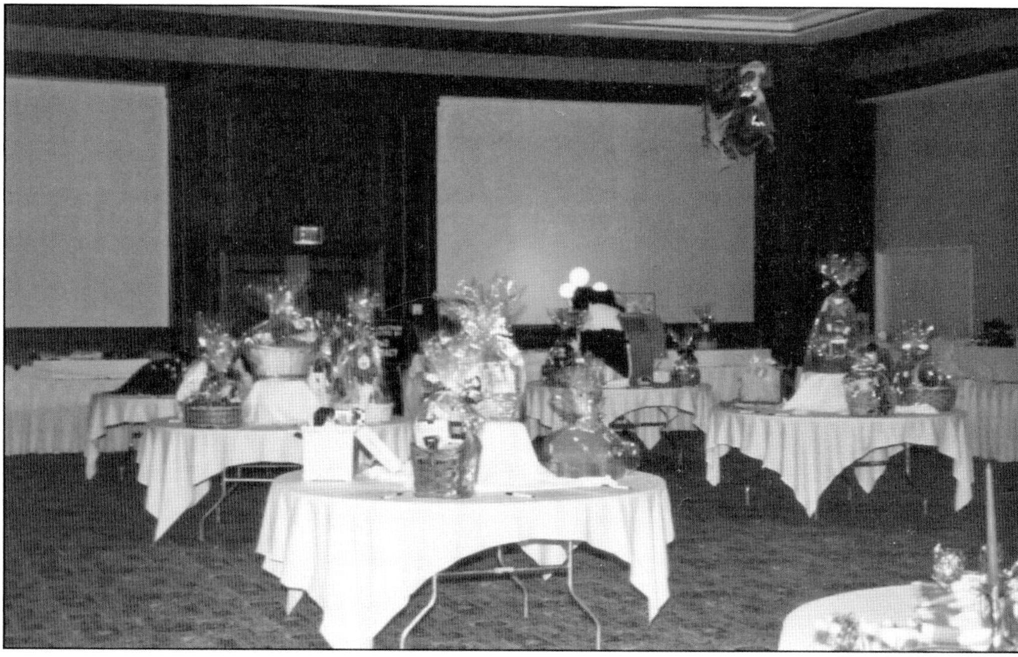

A benefit dinner and auction has been held for many years on behalf of Brother James Court. The event proves to be a very good fundraiser, and celebrity auctioneers help to bring in much needed funds for Brother James Court. This photograph of the 1999 dinner and auction shows the beautiful baskets of goodies that will be up for auction.

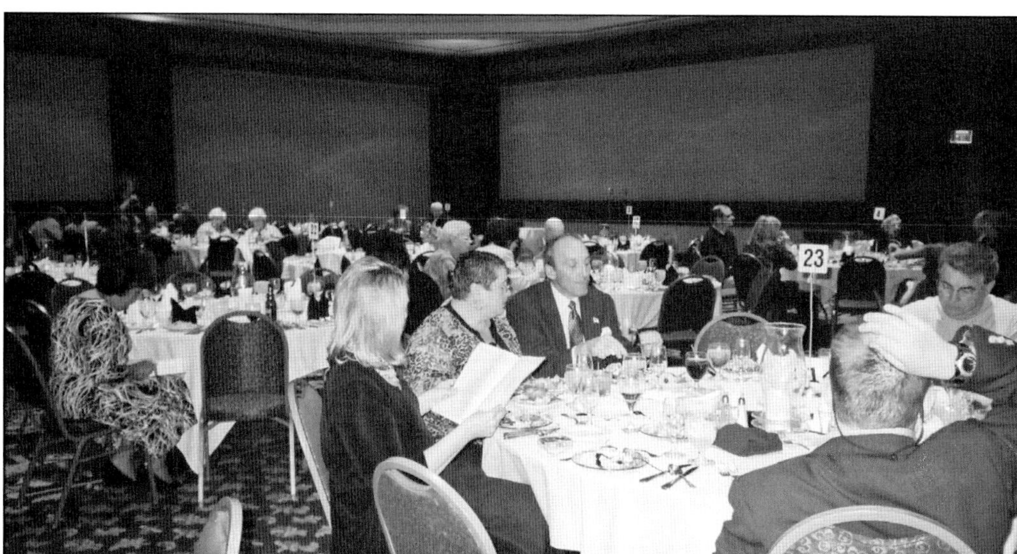

Tables filled with guests assure Brother James Court of a financial success for the evening. Hundreds of patrons and scores of the men who reside at Brother James Court would socialize and hold family reunions in celebration of the Brothers' work.

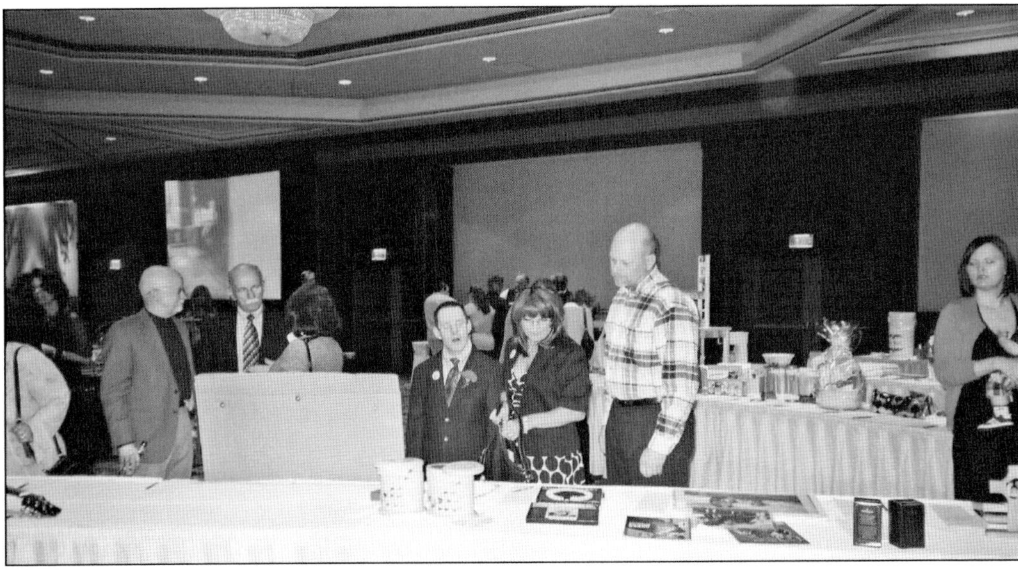

These images show more of the festivities at the 1999 benefit dinner. Above, guests peruse the items up for auction. Below, diners at table 16 enjoy each other's company and some good conversation.

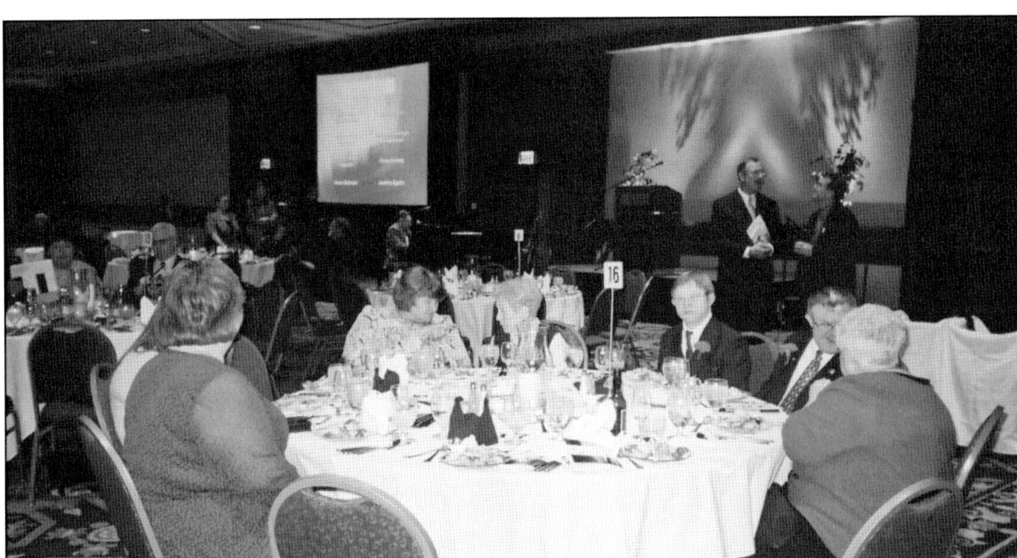

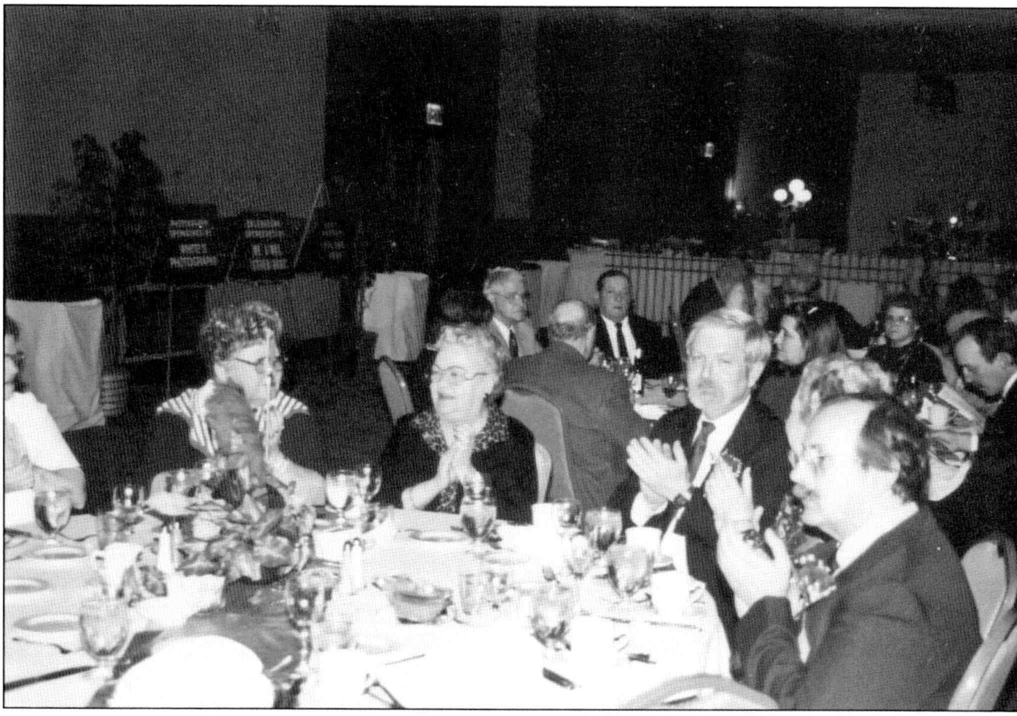

In these two photographs, diners at the 1999 dinner and auction take part in the festivities.

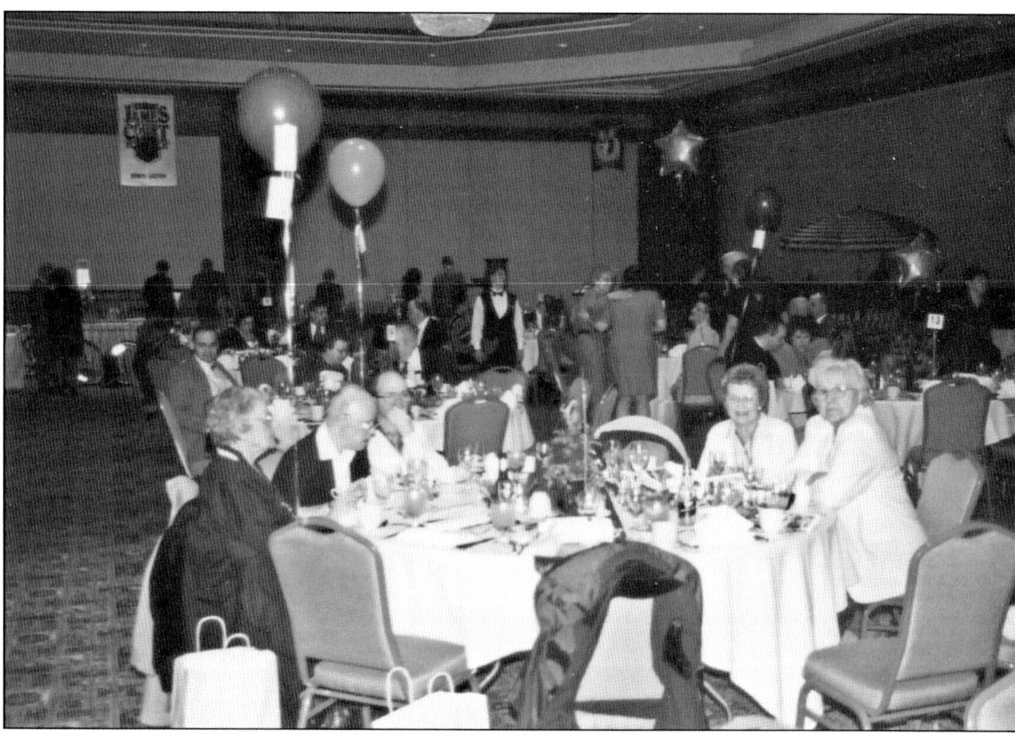

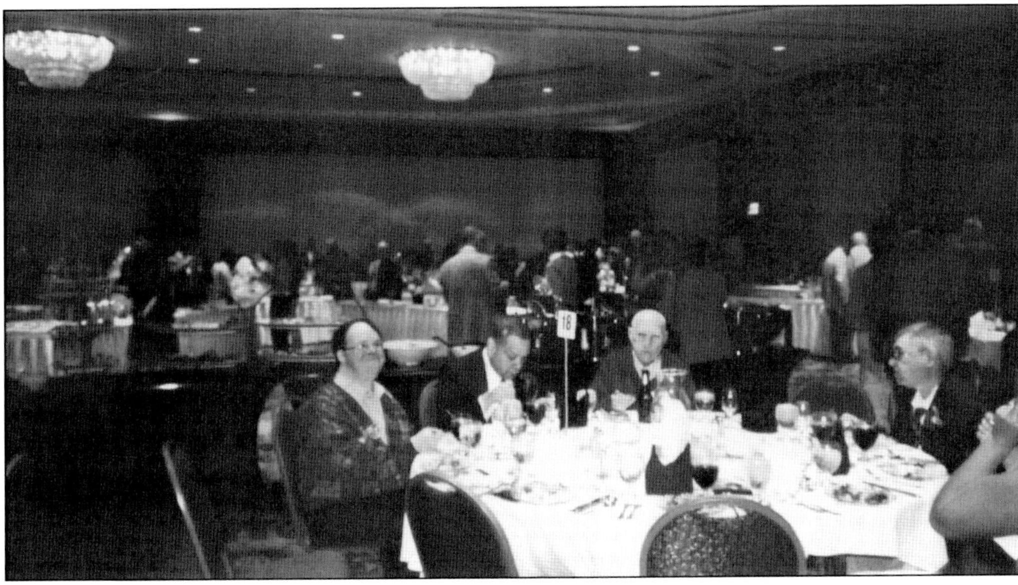

The April 2009 dinner and auction attracted a large crowd to the ballroom of a major hotel in Springfield. Below, Tim prepares for his upcoming vocal performance as patrons arrive during the reception. (Photograph courtesy of Laura Rape.)

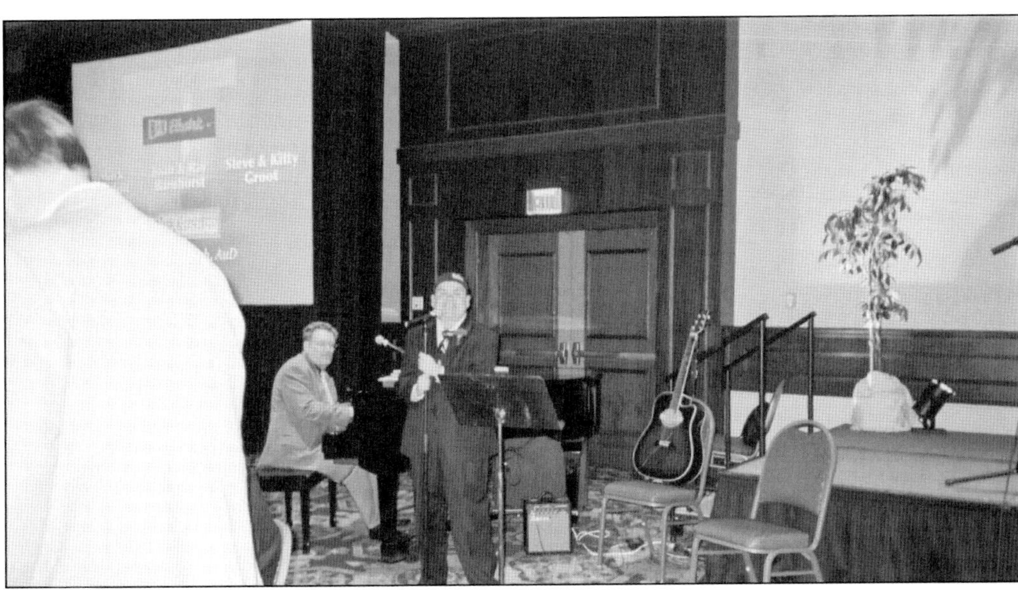

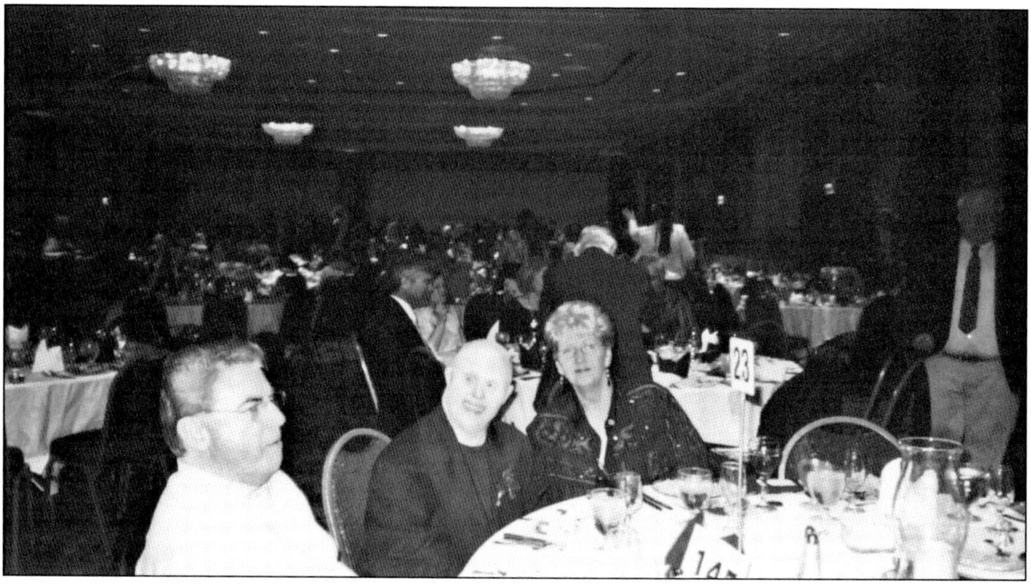

These photographs from the 2009 dinner and auction show the men of Brother James Court and their families. (Photographs courtesy of Laura Rape.)

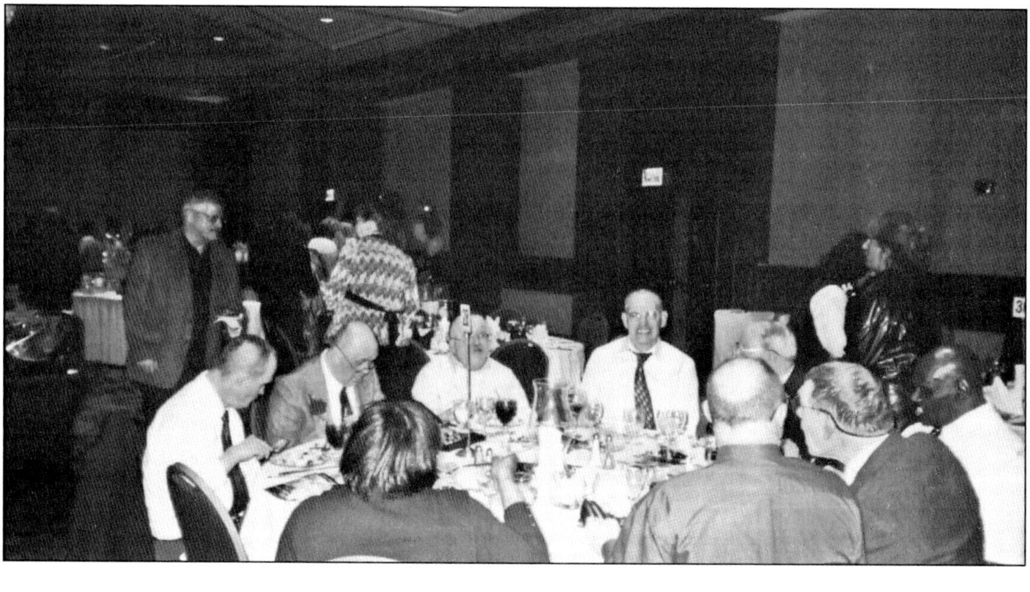

Four

OF CABBAGES AND KINGS

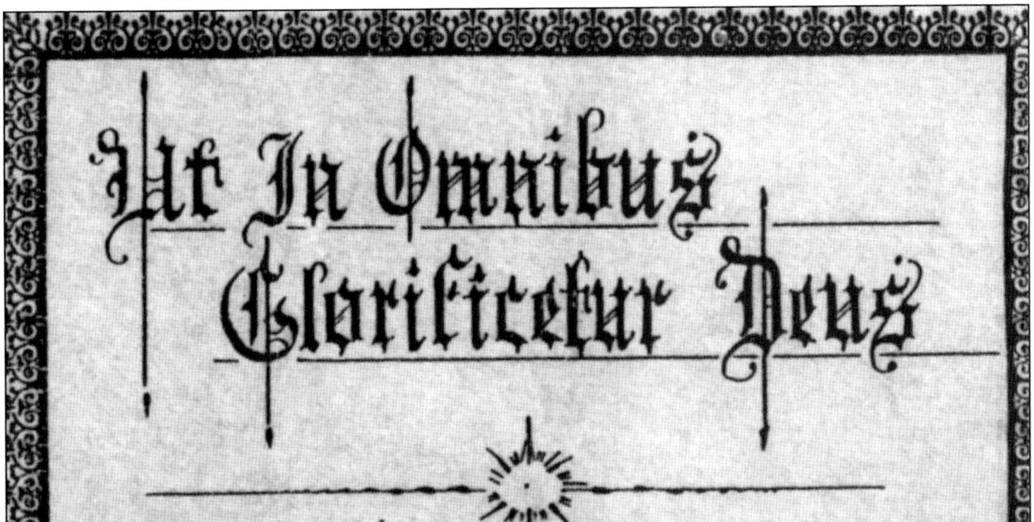

"That in all things, God may be Glorified" is the English translation of this Latin phrase.

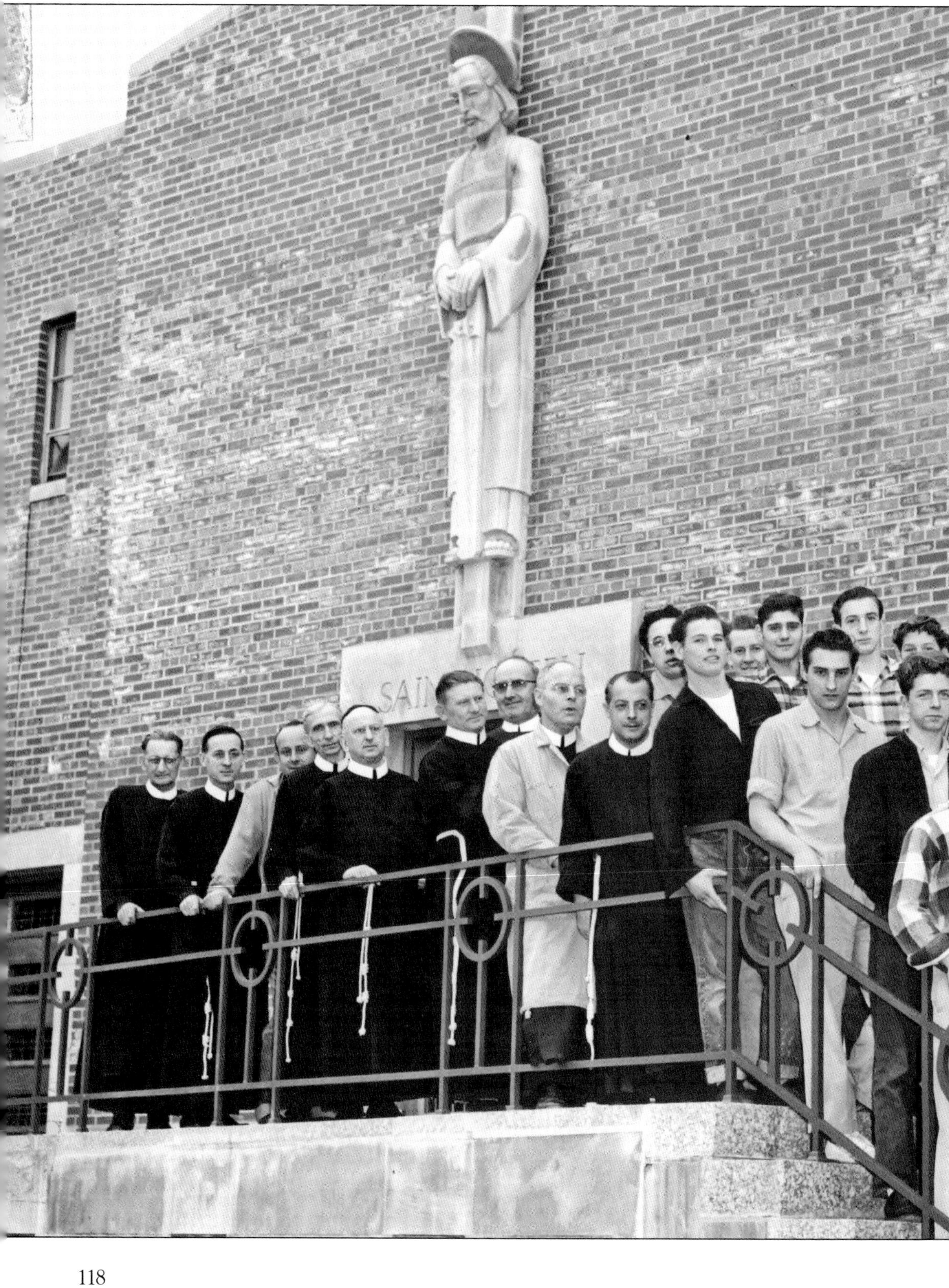

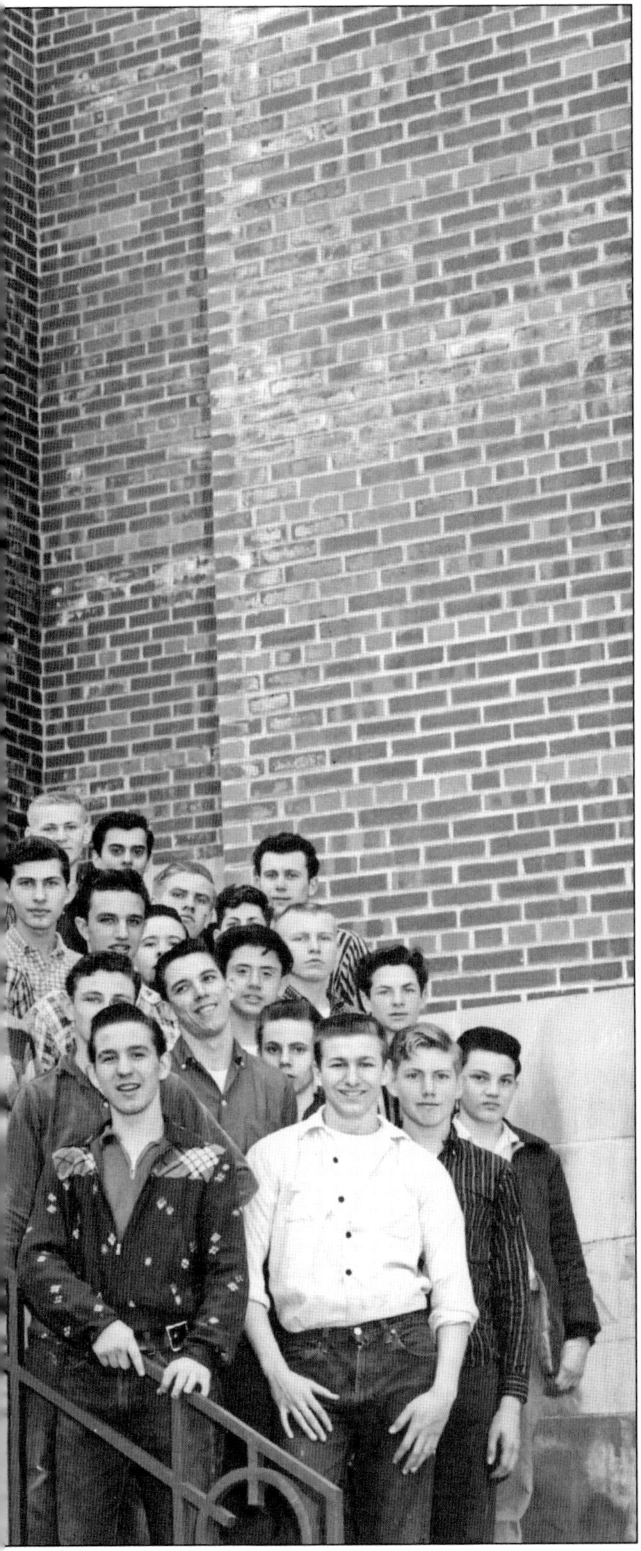

Here is the photograph pictured on the cover of this book, enabling all individuals to be seen and identified. On the steps of the Chapel of St. James the Worker are the brothers and students who built it. The brothers, from the left, are Brothers Theodosius and Aegidius, staff member Albert "Purgy," Purgatorio, and Brothers Placidus, Rembert, Elpidius, Justus, Falran, and Nestor.

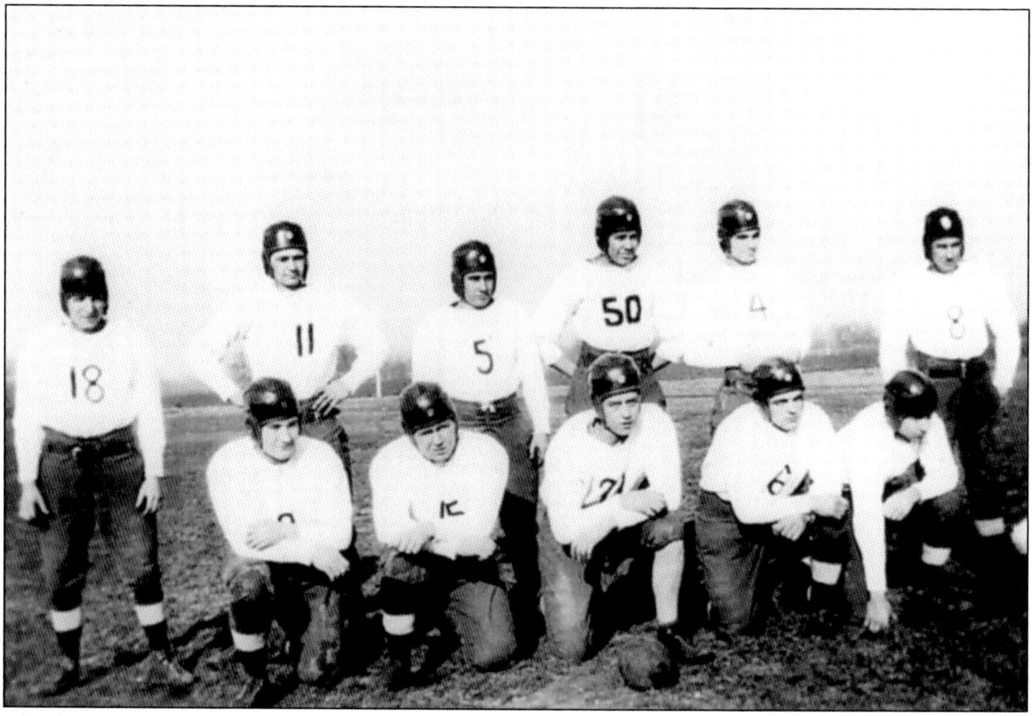

The first varsity football team posed for this photograph. The 1934 squad was made up of these 11 players plus three not shown. At the time the picture was taken, there were less than 25 boys in the school. September 22, 1934, marked the first football game St. James played and won, with a score of 6–0 against Springfield Cathedral Boys High School. Nick Todich scored the first touchdown in the history of the school on a four-yard run. The last game St. James won came on October 1, 1954, with a score of 28–12 against Nokomis High School. Scoring for St. James was Bob Doan with two touchdowns (5-yard and 25-yard runs) and two extra point runs; Bill Meny, one touchdown (15-yard run); David Brimmer, one touchdown (6-yard run); and extra point runs by Pat Capranica and Ed Capranica. The last game played was on November 9, 1956: St. James 13, Palmyra Northwestern High School 32. Scoring for St. James was Tom Guyon with two touchdowns (6-yard and 65-yard runs) and an extra point run by Joe Herman—the very last point ever recorded for the football team. Other coaches are profiled in chapter two, but another gentleman deserves to be recognized: Edward "Nonny" Selinger, who coached baseball, football, and basketball from 1949 to 1956. Selinger was a graduate of Springfield Cathedral Boys High School and St. Louis University. He had a long career as a certified public accountant in Springfield.

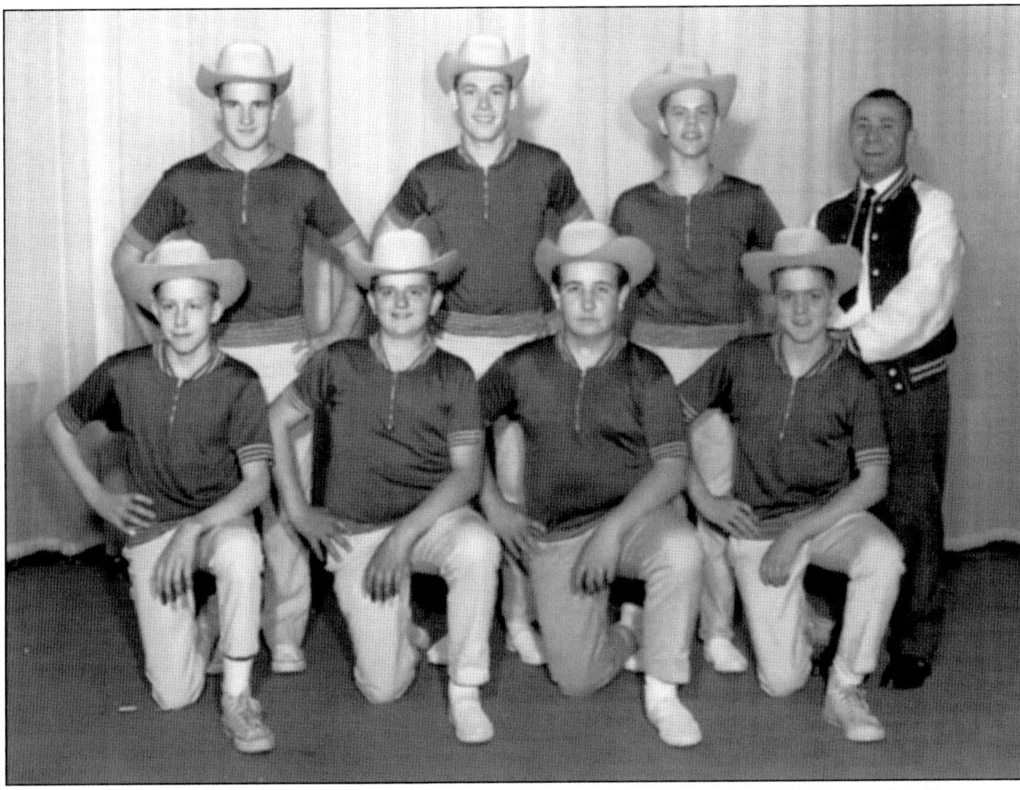

The first basketball game played was November 25, 1941, with a score of St. James 22, Waggoner High School 25. Tony Caruso scored 8 points for St. James, with Evaldo Baliva scoring 6, Joe Esela 4, John Bartolomucci 2, and John Kohlrus 2. St. James won its first game December 22, 1941, with a score of 37 to 25 against Stonington High School. Tony Caruso scored 14 points for St. James, with John Bartolomucci scoring 10, John Kohlrus 10, Evaldo Baliva 2, and Joe Esela 1. St. James won its final game February 10, 1970, with a score of 67 to 63 against Girard High School. Shane Cloyd scored 21 points for St. James, and Steve Antonacci scored 15, Mike Venturini 12, Jim Cour 11, Gerard Baulos 6, and Bill Tucker 2. St. James played its last game in the district tournament at Waverly High School on February 23, 1971. St. James lost with a score of 57 points to Divernon High School, who earned 85. Player Bill Tucker earned 19 points for St. James, while Harold Morrow earned 12, Jim Cour 10, Bruce Carlile 7, Terry Rapps 5, and Mike Valenti 4. Cheerleaders from 1964 are shown here with their advisor, William Croucher.

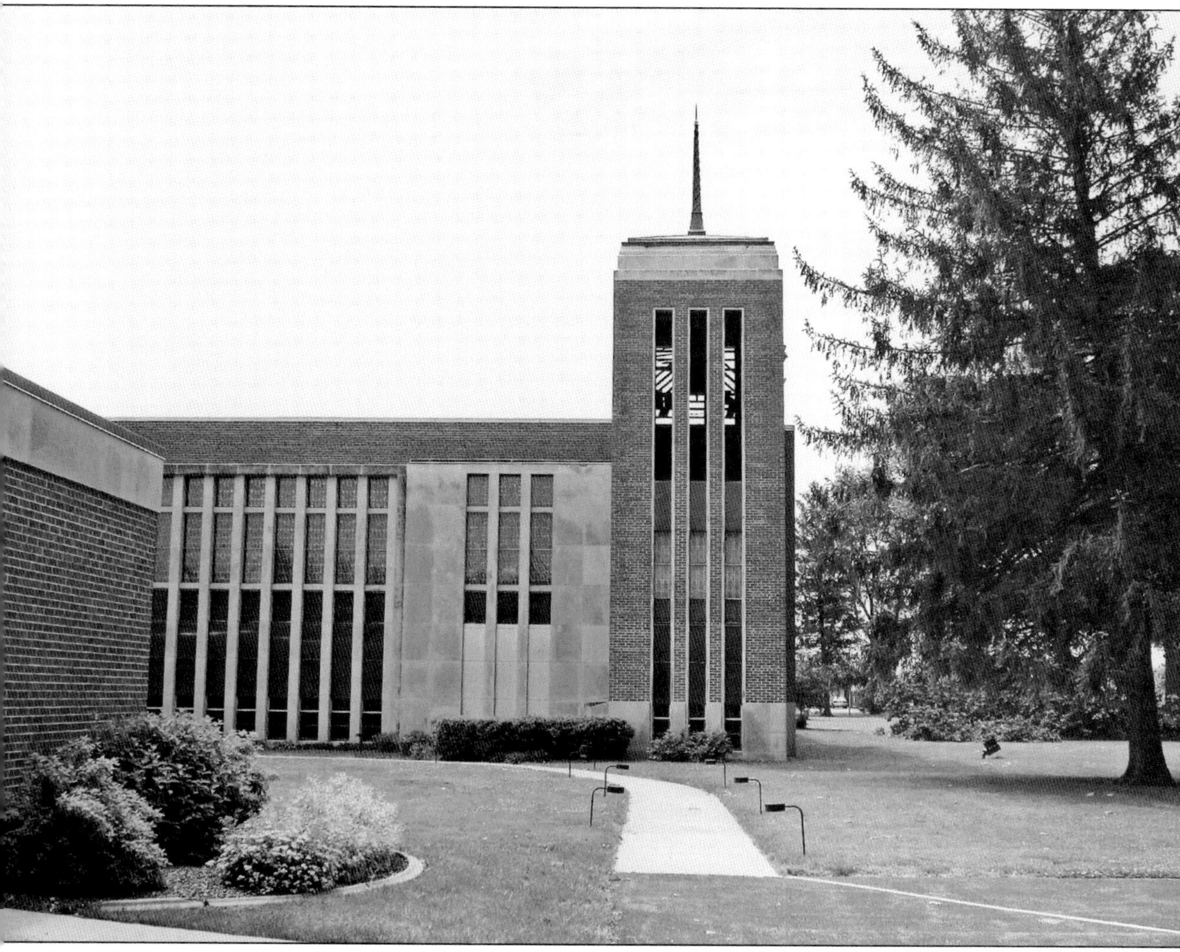

This current view of St Joseph's Chapel, looking south from the entrance courtyard of Brother James Court, shows the bell tower, which is still in use today 24 hours a day, seven days a week.

April 9,1947

Office of the Registrar QUINCY COLLEGE Quincy, Illinois

Rev. Father Fabian Merz, O, F. M.
St. James Trade School
Route 1
Springfield, Illinois

Dear Reverend Father:

In answer to your inquiry of April 2 I can give you the following information:

Quincy College will accept graduates from St.James Trade School if they present fifteen units as follows, with a general average of "C" or "77" (a unit represents five 45-minute class periods per week throughout a school year):

English (Composition & Literature)		3 year	3 units
Mathematics:			
	High-school algebra	1 year	1 unit
	Plane geometry	1 year	1 unit
Science:			
	General Science	1 year	1 unit
	Biology	1 year	1 unit
Social Studies:			
	World history	1 year	1 unit
	American history	1 year	1 unit
Electives:			
	(Shop work,mechanical drawing, religion, typewriting, etc.etc.		6 units

Your present curriculum needs a little strengthening in mathematics, otherwise it already meets all the above requirements. I think you can work in a year of algebra and a year of geometry without much difficulty.

Fraternally yours

(Signed) Fr.August Reyling, O.F.M.

Note: Our school has already complied with the above requirements.

(Signed) Br. Fabian

Brother Fabian,
Superior

This accreditation letter from Quincy College was sent to the brothers as a guideline shortly after the academic program began at St. James Trade School.

Copy

State of Illinois

Office of the Superintendent of Public Instruction

Springfield

Vernon L.Nickell
Superintendent

August 20, 1947

Br.Fabian
St.James Trade School
Sangamon Avenue - Sangamon County
Springfield, Illinois

Dear Brother Fabian:

Mr. Cruft and I enjoyed our visit with you, your principal Fahter Everest and other members of your staff yesterday.

We were again impressed with your excellent philosophy which seems to permeate the entire school and faculty. We believe you are making excellent progress vocationally and academically. We understand that you are carrying out the fourth year of your academic program as planned in our conferences in 1945 and 1946.

We shall be glad to call upon you again during the school year at your invitation to complete the annual report blamks which are necessary for recognition.

Again we commend you for your progress and interest in a broad and sound educational program.

Yours very truly

sig. C.C.Byerly

C.C.Byerly
First Assistent Superintendent
of Public Instruction

Pictured here is the Trade School Academic Review Letter from Public Instruction, which gave the brothers a much sought after endorsement of their new program.

AUTO MECHANICS

Fred Melich—Instructor **Charles Sonnenberg—Assistant**

Students—12

MACHINE SHOP

Brother Kolonat—Instructor

Students—11

BAKERY

Brother Juniper—Instructor

A. Caruso—Assistant

Students—10

CARPENTRY

Brother Rembert—Instructor

Brother Nicetius—Instructor

Students—10

BUTCHER SHOP

A. Altepeter—Instructor

F. Romano—Assistant

Students—7

TAILORS

Brother Nestor

Instructor

Students—4

AGRICULTURE

Brother Justus

Instructor

Students—3

FORGE

Brother Cherubim

Instructor

Students—3

DAIRY

Brother Sergius

Instructor

Students—2

FLORICULTURE

F. Huneke

Instructor

Students—1

SHOE SHOP

Brother Demetrius

Brother Adam

Instructors

Students—1

Pictured here is a June 1948 listing of the shop instructors and the numbers of students in each trade.

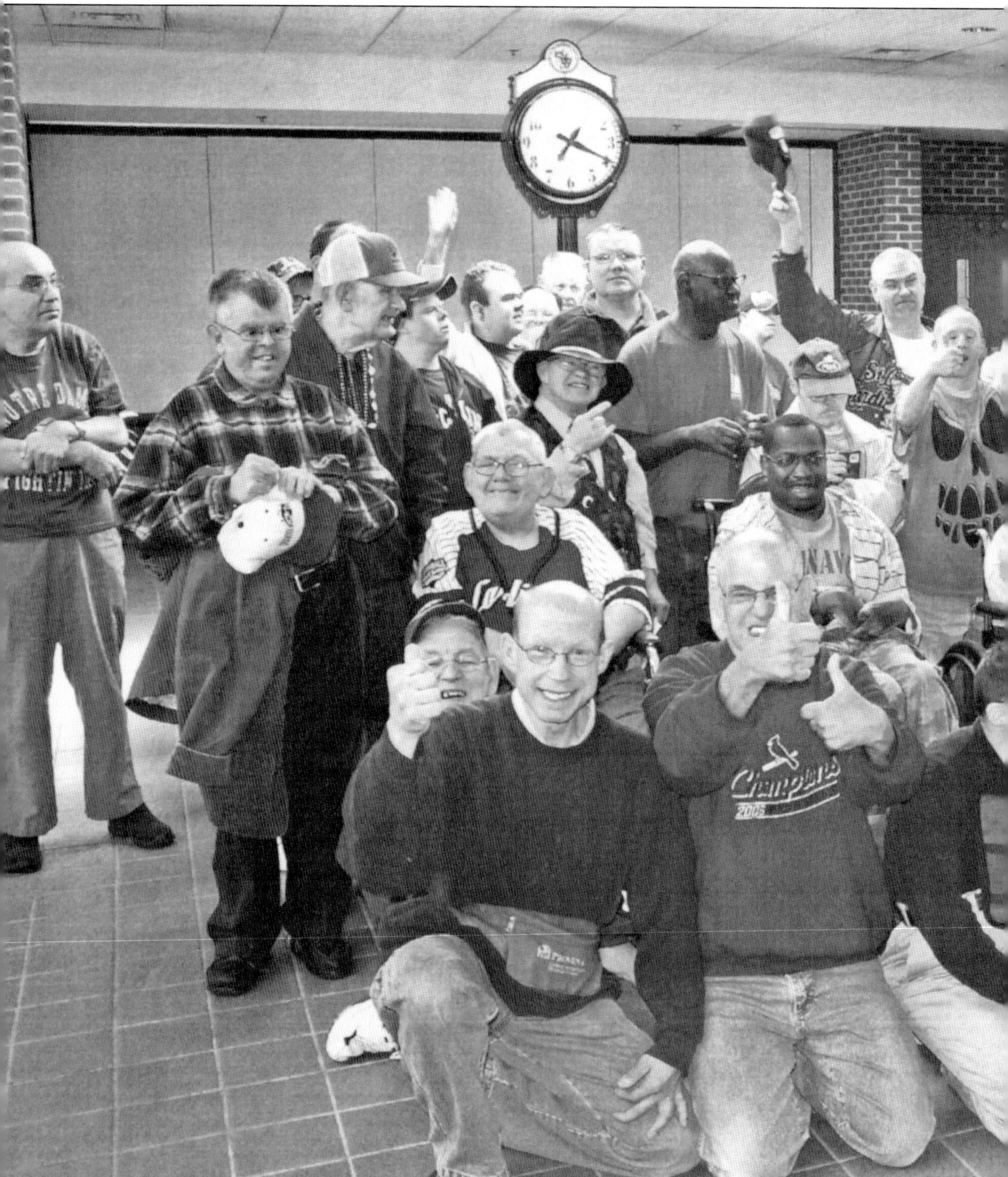

This group photograph shows many residents of Brother James Court in the fall of 2009. Their gratitude, appreciation, and frame of mind are evident in their facial expressions and body

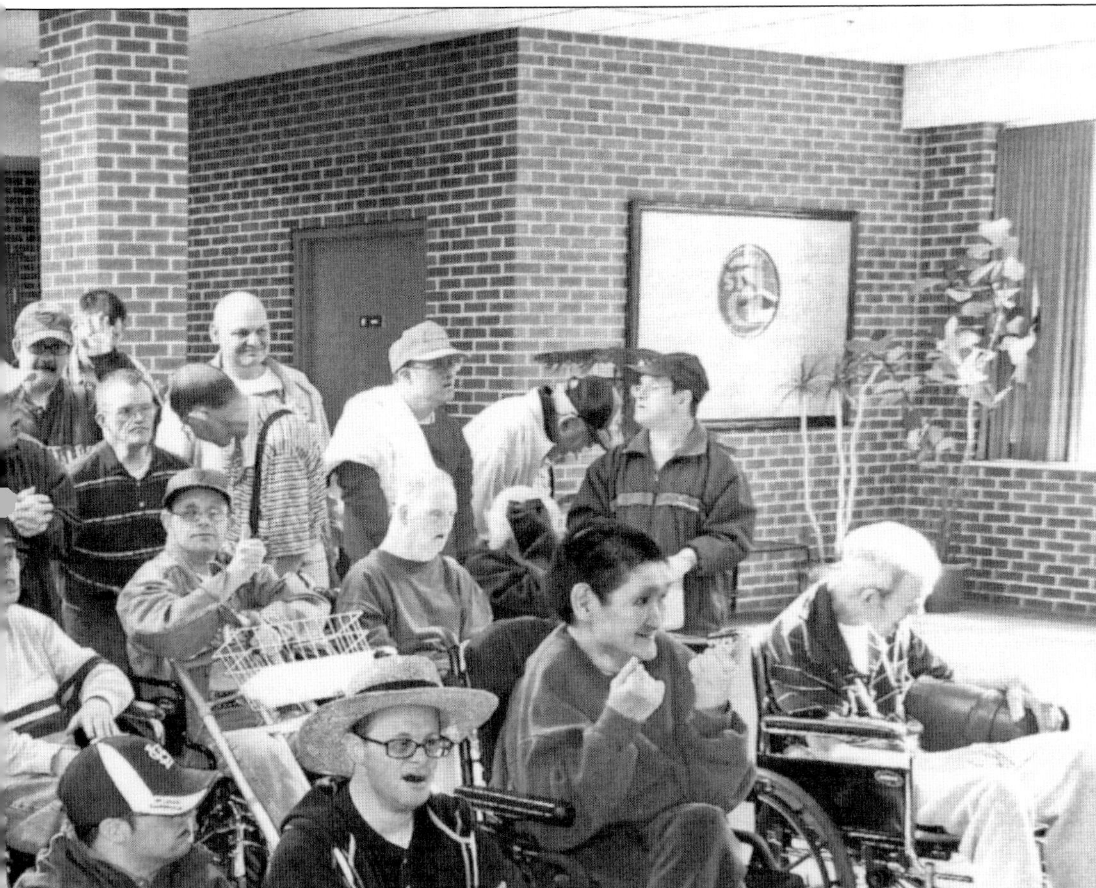

language, which for most is their most effective way of communicating "Thank You." (Courtesy of Bill Prose.)